AF497678

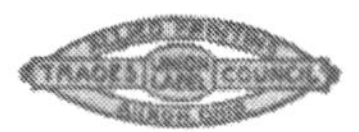

With the World's Great Travellers

Vol. III

Various Authors

Originally Published by
UNION BOOK COMPANY
1901

Contents

CONTENTS iii

THE CATHEDRAL, CITY OF MEXICO

VOLUME III

WITH THE WORLD'S GREAT TRAVELLERS.

THE WORLD'S GREAT CAPITALS OF TO-DAY.

London.

To the ordinary eye the moon and stars have at least prettiness, perhaps grandeur. To the trained astronomer, and the contemplative poet, the mighty firmament overwhelms the mind with the sense of human inability to grasp the vast. Knowing and loving the features and characteristics of London as a lover those of his mistress, it can be imagined how such a one despairs of doing justice, in a brief space, either to his subject or his own sane enthusiasm. He would fain impart his knowledge, insight, and what glimmerings of romantic fancy may add charm to the prosy exposition, but the showman's harangue is received as art without heart.

London is a hundred captivating sights and themes for our hundred capacities and moods. You go to it the first time with the child's enviable eye-delight in novelty, and are lucky if in a week you are not eye-sore, dazed, and jaded with the very monotony of new scenes and blurred impressions. You wisely fly to the lovely country lanes for restful change, and come back with new eyes and a clean slate. Then the mysterious quality which lifts visible London into the London of real romance and realizable antiquity dawns upon the mind. A third exploration reveals its almost omniscient and omnipotent headship as for three centuries the world's centre for the intellectual and material forces that have so largely built up our civilization. Continued observation brings other and endless aspects of the indescribable city, which is no city, but a Chinese puzzle of separately whirling worlds within each other.

This mystifying prelude may seem rather disheartening to the stranger, primed with rational curiosity to understand, as well as see, this unwieldy London. He will find, however, his curiosity whetted, deepened, elevated, in proportion as he takes with him a moderate grounding in the historical associations of the old city. This easily acquired information will prove to be a key that will unlock hidden places holding bunches of other keys, so that everywhere one may turn, the streets, buildings, and monuments recite their own fascinating stories.

We live in the day of big things, and sneer as we may at the superficiality of estimating quality by size, there is no escape from it when the purpose is only to kindle interest. Analysis can be undertaken afterwards. London "whips creation" in the number of its people, though its greatness is quite independent of this. The circle can be drawn to include four, six, or seven millions and it will still be true that the sustainers of its greatness come within a single million, possibly the half of that. Yet it has a few businesses useful for the novice to know. People have walked and ridden through the double tunnel under the wider part of the Thames since 1843. Its underground railway, costing five million dollars per mile to make, carries one hundred and fifty millions of people a year, and has been running forty years. The public are served by fifteen thousand cabs, which earn twenty-five million dollars a year. There are over one thousand omnibuses, not including tram-cars, on which there are roof seats, and you pay from two to six cents, according to distance. Steamboats afford a fine view of the city, at the same fares.

It has about five hundred theatres and music-halls, giving variety programmes. Many of these hold from three to five thousand and they are always well-filled. The roof of a famous music-hall built in 1870 slides off for a few minutes at a time, for ventilation on summer nights. The Crystal Palace entertains a hundred thousand people without being crowded, in its beautiful glass hall, 1,608 feet long, with two great aisles and transepts, and a charming pleasure park. In the palace are reproductions of ancient architecture, primitive peoples, extinct animals, everything in art and nature that can expand knowledge. The orchestra seats four thousand, the concert-hall four thousand, and the theatre four thousand, all under the same roof, yet their performances are simultaneous. The Palace cost over seven million dollars in 1854, and admission is twenty-five cents. The Albert Memorial Hall holds ten thousand. The Agricultural Hall covers three acres and a half, and holds audiences of twenty-five thousand.

There is not a day in the year without half-a-dozen or more public meetings, convened by religious, scientific, or other societies, a free field for the stranger to see distinguished people, hear average oratory, study character and customs, and lay in stores of useful knowledge with varied entertainment. "Doing the sights" is a matter of course, but they should be selected to suit one's mood at the time, also the usually unlovely weather, and above all, after some preliminary guide-book reading. The Tower is already familiar in story and picture, yet not every cockney is aware that its walls enclose a virtual town of over three thousand inhabitants. It has a hundred distinct interests for the leisurely-minded, besides that of being a great old fortress. The new Tower bridge equals the underground railway and sub-river tunnels as a triumph of engineering, lifting itself high above the tall ships' masts when they sail in and out of the port. Near by, the much maligned East End, the Whitechapel district beloved by horror-vending reporters, invites and will repay a visit.

Would you like to realize a dream of some magnificent pageant, in which the great notabilities of all the earth take a share? Take your stand where Rotten Row meets the Drive any morning or afternoon between April and July. Here meet the pink of fashion and the celebrities distinguished for honors won in art, science, diplomacy, statesmanship, and war. The outward and visible magnificence belongs to the horses rather than their riders and drivers, for plainness of attire and decoration is the rule among the great folks. This double daily parade is truly a unique spectacle, viewed by throngs of idlers of all nations, themselves a picturesque feature of the show.

A panorama with another sort of interest should be viewed ponderingly. Let the visitor approach Westminster Abbey from Victoria station along Victoria Street, once a worse than any Whitechapel nest of criminal slum-dwellers. Grouped into a picture unrivalled elsewhere in the world for architectural splendor combined with historic glory, he will see the hoary Abbey, not simply the stone record of a thousand years of human progress; not simply the petrified survival of druidicial worship in the forest groves, with its soaring tree trunk columns breaking into foliage as their tops meet to screen the sun and echo down again the ascending incense of prayer and song; not simply the stately temple which for ages has been the shrine of England's great ones, thirteen kings, fourteen queens, and the greater than these—the glorious array of its poets, musicians, statesmen, soldiers, sailors, and explorers, who, like Livingstone in his line and Chaucer in his, poured all their wealth of genius and power into the lap of their motherland, to make her happier and stronger. He will see through the mediæval stained windows the deeper meaning of the old church's story, the reddened sun-rays telling of the bloodshed that watered the growing plant of the nation's greatness, and the blue beams that figure Britannia's olden mastery of the seas, and the rainbow hues suggestive of her labors to give hope to the people that long sat in darkness till she brought the light of civilization.

Close to the Abbey's side stands the venerable St. Margaret's parish church, where Caxton printed the first book and is buried; where Ambassador James Russell Lowell's epitaph on Raleigh graces the window that honors the memory of Virginia's founder, whose headless body reposes in its precincts. Just behind the two churches stands Westminster Hall, as King William Rufus built it in 1099, though its great oak-beam roof was heightened by Richard II. Close behind it rises the majestic file of the Houses of Parliament, the great Victoria tower at one end, at the other the clock tower, with its minute-hand twelve feet long and its chimes that float around for miles. From its foot Westminster Bridge gladly crosses the Thames to the noblest of hospitals, St. Thomas's, founded in 1213. Its separate blocks corridored together, fitly match the Parliament building on the opposite bank of the river. When you stand on the Abbey sidewalk, near the Beaconsfield statue, you may feel you are standing in the true centre of the earth, for there will pass you in the course of a week in the season the picked leaders of most nations, the representatives of every faith and system of government, the ruling men of Asiatic empires and tribes, and travellers from the world's end to do homage to the mother of parliaments and the shrine of the immortal dead. And far in the distant haze hovers the dome of St. Paul's like a balloon ascending through the smoke clouds to the clear blue.

Starting westward from the Abbey, in this sacred bit of the great city, it is possible to walk seven miles on the grass and paths, through St. James's park, surrounded by Government buildings, stately old mansions, the home of the king when Prince of Wales, St. James's Palace, and Buckingham Palace. Then along Constitution Hill, across Piccadilly into Hyde Park, along Rotten Row (from *Route du Roi*) to Kensington Gardens with the house Victoria was born in, and so on, with a few breaks. The group of palatial museums at South Kensington tempt the stranger, whatever his tastes or culture, to spend a year there, and each year so spent will need another to do justice to their marvellous contents.

Turn back now, along Piccadilly, a unique panorama in itself, pass the cluster of great restaurants, theatres, music-halls, and other pleasure places that reach half a mile or so towards the Strand, where the hotels range round Charing Cross. Along this narrow but brilliant highway lie more theatres and a famous church or two, and the cold bath in use since the Romans made it two thousand years ago. Then up Fleet Street, whence the daily papers flutter morning, noon and night, until St. Paul's crowns the highest bit of the city. Its interior, and the monuments to the nation's naval and military heroes, will impress the visitor, though hardly so much as the exquisite singing at the short services of morning and afternoon, the strains of vocal and organ music floating and billowing in the great dome and along the lofty aisles.

Between St. Paul's and old Bishopsgate lies "the city," that is, the square mile or so given up to business, with no private houses left in it. Still going eastward the route passes through the Billingsgate fishmarket quarter, where its famous language still flourishes. Here stands "the Monument," a column surmounted with a gilt frame, commemorating the great fire of 1666, which began at this spot. If we take our stand far away on Blackfriars Bridge some thirty-five church steeples may be counted, each with its upper part painted black. The dome of St. Paul's is one of these. They mark the area of the fire, as each rebuilt church had to bear this memorial. But for this law St. Paul's would have had a gilded dome. Soon we come to the Tower, and then the long line of docks, covering thousands of acres, and stretching miles down the river. Here the merchant wealth of the country, and of the world, is realizable as nowhere else.

London shows both sides of its shield: incalculable wealth, poverty that defies description. Years of familiarity with its slums, before slumming was invented as a fashionable fad, only deepened the conviction that all the noble efforts to eradicate the worst evils in the situation are utterly hopeless. The breed flourishes faster than the mild measures to improve it can operate.

The homes of aristocracy in Mayfair, the heart of the West End, disappoint those who expect magnificence—long rows of houses in narrow streets, once red brick, now dingy black and musty-looking, the monotony broken here and there by a newer and more pretentious stone mansion. The great Squares are a brighter feature. The same sooty brick houses, large and small, make the quadrangle, each having a key to the gates that enclose the park, in which nursemaids exercise the children and pet dogs, and an occasional game of croquet is ventured by country cousins. The coating of soot on every branch and leaf is fatal to clean hands and summer costumes. The newer streets, and the region around the South Kensington Museums, make a better display of architecture. A little experience will reconcile the stranger to the general dowdiness of house exteriors, when he learns that the English climate has caused the English people to think most of the home within. The contrast on entering these plain structures is startling and gratifying. While this home love and home pride with homely ways are the strongest characteristics of the people, the saying of Charles the Second is still true, that there is no other country in which one can spend so many hours the year round in the open air. They spend as much of their daylight as possible out of doors and their evenings at home have a hearty, informal, delightful charm, wholly in contrast to the stiff and stagy receptions known in other cities.

The innate love of country life is shown by rich and poor alike. On the four legal bank holidays, the Monday after Christmas, Easter Monday, Whitsun Monday, and the first Monday in August, all business is suspended throughout the land, in most cases from the Friday evening until Tuesday morning. Then the masses come forth in all their might and finery, they take possession of the street vehicles, the railways and boats. The "upper" and "upper middle" classes religiously stay at home on those days, dreading the uproarious throngs of 'Arries and 'Arriets, who jam themselves ten deep into seats for five and monopolize every place of amusement. Yet it is a cheery sight to see all these hundreds of thousands of London toilers hurrying on wheels of all sorts away to Epping Forest, kept in its virgin state these four hundred years, and to Hampstead Heath, the Crystal Palace, the great parks, and similar handy breathing places, not to mention the favorite resorts within a twenty-mile radius. You will smile at grown folks playing skip the rope the whole day long, and kiss in the ring, and such like primitive games, but it is a wholesome sign when a whole population can find hearty pleasure in romping on the grass, for simple delights gained by healthy open-air exercise yield a more lasting happiness than is to be got by paying money to sit still and see hirelings make antics for you.

These outlying places are the crowning glory of London. Beautiful Windsor, Richmond Park, Kew Gardens, Epping Forest, and the ideally delightful Edens that nestle along the bends of the upper Thames, are all within the twenty-five mile circle, though one can find fifty fairy-grounds within five miles from any city station, where one can sprawl on the velvet grass beneath some spreading oak, and drink in the balmy scent-laden air, out of sight and sound of bricks and mortar. You may, certainly, be disturbed by the carolling of larks, linnets and others of the feathered choir, and perhaps by the waftings of some village church's silvery peal of bells, celebrating a wedding on the general holiday merrymaking. Even in the very heart of London's busiest quarters one can instantaneously step from the streets into grassy enclosures with great old trees, as silent and restful as if we were in some monastic cloister a century or two back. Until it has been experienced it is impossible to realize the beauty and mental relief of being able to turn from the rush and roar of the great city into one of these lovely retreats, or into the Cathedral, or Abbey, or nearest old church, where "the dim, religious light" of the stained windows, and the poetry of design and associations, and perhaps the pealing organ, waft the jaded senses into lotos land.

Coming back to details of another kind it is to be remarked that for noise, we can conscientiously claim our own New York as champion unrivalled. This item of metropolitan noise in some wise hits off the characteristics of the nations. New York has its fearsome rattle-clatter, sharp, pungent, nerve-racking, incessant, typical of the ceaseless "hurry-up" of its folk, in talk and motion. All is "rapid-transit" rush, anyhow, anywhere. Paris has its light, flitting, skipping, pittypat noise, as of a million chattering magpies busy shifting quarters. London has altogether another noise—a deep, soft diapason, Niagara-like in its immensity and pitch—a low melodious roar, the noise of "the roaring loom of time"; noises of the past; great booming echoes of dead centuries; the wailings of populations crushed by endless wars, oppressed by dynasties of tyrants, crowned and uncrowned; smitten to death by plagues; swept out of life by Ignorance, Poverty, Evil Fate. Great London has gathered the voices of the peoples in a thousand years of matchless history, and he who listens aright can hear them all as they go up to heaven in the mighty volume of its sun-dimmed incense of smoke.

This London is a miniature world. It is made up of representatives of every nationality; is the hive of every land's industry; the market-place for every country's products. It is the mart where traders from all the ends of the earth transact their business; the bank to which every nation and tribe intrust their gains; the parlor, the parleying-place, the parliament of the earth, where rulers and subjects, races and clans, leaders and followers, explorers, travellers, scholars, reformers, do their best talking, most of it in the hearing of all peoples who use the English tongue.

LONDON BRIDGE

London is more than all this. It is the purgatory and the elysium of generations of Britain's great souls. As the centuries have cast their hallowed tints of sombre gray over her dumbly eloquent stones, they have seen a long procession of sad figures threading the old, quaint, crooked byways and highways, figures of gaunt men and weary women, dropping out from the ranks here and there from sheer want of the wherewithal of life. These have been the forerunners, the seed-sowers, the pioneers of England's greatness—singers and seers, planners and day-dreamers, toilers with hand and brain, potential Cæsars and Alfreds, Shakespeares and Arkwrights, Wrens, Reynoldses and Wellingtons, without a ray of the ripening sunshine. Old England had its genius-breeders long before the luckier later sons were born. Not a stone of St. Paul's that glorifies the powers of its designers but is also, when you rightly look, a tombstone to the memory of some unknown toiler whose brain, heart, muscle or blood was spent to make that cathedral sublime; nor can you pick up a page of your Chaucers, Shakespeares, Miltons, Goldsmiths, and Tennysons but, if you scan it closely enough, you will find it stained with the tears of countless strugglers, who wrought themselves sore in the cause of man's elevation, only to earn a nameless grave for themselves. Pioneers, they sank, but their bones so enriched the soil that the London which was a purgatory to them is an elysium to us to-day, pacing whose witching shades we may see, if we close our eyes on inferior sights, the ghosts of the legion of Greathearts who haunt the old home, whose coldness to them in their own day they have avenged by making it glow with the glory of their names and works.

This is the crowning charm of London the unique—that we tread on ground every inch of which has its thrilling story to tell. There Shakespeare trod. Here Marlowe fell. Here Otway died, starved. Here Carey fainted, foodless. Here Goldsmith trailed footsore, hungry, despairing of fame. Here Johnson and Savage tramped the street all night with three cents between them for coffee at the street stall in the early morning. Here gentle De Quincey slept on the doorsteps. Hear him: "So then, Oxford Street, stony-hearted stepmother, thou that listenest to the sighs of orphans and drinkest the tears of children, the time was come at last, that I no more should pace in anguish thy never-ending terraces; no more should dream, and wake in captivity to the pangs of hunger. Thou, Oxford Street, hast echoed to the groans of innumerable hearts!" Aye, and still do thy throbbing streets, O glorious, pitiless London, reverberate with the wails of unsuspected thousands! To-day, this very day, the artist, the poet, the scholar, the inventor, the helpless sons of genius may perish, and most literally do perish, die of the heart-break that is born of hunger, in the wilderness of merry London. Who cannot readily recall a score of these tragedies, within any past score of years, where genius, talent, worth, character, industry, patient effort, failed to win recognition for the ill-fated ones—until the day *after* their lamentable death?

Glasgow, Dublin, Liverpool, Manchester.

London is not the typical English city, though types of almost every city in the eastern hemisphere can be unearthed in its mazes by those who know. The traveller who would get an understanding view of the United Kingdom must visit the great centres of industry in England, the sources of its modern strength, and take a look at the chief cities of Scotland and Ireland. But if he would penetrate deeper into the heart of the nation he will do well to halt by the way and get in touch with the unpretentious towns and lovely country scenes from whose old-fashioned folks most of the makers of the great cities have sprung.

Leaving London for the north a passing thought is due to Birmingham, the most American of English cities in its marvellous activities, metal work of every kind especially, from "ancient" idols for pagan temples in the East to exquisite altar-plate and prayer-book bindings for the institutional foes of idolatry. The local corruption of the name into Brummagem has added a descriptive term to the language, and it also illustrates the interesting fact that these local pronunciations usually preserve historical fact, as the now important city used to be no more than a hamlet adjoining Bromwich, hence Brumwich-ham. It showed the way, in the early seventies, how municipalities of unsalaried and unselfish citizens can acquire their own lighting and waterworks and otherwise carry on the town's business at an immense saving over the ordinary system. A new city has arisen out of the old one and the running expenses are lower than ever. Sheffield, the centre of the cutlery industry, is well worth studying for a day, for its activity, the surrounding scenery, and the effect of foreign competition upon its staple trade.

Manchester is familiar as the mother of the cotton trade. Its fortune was made by its spinning and weaving enterprises, by its quick utilization of the steam-engine and the inventions of mechanical genius. The first working railway was that which ran between Manchester and Liverpool in 1830. It first gave England the honor of being regarded as the workshop of the world. The wider adaptations of steam power and the establishment of free trade enriched its capitalists and merchants beyond the dreams of their fathers. Many a Lancashire millionaire could not write his name. Within the memory of middle-aged men there have been great enterprises, princely philanthropies, and striking public speeches by self-made magnates who could not compose letters nor speak gracefully without help from others. The city is marked by its pillar of smoke by day and of furnace fire by night. Its wise people carry their umbrellas as constantly as their pocket-books, for "the rain it raineth every day," at least drizzleth. The population of Manchester and its twin city, Salford, touches three-quarters of a million, sturdy and stern Britons, proudly dubbing themselves "Manchester men," in distinction from "Liverpool gentlemen."

Its murky air, ungainly factories and buildings generally, impress the stranger with its intensely practical spirit. The poetry of existence reveals itself in the cosy interiors and the charming outskirt residences. It has romance in its history and associations. Mancastra was a Roman camp in the reign of Titus. Under the Saxons and the later Normans it fashioned itself to the times just as it did to the magic wand of the nineteenth-century genius. It fought for the Parliament against the Royalists. For more than three centuries it led in woollen and, latterly, cotton manufactures. Its district is rich in coal-mines. The Bridgewater Canal dates from 1761, the principal one in the country. A greater, though apparently a less wise, because unprofitable, enterprise, has been the ship-canal. American cotton has always been unshipped at Liverpool, by which its brokers have greatly profited. To save tolls, delays and cost of rail transport, Manchester men made an imitation Suez Canal by deepening and adapting certain waterways, by which ships can pass into the new port of Manchester without troubling Liverpool. It may be hard to realize that Manchester can scarcely hope to become again the world's cotton factory, seeing that she has not only taught other nations how to do her work, but has long been selling them her machinery and coal for that purpose. A momentous sign of the times is the rapid migration of her capital and brain to Japan and India, where operatives of sufficient skill are content with a mere fraction of the home-workers' wage, and ocean transport is saved.

The sight-seer will be charmed by the noble city hall with its tall tower, its peal of twenty-one bells, and the public recitals on its great organ. Manchester possesses the oldest free library in the world, Chetham's, with 40,000 rare old books ranged on the shelves in the old mansion rooms where some of them have reposed for nearly three hundred years. It also has the first of modern free libraries on the grand scale, opened in 1851, a gift from a citizen, greatly enlarged since. Its famous Free Trade Hall has echoed with the eloquence of the world's famous men and women, in speech and song. Scarcely an American statesman or orator of note, being in England since 1856, but has been cheered by its audiences. The public meetings of all kinds in this hall have been among the most valuable educational influences of the half century. It was said by Lord Salisbury, many years before he became Premier, that "as Manchester thinks to-day, England thinks to-morrow," and it used to be true.

The traveller should try to be in Manchester in Whitsun Week, to see its most striking characteristic. It is the Sunday-school children's gala time and all business is demoralized in their honor. On the Monday twenty or thirty thousand Church of England scholars march with bands to a service in the Cathedral, the whole town and country around crowding the streets. Tuesday is the only off-day. Every other one is a half-holiday for those who do not take whole ones. Each church gives its scholars picnics in parks or on local farms in the afternoons, and a whole day's country outing on one day. Friday is the grown folks' picnic day, and on Saturday the Total Abstainers' parade. They are called Tee-totallers, because one of the founders, a Lancashire man, happened to stammer in a speech in trying to say *total abstinence.*

The Cathedral is not a great edifice, but has many remarkable fifteenth-century carvings and side chapels. It is affectionately known, in the local vernacular, as "t'owd church," the old church. On Easter Mondays the villagers and working folk used to crowd in to be married, as many as two hundred couples being despatched at a blow, the same service answering for all simultaneously. The city may be proud of its Victoria University, the development of Owen's College, founded in 1847. Of its many famous characters, the names of De Quincey and Harrison Ainsworth are perhaps the best known in literature.

Liverpool is thirty-six miles from Manchester and three from the sea. Its first charter was granted in 1229 and it sent two members to Parliament in 1296, yet its population until the seventeenth century was only about one thousand. It has the distinction of having made the first dock, penning up with flood-gates sufficient water to keep ships afloat between the fall and rise of tides. This was built in 1709. It is unkind, though true, to record that Liverpool's first fortune was made in the slave-trade. Its ships went to the west coast of Africa and took in cargoes of natives whom they then transported to the West Indies as slaves, being paid for by cargoes of sugar and rum, brought home to Liverpool. This traffic began about 1720. It was suppressed by Parliament in 1807, the number of ships then engaged in it being 185, carrying over forty thousand slaves annually. A good deal of privateering was carried on during the eighteenth-century wars, an echo of which survived until the American Civil War of 1861-65.

Liverpool has many unique features of interest. It has not many manufactures, and only four or five ship-building establishments, for reasons which will appear in the pages on Glasgow. Its commercial growth has been extraordinary. In 1800 the population was under 78,000; in 1900 it was about 750,000. In the first-named year the tonnage of its ships was 450,000, and is now nearly 10,000,000. Its commerce is chiefly with America. A magnificent sight is its endless array of docks, stretching along both shores of the Mersey in a line, measured continuously, of over thirty miles. Many a stately procession of great ships glides up the spacious river, laden with precious cargoes not to be estimated by statistics. Over fifty thousand Americans, it is said, visit England each summer, entering by this majestic water-gate. Who shall tell the influence of this mingling of kindred peoples, the moral and national worth of all they bring and all they take?

It is a new city, as towns go in the old country, with few visible marks of its history. The public buildings are not specially imposing, but St. George's Hall stands on a commanding site and in exterior and interior holds its own with the best civic temples, in spaciousness and grace. The great public library near by does honor to the city and to its donor. The art gallery is remarkable for its construction, as for its exhibits. It has a circular floor of one hundred feet in diameter without columns or any intermediate support, and beneath it is an amphitheatre, used for lectures, with its benches hewn out of the solid rock.

To ferry across the river to Birkenhead and Bootle, and down to New Brighton and other popular resorts, is an excellent way to appreciate the greatness of this famous port. As a city it has little charm, except in its surroundings.

All the excitements of the transatlantic voyage may be had in miniature (except the *mal de mer*) in crossing the lively channel to Dublin. The metropolis of Ireland must not be judged by commercial and cosmopolitan standards.

A city of many contrasts, stirring associations and poetical interest, two patriotisms, two grand divisions of its community, are discernible in the air. On the one hand is the Castle, lacking the castle feature and charm, with a pervading sense of royalism *minus* the outward symbols of state which give it popularity and influence. On the other is the vibrant nationalism which, in many tones and by a hundred tokens, expresses its hostility to the emblems of what it regards as alien dominance. Pathetic in its way is the decay of once fashionable, not to say aristocratic, districts, that have lapsed into commonplace, and many fine streets hobnob with veritable slums. This gradual decline of much residential property impoverished old families and added to the sum of general discontent. Dublin has never taken kindly to the idea of becoming a commercial city, such as Liverpool. The intellectual head of the island, it prides itself on the genius of its professional people.

Irish eloquence shines as brightly as ever in its pulpits, in the law courts, and, indeed, wherever public speech is heard. The Four Courts enshrine the fame of many a gifted patriot orator and wit. Trinity College, founded by Queen Elizabeth, has made its mark not simply in the island and kingdom but all over the world. The same is true of its colleges in general.

The city lions are these buildings, the Castle, Phœnix Park, St. Patrick's Cathedral and sundry monuments. One world-important industry has done wonders for the city. The Guiness product rebuilt the Cathedral out of its decaying remains. A local distillery has contributed nobly to the city's reputation for progress. Singular it certainly is that the most appreciated malt liquor of the kind known as stout, should be produced in three cities, Dublin, London, and Philadelphia, each of which can boast the filthiest river in its country, the Liffey, the Thames, and the Schuylkill.

Dublin earth quickly turns to black bog under the frequent rains. Yet neither its mud nor its political differences can damp the cheery spirits of its natives. This is one great delight of a journey to the island. Usually we see what we set out to see anywhere. No matter whether our quest is for city shows or the lovely rural scenery, or the sports on the Curragh, or the woes of the impoverished masses, we cannot pass a single hour without marvelling at the native good-humor and good wit of even the most distressful-conditioned people. Where less gifted sufferers grow melancholy-visaged, the Irish greet misfortune with a continual smile, in which fact lies a world of hope, and not a little envy.

Up in Belfast the austere-faced Ulstermen have made a commercial centre of the first rank. Ship-building and the flax industry, with others, flourish, and the city might be a civic paradise if faction warfare could be cooled down.

Passing now to Glasgow we find ourselves in a city of comparative palaces. Its buildings are of sandstone, its streets handsome, its municipal government so admirable as to have become the model for American cities. The canny Scot may be trusted to make the citizen's penny bring a full pennyworth. The city authorities own their plants for providing the people with light, and for bringing the pure waters of Loch Katrine into every home. They went a step farther and bought the public tramways and cars, giving the people cheaper travel than had ever been known.

Glasgow stole the greater part of Liverpool's ship-building business and Belfast a goodly share. Miles and miles of the banks of the Clyde are decorated with skeletons of new vessels waiting to be clothed in steel or wood garb. Every variety of craft is to be seen, from the battle-ship to the racing yacht. But Glasgow turns its hands to everything makable and salable. Its three-quarters of a million inhabitants work at innumerable trades. Their success shows in the substantial build of their city, which has more than a liberal allowance of splendid structures. Modern and up-to-date, its whirl of daily life recalls New York in certain aspects. This modernness in architectural effect is the more striking when we stand in the High Street and reflect that the grand national hero, William Wallace, fought a battle with the English on this spot in 1300. The city's patron saint, Kentigern, gave it its name in the sixth or seventh century, *glasgu*, the dear family, after a band of his disciples settled there. Its cathedral, old St. Mungo's, takes its name also from Kentigern's *munghu*, or most loved friend. Its charter, authorizing the holding of a free market, was granted in 1175. Commercial development dates from 1707, when the union with England was settled. Glasgow University traces its beginnings to 1450. In making a new dock recently the diggers brought to light a boat, formed out of the trunk of a tree, a relic of primeval seamanship. The scenery of the Clyde, and for miles beyond its banks, has been the theme of many a poetical description by American travellers. The reader of Scott needs no reminder of its richness in historic story. But is not all Scotland a picture-poem of stirring romance?

"Auld" Edinburgh is written of elsewhere in this volume by its brilliant son. American newspapers that lop off the final letter, also objected to in Pittsburgh, are evidently unaware that it is pronounced Edinborough (burrow). The unrivalled queen of British cities, the uncommercial capital of Scotland, its ancient capital and its present glory, is worth the pilgrimage, even from old Athens and Rome. The towering castle was begun twelve centuries ago. St. Giles's church dates from 1110. It was a walled town in 1450. Progressive in the sleepy old days, it set up its first printing-press, one of the world's first presses, in 1507, and has been literary ever since. The early rulers brought musicians and scholars from abroad to delight their courts, and many jealousies they caused.

KENILWORTH AND WARWICK CASTLES.

ELIHU BURRITT.

[Elihu Burritt, the "Learned Blacksmith," wrote two works of mingled description and economic observation in the British island, these being "A Walk from John O'Groat's to Land's End" and "Walks in the Black Country and its Green Border-Land." It is from the "green border-land" section of the latter that we take the following description of two of England's most famous ancient castles.]

Between Coventry and Warwick, in a green, quiet rural district, stands Kenilworth, and Kenilworth is a castle which absorbs into itself all of space, population, and history that belongs to the name. Not only novel-readers, but practical history-readers at a distance, never think of anything but the castle when the name is mentioned or suggested.

Still, there is a goodly, tidy, and comfortable village near the ruins worth visiting, without the lion which attracts so many thousands a year to pay their homage and their admiration—to the genius of Sir Walter Scott. All the ordinary trades of a practical business community are carried on in this village; and a tall, taper chimney of a tannery, as high as any church steeple, smokes its pipe in the face of all the romantic antiquities of the place. Still, the people would probably confess that the principal source of their income is derived from their vested interest in Sir Walter Scott's "Kenilworth," not in the real castle walls. Take away that famous novel, and, with all the authenticated history that remains attached to them, not one in five of the visitors they now attract would walk around them with admiration. In fact, they are more a monument to the genius of the great novelist than to the memory of Elizabeth and the Earl of Leicester. If any community ever owed a statue to the honor of a benefactor for money value received, the Kenilworths owe one to the celebrated Scotch writer. One might reasonably estimate that his book has been worth ten thousand pounds a year to them for the last quarter of a century or more.

There are observatories, barometer and anemometer stations around the coasts of England, where rain-falls and wind-blows, tide-risings and star-showers are registered. There are other observation-stations where the self-registering offices of human fames and reputations are kept, and where these are measured spontaneously. Go to Stratford and look at the inner walls of Shakespeare's house and the record kept there, and count the names from the four quarters of the globe written there in homage of the great bard; go to Abbotsford, and consult the day-book of that great memory; go to Olney, and see what manner and multitude of names cover and re-cover the little garden summer-house in which Cowper wrote, and you will have this self-registration of human genius and its appreciation. So at Kenilworth, the visitors' day-book at the hotel will show how many come from both hemispheres and all their continents to see the scene of Sir Walter Scott's romance.

I was favored with a bright day on the sunny edge of autumn for my visit, when the very sky imparts a radiance to the ivied ruins of old castles and abbeys. Kenilworth shows its successive ages and uses in the various departments of its structure. From the ground it occupied, one would hardly conceive it to be a fighting castle. But when you come to look at the massive Cæsar's Tower, you will be impressed with its impregnability in the bow-and-arrow period of English warfare. Its lofty walls hold their frontage and perpendicular lines as true and even as if they were a last-year's structure. It is seemingly composed of several towers connected by walls sixteen feet thick, perforated by window-holes which look like so many archways. It is built or faced with hewn red sandstone, and is a perfect specimen of mason-work. The Insurgent Barons stood a siege of six months against Henry III. behind these strong walls, and in the reign of Edward I. Roger Mortimer, Earl of March, presided over a grand tournament beneath them.

In a later century the castle passed into the hands of John o' Gaunt, who added the noble structure called the Lancaster Buildings, or banqueting-hall. This must have been one of the finest specimens of architecture of his time in England, and, in ruins, presents the graceful proportions and embellishments of its structure. Under the *régime* of that celebrated nobleman the castle began to put on a civilian dress over its coat of mail, and to echo with the music and mirth of dancing and feasting, instead of the clangor of arms.

But Robert Dudley, Earl of Leicester, completed the transformation into a residential palace. He not only added the wing called the Leicester Buildings, but he renovated and embellished all the old portions of the huge pile. He erected an ante-castle, or a great gate house, which is a noble structure in itself. Never did a subject build, and rebuild, and embellish on such a scale as he did to receive his sovereign.

Three times Elizabeth was his guest. Her last visit was in July, 1575, and lasted seventeen days. Of the festivities and princely entertainments he prepared for her on this occasion Sir Walter Scott has written with all that natural enthusiasm and predilection with which, perhaps, above all other

English novelists, he dilated upon such a subject. His graphic descriptions of these scenes are so familiar to the million that I will not venture to go behind his brilliant fictions in search of actual historical facts of duller interest. The day of such favorites has gone by, like the beauty and glory of this once gorgeous fabric. The sun of Christian morality and civilization has risen to a purer flood of light, and such broad-faced gallantries would now be looked out of countenance in high places....

The facing of the massive and lofty Cæsar's Tower must be nearly three centuries old, and it is wonderfully perfect. The perpendicular lines from base to battlement are as straight as if the walls were run in a mould; the eye cannot detect a deflection of a hair's breadth, nor has time been able to eat into the smooth and even surface. I noticed, however, that "the brave old ivy green," which braids such bandages for the wounds made by time and human violence in abbeys and castles, had wound around the front of this huge tower such a thick spread that it had deadened the skin of the wall and was eating into the solid body of it like a caustic blister. There were men at work on tall ladders, removing this thick green bandage and letting the sun in upon the stone, which had not seen its light for years.

The Gate House is in excellent preservation, and is occupied by a tenant of the Earl of Clarendon. The towers are supported by old pear-trees that clasp their long arms around the stone-work and hug it so tightly that you may see their impress in the wall. It is a pleasant sight, which a poet might make something of, to see them hanging their clusters of luscious fruit up and down, as if, like the idea expressed in Solomon's Song, they were staying the venerable building with apples and cheering delicacies. Indeed, for its historical associations, as well as for the architectural character disclosed in its picturesque ruins, Kenilworth, perhaps, stands at the very head of all old English castles as an object of popular interest. If a self-registering apparatus could be put in operation at the gate opening to it, which would number and record the human feet, just as some instruments register the rain-drops that fall, doubtless no other castle in England would show such a census of visitors as this.

Warwick Castle! England and all who speak its language owe the successive inheritors of this great living pile of buildings more than they have ever acknowledged; for it is really the only baronial castle that has survived the destruction or decay of all the other monuments of the feudal ages of the same order. We should not know what they were in their day and generation were it not for this. It helps our fancy to fill up the vast breaks in the walls of Kenilworth, Dudley, and Chepstow; to reconstruct their banqueting-halls, their drawing-rooms, galleries, crypts, and kitchens, and to reproduce them entire in their first and fullest grandeur. By the light of Warwick we can not only rebuild and roof the broken walls of these old castles, but bring into the vista of the imagination their interior embellishments, their carved cornices and wainscoting, their luxurious furniture, tapestry, paintings, and other works of art. Thus, Warwick represents to us in its living being and form of to-day the hundreds of castles that were planted over the island in the first century after the Conquest. Schamyl in his native costume and dignity could not represent better at St. Petersburg the leaders of the Circassian race and country than does this grand home and fortress of the Warwicks the embattled citadels of the old English knights.

Warwick Castle, the fortress of one of the stoutest and grimmest of the old English fighting knights, did not put on the armor of nature to help out its own. It did not take advantage of perpendicular rocks or river-sides like Stirling, Edinburgh, or Chepstow. At first thought one might fancy the founders of it selected the location more for fishing than fighting. And now, in these quiet sunny days of peace, with its venerable mane of cedar-trees, it looks like a grand old lion lying down with its paw tenderly over a tired lamb. Or, it basks its broad side on the bank of the Avon, which photographs its walls and towers and turrets every bright day in the centuries. The castle is all intact and entire, with no part clean gone or going to ruin. Inside and out, from end to end, it is the harmonious growth of many ages, and registers them in distinctive illustrations. It shows what can be done by a dozen generations of wealthy men, inheriting an estate that doubles in income every half-century. Here each branch of the wide-spreading family tree has hung in festooned clusters the foliage of its life, genius, and taste. Each has contributed its contingent to the magnificent whole to be handed down to a posterity which should cherish and adorn the heirloom of illustrious ancestors, and send it down the line of the future with added wealth and beauty.

With such an anchorage to moor a family name and estate to, there is no wonder that both should attach their being, life, and treasures to it with a proud ambition of perpetuity. The name holds on as everlastingly as the estate. For the poorest man on earth must have some distant relation, and the richest man's son would take the name of the twentieth cousin to inherit the title and castle of Warwick. However thin and attenuated may be the line of blood relationship between these families, the favored heir to this baronial rank and wealth gathers within his coronet all the memories and distinctions and even relationships of his predecessors all the way back to the Conquest. He is the heir of all of them; Saxon, Dane, and Norman converge into his *status* and blend in his being....

The great body of the castle itself, viewed detached from its grand surrounding walls and towers, presents no very salient features. It is a long range of buildings, with a straight front on the river. It never had the imposing or varied frontage of Dudley Castle in its day, or the palace halls that flanked the great tower of Kenilworth. But in its large straight suite of lofty apartments you have a museum of objects illustrating the tastes, habits, fashions, luxuries, and arts of all the ages and generations which those massive walls have seen. Passing from end to end, you may gauge English history for seven centuries with an observing glance through these objects. Here the white-winged dove of Peace has made her nest in the rusty and battered helmet of grim-visaged war.

On entering the Great Hall one is deeply impressed with its capacious faculty of hospitable entertainment. Truly, if tables were ever spread from end to end, a regiment of guests must have sat down to the banquet. It is sixty-two feet in length by forty in breadth, and the roofage of it is lofty and done in elaborate Gothic, rich in carving and other ornament. Here are the coronets and shields of all the earls back to Henry de Newburgh, who seem to look down upon the company below through their cognizances, as if represented in and countenancing all the generous hospitalities their living heir is disposed to give. The walls are wainscoted with the brave old English oak, far advanced in its seeming transformation into ebony. All you ever read in romance or veritable history about walls hung with armor of crusaders and other knightly raiders, interspersed with spoils of the chase, is here realized in full; and you see that even Sir Walter Scott has not exaggerated the fact in this respect. Conspicuous on the genealogical tree of these weapons and outfittings for war is the helmet usually worn, says the loyal guide-book, by the usurper Cromwell. Here, too, is the doublet in which Lord Brooke was killed at Lichfield, in 1643.

Three great Gothic windows are set out in deep recesses, as if to embrace and welcome the first and last light of the day, and to soften and diffuse it, a tinted smile, over the spacious apartment and its embellishments. But if the outside world smiles inward through these great windows so graciously, their outward vision opens upon a scene of exquisite beauty, which few can be found to equal. Here a vista deploys before the view full of all the attractions that nature and art can give to a landscape. What a pier-glass is to the richest drawing-room, the gentle and classic Avon is to this variegated scenery, as a portion of it, and as a reflecting medium of all its other features. It meanders through the landscape as a limpid hem to lawn, field, grove, garden, and forest, now flashing a silver radiance, now one of gold, upon the robe it adorns, just as the sun's rays vary in their fall and flood. Right before the face and eyes of the castle, the river forms a great brooch of emerald, or a little green island, which may be taken for its coat of arms, or *cognizance*, much older and nobler than any hung up in the Great Hall. Then the soft and level river, looking half asleep, or checking its flow in the presence of these human antiquities, just below them arises and stands on its feet, showing a stature one hundred feet high in a cascade that sings a kind of lullaby to the by-gone ages whose spirits haunt the castle.

It was in these grounds that, in 1846, I saw for the first time a real cedar of Lebanon, and I never shall forget the impression it made upon me. Here they stood, grand and venerable, with their long low arms extended as if pronouncing "a benediction after prayer" upon the green lawn that mirrored their august entourage. Here they stood, singing the same old song they sang to David on Mount Lebanon. It was a mere fancy; but I listened to the soughing murmur with the thought that they were reciting to each other some of his best psalms of praise and thanksgiving.

From the Great Hall you have a vista of state rooms on one side, and private or family rooms on the other, extending in a straight line for three hundred and thirty-three feet. All these apartments, large and small, are adorned and enriched with specimens of high art and high labor, collected by all the families that have owned and occupied the estate. In some respects each room, if not the museum, is the mirror, of its age. Armor and articles of luxurious or antique furniture divide with pictures of the same dates the admiration of the visitor. Here is the celebrated painting of Charles I. by Vandyke, for which Sir Joshua Reynolds offered to pay five hundred guineas in his time. How much it would bring under the hammer to-day those who know the existing *furore* for the old masters may easily estimate. And all the old masters are here, represented each in several of the pictures that made their fame. In fact, a national gallery of paintings, of creditable number and variety, might be filled from the treasures of art exhibited in these splendid apartments. Here figure Rubens, Rembrandt, Vandyke, Salvator Rosa, Guido, Murillo, David, and other great artists of different ages, schools, and countries.

Then, as the framework of all these pictures, you see the artistry of the chisel, or carved work in wood and stone of contemporary schools in that department. Then the garnered treasures collected by these various branches of the family, purchased in different centuries and countries, are arranged in happy taste and harmony with the pictorial adornments. Wardrobes, cabinets, tables, and all the articles of luxurious furniture found in palaces, English or Continental, modern or ancient, are here in all their variety and curious workmanship.

The "Kenilworth Buffet," a work which attracted so much admiration in the Great Exhibition of 1851, is a masterpiece of design and execution. It is Kenilworth and its romantic history, with the principal acts and actors of its Elizabethan drama, carved in oak from a tree that stood a green, tall sentinel of nature at the time to witness the festive scenes. Even Elizabeth's meeting with Amy Robsart, and her interview with Leicester after the exposure of his faithlessness, are done to the life by the carver's chisel.

Two objects connected with Warwick Castle every one, young or old, who visits it, will remember perhaps most distinctively. They are the "Guy's porridge-pot" and the great marble Vase. Both are of prodigious capacity, the very Gog and Magog of all hollow-ware. The Irishman who called the donkey the father of all rabbits would call this large porridge-pot the father of all kettles. Its history cannot be got out of it by the grave and solemn thumpings that the old woman gives its massive sides. So it is ascribed to the great Guy's time and to his personal use. As ornithologists deduce the size and habits of some prehistoric bird by a single foot-track in petrified clay, so the size, strength, and other capacities of that legendary giant are deduced from the size of this remarkable pot. The analogy might seem reasonable to many simple-minded people. Surely no man could be less than eight feet and a half high who needed such a kettle for cooking for himself and family, even if his children were nearly as large as himself. And this is the size accorded to that prehistoric hero. He was one of those amphibious beings who, like King Arthur, have lived in the misty border-land of history, half substance and half shadow, but projecting a full human outline upon the spectrum of by-gone centuries.

The history of the Great Vase is more ancient and uncertain still. It is of white marble, executed in the purest Grecian order of conception and art. It is truly a mighty goblet, with two handles of intertwisted vine-branches and wreathed and crowned with the tendrils, leaves, and clusters of the vineyard. It was fished up from the bottom of a lake near Tivoli by the British ambassador then at Naples, from whom it passed into the hands of the father of the present earl, who conveyed it to England and placed it in its present position.

The high and solid walls that enclose the castle and their great towers impress you with the realities of the ages they represent. Erected before gunpowder had been brought into the field of battle, they still look as if the builders anticipated its introduction and power, and they would stand a heavy battering now, old as they are, by common cannon. In a word, Warwick Castle is a structure which must grow more and more interesting from decade to decade. It is the only feudal palace left intact in England. It was ranked among the very best of them when they were all alive and strong over the land. It is associated with a name that stands among the first in the Norman aristocracy. Its location in itself is deeply interesting. Shakespeare breathed an inspiration upon the little Avon that laves its foundations, and gave to its name an immortality more vital and beautiful than the Tiber's. All these aspects and associations are becoming more and more widely appreciated; and the footfall of visitors from distant countries crossing the threshold will grow more and more frequent as the readers of English history and romance increase in both hemispheres.

WINDSOR FOREST AND CASTLE.

ANONYMOUS.

[It is to the author of "English Forests and Forest-Trees," who fails to give his name on the title-page of a work whose authorship is amply worthy of acknowledgment, that we owe our present selection. Among the various historic forests of England, that of Windsor ranks high, and the adjoining castle was the seat of many interesting episodes of English history. The selection we give is mainly confined to the scenery and traditions of the forest.]

Windsor forest and castle are dear to all Englishmen. Few palaces have grouped around them so many associations, both legendary, historical, and poetical, from the time of Arthur and the knights of his Round Table to those of the royal house of Hanover. The castle has been the abode of royalty from the time of the Saxon kings. It was while King John lived at Windsor that the barons obtained from him the Magna Charta. Cromwell has held his courts within its walls, and Charles I. lies buried in its chapel. A Scottish king has been a captive here, and here have been celebrated some of the most splendid pageants and courtly ceremonies recorded in history. The forest, though it can scarcely be said now to exist, has also some "legends of woe and dread," and other associations.

The forest was once of enormous extent, comprehending a circumference of one hundred and twenty miles.... In the lapse of time, however, it dwindled away; for we find that in the reign of James I. its circumference was estimated by Norden at only seventy-seven miles and a half, exclusive of the liberties extending into Bucks. At this period there were fifteen walks within it, each under the charge of a head keeper, and the whole contained upward of three thousand head of deer. This extent was somewhat diminished in later years; for in a subsequent map, by Roque, the circuit is given as fifty-six miles.

In the year 1813 an act of Parliament was passed for its enclosure. The portion which had been previously enclosed, known as Windsor Great Park, was of small extent compared with the whole range of the forest. The area of the park was less than four thousand acres, of which two thousand were under cultivation; while the open unenclosed forest amounted to twenty-four thousand acres. Scarce a vestige of the forest is now left, except what has been apportioned to the crown, adjoining the Great Park.

The view from Windsor Castle is one of the finest in England. A vast panorama extending as far as the eye can reach. All flat,—the faint blue horizontal line, scarcely discernible from the clouds, so distant is it, as straight as the boundary of a calm sea,—and yet how infinitely varied! What would such an expanse of land be in any other country? A mere drugget compared to this Field of Cloth of Gold. A lovely river, to which the hackneyed illustration of molten gold might well be applied from the silent roll of its glittering waters, as if impeded by their own rich weight; now flashing like a strip of the sun's self through broad meadows whose green is scarcely less dazzling, now lost in shady nooks of wonderful and refreshing coolness. Trees of every sort and growth, singly, in clumps, in rows, everywhere. Little bright-looking villages, with their white spires or gray towers, dotted all over the scene. Everything is in perfect harmony. The gentle murmur of human life, reaching us from the distance, is no more injurious to the effect than the rustling of trees or the chirping of the birds....

Our first homage is to Nature. The influence of the beautiful is predominant over all others. We think only of the scene before us, and must thoroughly enjoy it for its own sake before we can bestow a thought on a single association connected with it. We forget all about the walls we are standing on. We do not even reflect that the golden river is our old friend the Thames. It never strikes us that that expanse of green out there to the right, so thickly planted with massive elms and chestnuts, is a very celebrated place called the Home Park of Windsor, or indeed that it is called anything else—or anything at all. We are (metaphorically speaking) rolling in that grass with a republican contempt for its patrician connections, and picking out the best of those trees with an ungrateful heedlessness of what royal hand may have planted them there for our gratification.

[The author proceeds to describe some notable places surrounding. To the left, across the river, is Eton College; immediately facing is the town of Slough, where the Herschells made their residence; to the right is Stoke Poges, the scene of Gray's "Elegy"; to the extreme right is Runnymede, where King John signed Magna Charta; and nearer at hand is the village of Datchet, the scene of Falstaff's ducking, in the "Merry Wives of Windsor."]

And now, reader, it is high time we turned our attention to the forest side of the question.

By the forest we must be distinctly understood to mean, not merely the dense collection of wood to which the term is usually applied, but that aspect of nature generally wherein the wild and unchecked growth of forest-trees forms the principal feature. The so-called Windsor Forest has almost entirely disappeared, a few insignificant plantations alone retaining the title. The

Great Park, however,—indeed, the whole country south of the castle for several miles,—presents every variety of the class of scenery which it is our business to treat.

Our way into the Great Park lies along the celebrated avenue known as the Long Walk. This is no less than three miles in length, extending in a perfectly straight line from the castle, in a direction almost due south, to Snow Hill, a natural elevation surmounted by an equestrian statue of George III.

We have two good miles before us ere we can meet with an outlet that will enable us to ramble among the trees to our hearts' content. The Long Walk, however, is a very fine sight, in spite of its dire straightness. A splendid road, three miles long, bordered by double rows of giant elms, is not without interest. The regularity is not unpleasing, because not overstrained. The trees, once pressed into the service of order, have been allowed to grow their own way, instead of being clipped and cropped as they would be under similar circumstances in some countries,—France, to wit. Here we have Nature with her hair combed merely; there we should find her with her head shaved. The monotony of the perspective is nicely broken by the undulations of the ground. It is pleasant to turn occasionally into the aisle-like sidewalks, and look up at the cool green roof of trellis-work formed by the interlacing trees. Besides, the castle, as we look back at it receding from us, begins to recover something of its original character: Edward III. and William of Wykeham are resuming the ascendancy. The gradually deepening stillness, too, is exactly what we could wish. The rooks, hovering over us eternally, afford very agreeable companionship; and we consider their quiet, though apparently cynical, observations very much to the purpose indeed.

Ere we proceed far on our way, an object of once agreeable, now melancholy, interest attracts our attention. This is the famous Herne's Oak, which stands in the enclosure known as the Little Park, to our left. It is contended by some authorities that the veritable Herne's Oak was cut down by some orders of George III., delivered in a mistake as to its identity. Others, with a natural reluctance to believe so sagacious a monarch capable of such a blunder, maintain that the rumor originated in the fact of his majesty causing some similar trees in the vicinity to be cleared away, that the oak itself might occupy a more prominent position.

The agreeable interest attached to this famous tree is well known. It is supposed (though there has been much controversy as to its authenticity) to be the identical tree immortalized by the mention of Shakespeare as the scene of Herne the Hunter's unamiable exploits:

"There is an old tale goes, that Herne the Hunter,
Sometime a keeper here in Windsor forest,
Doth all the winter time, at still midnight,
Walk round about an oak, with great ragged horns;
And then he blasts the tree, and takes the cattle;
And makes milch-kine yield blood, and shakes a chain

In a most hideous and dreadful manner."

The interest we have alluded to of a melancholy description is of a more recent date, and is derived from the tantalizing fact that *Herne's Oakis no longer visible to the public*, the portion of the park in which it stands having been recently enclosed as an addition to the private grounds of the Duchess of Kent's residence at Frogmore.

We tried hard once to tempt an inflexible gate-keeper to let us in,—just to have a look at it. It was of no use. We assured him we should do no harm, and (as the most delicate means of suggesting a recompense) offered to pay the expenses of any trustworthy person he might choose to send to look after us. He was adamant,—no strangers were allowed in. We appealed to his feelings,—like Rolla and the sentinel,—asked him (in terms we considered adapted to his mental cultivation) how he would like to be a poet wrecked in sight of inspiration. His expressed opinion was that we were making fun of him.

He was not, however, a bad fellow; his sternness was a matter of duty, not constitution. He was touched by our disappointment, and sought to console us by the assurance that we had lost nothing; "that there was nothing to be seen in the tree; that it was about the ugliest he ever see in the whole park; and as for Herne the Hunter, it was nothing but a pack of old woman's rubbage."

However, neither our niggardly exclusion from the sight of the old tree, nor the materialist consolations of our friend the gate-keeper, can efface the impression on our mind of the grim forest-fiend haunting the old park like a family spectre.

There is no satisfactory legend of Herne the Hunter. Vague tradition states that he was a keeper in the forest in Elizabeth's reign, who, having committed some crime which occasioned his dismissal, hung himself on the tree. This is a view of the case we cannot think of taking. The idea of a discharged flunkey committing suicide on a mere sentimental consideration of wages and perquisites is a sorry foundation for the magnificent "demon business" indicated by Shakespeare. Our notion is of something far more weird and fiendish,—a story of fearful crimes and unhallowed compacts; something in the nightmare German ballad style....

It is a long lane that has no turning; we mean the Long Walk is. Passing through a handsome pair of lodge-gates, we emerge fairly into the Great Park.

Now we are in the Forest.

When we inform our reader that our first impulse is to run as fast as our legs can carry us, he will doubtless require an explanation.

Assuming that it is a fine day we have chosen for our ramble, in the first place we are surrounded by a bright and rarefied atmosphere, whose inhalation, to quote a lamented writer, is a process something between breathing and drinking. The scene has changed, as if by magic. The barrier we have just passed would seem to be a fairy circle, shutting out all matters pertaining to human life. Castles and towns are things we must have dreamt of somewhere long ago. We are in a vast solitude of grassy mounds and giant trees, in all their native luxuriance, spreading as far as the eye can reach. The stillness would be appalling but for the clamor of a million birds. We have heard of a native of Piccadilly, who, spending a night in the country for the only time in his life, declared that he had been unable to sleep, the confounded birds made such a noise. If we had a grudge against that native (and doubtless if we knew him we should not be long in forming one, as we certainly should not like him), and had it in our power to punish him in our own way, we should condemn him to sling a hammock on one of the trees in Windsor Great Park, and roost there for a week; for the birds in Windsor Great Park are the noisiest in the world.

These are the combined causes of an effect similar to that of laughing-gas, or something to drink, leading to gymnastic results such as we have indicated....

The rabbits of Windsor Park, by the way, are endowed with matchless impudence. They treat you with a familiarity which borders too close on contempt to be gratifying. They will scarcely get out of your way. They sit comfortably before their holes, lazily watching you go past with as much indifference as a country gentleman seated at his own door would the passing of a travelling tinker. The same may be said of the game generally with which the park abounds. The flocks of deer will go on browsing comfortably till you almost tread on their little black noses. Then there will be a short listless consultation as to whether you are a person to be tolerated or not. The leader will probably give a verdict in the negative, and they turn slowly round, all showing their powder-puffs of tails at once in the most insulting manner, and strut a few yards off, when they recommence their endless meal, merely regarding you as something of a bore and a nuisance, but in no serious light whatever.

Once we started a pheasant; he would not even pay us the compliment of flying. We ran at him violently; he ran a few yards off, and commenced pecking at something. We threw a stone at him; he ducked his head a little,— no more. We waved our hands and cried "Shoo!" in the most approved manner, demonstrations to which he would not condescend to pay the slightest attention. We ran towards him again; he ran away from us a short distance, and then before our very eyes roosted on an old rail with unmistakable intentions of going to sleep. This was insufferable. We could almost have knocked him down with our walking stick, and were sufficiently exasperated to think of trying, when the appearance of a game-keeper on the horizon suddenly made us look in an opposite direction, and commence a careful search for botanical specimens.

This tameness, which is shocking to us, is very different from the trusting innocence of Alexander Selkirk's happy family, who were

"So unaccustomed to man."

It is the insolent security of a privileged class. They know you are not allowed to shoot them, and the airs they give themselves are intolerable....

Descending a cool valley densely wooded with magnificent Scotch firs, we come to a bridge crossing a placid-looking lake of considerable dimensions. The stranger generally thinks this is Virginia Water; he is a little disappointed,—thinks it hardly merits the reputation it has earned for beauty,—but, on the whole, is not dissatisfied. He thinks it is probably a little better farther on, on one side or the other; he wonders which he ought to try; he is, however, loath to explore either till he has ascertained whether there is really anything to be seen or not (for your speculative sight-seer is a cautious fellow, and has a great objection to being taken in). Seeing a lodge-gate a little ahead, he proceeds there to ask whether there is any more of Virginia Water than what he has just left; not but what that was very delightful,—he merely wishes to know. The lodge-keeper laughs sardonically, and, good-naturedly blessing the stranger's eyes, tells him that is none of Virginia Water; then, with a look of contemptuous pity, seizes him by the arm, leads him impatiently to a little gate opening on to a thick wood, thrusts him in, and, bidding him follow his nose, returns to the lodge, satisfied at having nothing more to do with a person of *that* scale of intelligence.

Our plan is to follow the lodge-keeper's precept and the stranger's example. We pass through the little gate, and after a few seconds' walk through the wood, come unexpectedly on a very novel and delightful scene, of which we cannot speak in higher terms than to say that it fully merits the florid eulogium of the original edition of the *RoyalWindsor Guide*, already quoted.

We are standing on the brink of an immense lake, whose extent alone is sufficient to do away with all ideas of its artificial origin. This is completely enclosed by densely wooded acclivities, rising almost from the water's edge, one above the other, in agreeable perspective, so as to exclude the slightest glimpse of the world beyond. On one side of the lake a broad pathway of dark-green grass, yielding like a rich Turkey carpet to the tread, extends from one end of the lake to the other. Immediately on the left, the shelving woods begin to rise. There is not a sound to be heard except a gentle murmur of the trees, that never ceases.

The scene is not very romantic; but there is no earthly reason why it should be; it is very peaceful and very charming, suggesting all sorts of pleasant quiet-life recreations. The lake would not have suited Wordsworth, but it would have been the very thing for Izaak Walton. You could not get much poetry out of the woods, but you could get capital picnics in them; and there be those who despise poetry, but where is the ascetic who would turn up his nose at a picnic?

As we proceed, the view of the lake gets more extensive. The cool breeze from it, and the soft springy turf scarcely six inches above the level of the water, make the walk very agreeable. One feature is particularly worth mentioning; some of the largest and most beautiful specimens of that most dainty of English trees, the silvery birch, are to be seen gracefully dipping their light branches into the lake. At length the pathway takes a turn up into the wood, from which we soon emerge into an open space, where we come across an object that really startles us,—a classic temple in ruins!

These ruins are of course not genuine. At a second glance we recognize the masquerading tendencies of George IV., as developed by Sir Jeffrey Wyattville. There is, however, no objection to the exercise of such a whim in what was never intended to serve any other purpose than that of a gentleman's pleasure-ground. Moreover, the ruin has some claims to be considered as a work of art of no mean merit. The design is admirable, and the semblance of decay is wonderfully imitated. The broken columns seem to have lain there for ages. Huge trees obtrude themselves between the shattered fragments as if they had grown there since the building had fallen to ruin. Some portions are completely hidden by masses of ivy and lichen, apparently the growth of centuries. Altogether the thing is admirably "got up," and makes us think what a stage-manager Sir Jeffrey Wyattville would have made for arranging a Christmas spectacle.

We should remark that the materials, consisting of columns of red and gray granite and porphyry, and several marble statues, are of veritable antiquity. The greater portion were transferred from the outer court of the British Museum, the remainder being from the Elgin collection. The reason of the building being called the Temple of Augustus was probably because Sir Jeffrey thought that name would do for it quite as well as any other, in which case we quite agree with him....

The Great Park is rich in varied woodland scenery. There are not only fine thriving oaks, throwing out their gigantic arms, but sturdy pollards without end, which seem to have set time and season and decay at defiance. They are gnarled and knotted, twisted and distorted, yet at the same time sound and vigorous at heart. The beeches, too, may be seen of all ages and sizes, picturesque and beautiful in their decay, but while in full vigor, and dotted with their sparkling leaves, they are the richest ornament of the wood.... The size of some of the trees is enormous; one beech-tree, near Sawyer's Lodge, measuring, at six feet from the ground, thirty-six feet round. It is now protected from injury, and nature seems to be doing her best towards repairing the damage which its exposure to the attacks of man and beast has produced. It must once have been almost hollow, but the vacuum has been nearly filled up. One might almost fancy that liquid wood, which had afterwards hardened, had been poured into the tree. There is no bark on this extraneous substance; but the surface is smooth, hard, and without any appearance of decay.

THE ASPECT OF LONDON.

HIPPOLYTE TAINE.

[Taine's "English Literature" has in itself added a new work to the world's best literature of far more value than many of those with which it deals. In his "Notes on England" he gives us thoughtful impressions of the country itself, from which we select his pen-picture of the great city on the Thames. The picture is not an inspiring one. He could not avoid comparing in his mind this fog-haunted capital with the brighter aspect of his native Paris.]

Sunday in London in the rain; the shops are shut, the streets are almost deserted; the aspect is that of an immense and a well-ordered cemetery. The few passers-by under their umbrellas in the desert of squares and streets have the look of uneasy spirits who have risen from their graves; it is appalling.

I had no conception of such a spectacle, which is said to be frequent in London. The rain is small, compact, pitiless; looking at it, one can see no reason why it should not continue to the end of all things. One's feet churn water; there is water everywhere,—filthy water impregnated with an odor of soot. A yellow, dense fog fills the air, sweeps down to the ground; at thirty paces a house, a steamboat appear as spots upon blotting-paper. After an hour's walk in the Strand especially, and in the rest of the city, one has the spleen; one meditates suicide. The lofty lines of fronts are of sombre brick, the exudations being incrusted with fog and soot. Monotony and silence; yet inscriptions on metal or marble speak and tell of the absent master, as in a large manufactory of bone-black closed on account of a death.

A frightful thing is the huge palace in the Strand which is called Somerset House. Massive and heavy piece of architecture, of which the hollows are inked, the porticoes blackened with soot, where, in the cavity of the empty court, is a sham fountain without water, pools of water on the pavement, long rows of closed windows,—what can they possibly do in these catacombs?

It seems as if the livid and sooty fog had even befouled the verdure of the parks. But what most offends the eye are the colonnades, peristyles, Grecian ornaments, mouldings, and wreaths of the houses all bathed in soot. Poor antique architecture, what is it doing in such a climate? The flutings and columns in front of the British Museum are begrimed as if liquid mud had been poured over them. St. Paul's—a kind of Pantheon—has two ranges of columns: the lower range is entirely black; the upper range, recently scraped, is still white, but the white is offensive: coal-smoke has already plastered it with its leprosy.

These spots are melancholy, being the decay of the stone. And these nude statues in memory of Greece! Wellington as a fighting hero, naked under the dripping trees of the park! That hideous Nelson, stuck on his column with a coil of rope in the form of a pig-tail, like a rat impaled on the top of a pole! Every form, every classical idea, is contrary to nature here. A swamp like this is a place of exile for the ark of antiquity. When the Romans disembarked here they must have thought themselves in Homer's hell, in the land of the Cimmerians. The vast space which, in the south, stretches between the earth and the sky, cannot be discovered by the eye; there is no air; there is nothing but liquid fog; in this pale smoke objects are but fading phantoms. Nature has the look of a bad drawing in charcoal, which some one has rubbed with his sleeve.

I have just spent half an hour on Waterloo Bridge. The Houses of Parliament, blurred and indistinct, appear in the distance but a wretched pile of scaffolding; nothing is discernible, and, more particularly, nothing is living, except a few steamboats skimming along the river, black, smoky, unwearied insects. A Greek watching their passengers embarking and disembarking would have thought of the Styx. He would have found that to exist here was not to live; in fact, life here is different from what it is in his country; the ideal has altered with the climate. The mind quits the without to retire within itself, and there creates a world. Here one must have a comfortable and well-ordered home, clubs, societies, plenty of business, many religious and moral preoccupations; above all, instead of abandoning one's self to the influence of exterior impressions, it is necessary to extrude all the sad promptings of unfriendly Nature, and fill up the great void wherein melancholy and tedium would take up their abode.

[After this gloomy image of a rainy London, and a description of the Sunday church services, the writer proceeds in a more complimentary vein.]

The population numbers three millions and a quarter; that makes twelve cities like Marseilles, ten cities like Lyons, two cities like Paris, put together; but words upon paper are no substitutes for the sensation of the eyes. It is necessary to take a cab several days in succession, and proceed straight on towards the south, the north, the east, and the west, during a whole morning, as far as the uncertain limits where houses grow scanty and the country begins.

Enormous, enormous,—this the word which always recurs. Moreover, all is rich and well ordered; consequently they must think us neglected and poor. Paris is mediocre compared with these squares, these crescents, these circles and rows of monumental buildings of massive stone, with porticoes, with sculptured fronts, these spacious streets. There are sixty of them as vast as the Rue de la Paix. Assuredly Napoleon III. demolished and rebuilt Paris only because he had lived in London. In the Strand, in Piccadilly, in Regent Street, in the neighborhood of London Bridge, in twenty places, there is a bustling crowd, a surging traffic, an amount of obstruction which our busiest and most frequented boulevard cannot parallel. Everything is on a large scale here: the clubs are palaces; the hotels are monuments; the river is an arm of the sea; the cabs go twice as fast; the boatmen and the omnibus conductors condense a sentence into a word; words and gestures are economized; actions and time are turned to the utmost possible account; the human being produces and expends twice as much as among us.

BANK OF ENGLAND

From London Bridge to Hampton Court are eight miles,—that is, nearly three leagues of buildings. After the streets and quarters erected together, as one piece, by wholesale, like a hive after a model, come the countless pleasure retreats, cottages surrounded with verdure and trees in all styles,—Gothic, Grecian, Byzantine, Italian, of the Middle Age, or the Revival, with every mixture and every shade of style,—generally in lines, or clusters of five, ten, twenty of the same sort, apparently the handiwork of the same builder, like so many specimens of the same vase or the same bronze. They deal in houses as we deal in Parisian articles. What a multitude of well-to-do, comfortable, and rich existences! One divines accumulated gains, a wealthy and spending middle class quite different from ours, so pinched, so straitened. The most humble, in brown brick, are pretty by dint of tidiness; the windows sparkle like mirrors; there is nearly always a green and flowery patch; the front is covered with ivy, honeysuckle, and nasturtiums.

The entire circumference of Hyde Park is covered with houses of this sort, but finer, and those in the midst of London retain a country look. Each stands detached in its square of turf and shrubs, has two stories in the most perfect order and condition, a portico, a bell for the tradespeople, a bell for the visitors, a basement for the kitchen and the servants, with a flight of steps for the service; very few mouldings and ornaments; no outside sun-shutters; large, clear windows which let in plenty of light; flowers on the sills and at the portico; stables in a mews apart, in order that their odors and sight might be kept at a distance; all the external surface covered with white, shining, and varnished stucco; not a speck of mud or dust; the trees, the turf, the flowers, the servants, prepared as if for an exhibition of prize products.

How well one can picture the inhabitant after seeing his shell! In the first place, it is the Teuton who loves nature, and who needs a reminder of the country; next, it is the Englishman who wishes to be by himself on his staircase as in his room, who could not endure the promiscuous existence of our huge Parisian cages, and who, even in London, plans his house as a small castle, independent and enclosed. Besides, he is simple, and does not desire external display; on the other hand, he is exacting in the matter of condition and comfort, and separates his life from that of his inferiors. The number of such houses at the Westend is astonishing. The rent is nearly five hundred pounds; from five to seven servants are kept; the master expends from twelve to twenty-four hundred pounds a year. There are ten of these fortunes and these lives in England to every one in France.

The impression is the same when visiting the parks; the taste, the area are quite different from what is the case among us. St. James's Park is a genuine piece of country, and of English country; huge old trees, real meadows, a large pond peopled with ducks and water-fowl; cows and sheep, in an enclosed space, fed on the grass, which is always fresh. There are even sheep in the narrow green border that surrounds Westminster Abbey; these people love the country in their hearts. It is sufficient to read their literature from Chaucer to Shakespeare, from Thomson to Wordsworth and Shelley, to find proofs of this. What a contrast to the Tuileries, the Champs-Elysées, the Luxembourg! As a rule, the French garden, that of Louis XIV., is a room or gallery in the open air, wherein to walk and converse in company; in the English garden, such as they have invented and propagated, one is better alone; the eyes and the mind converse with natural things. We have arranged a park on this model in the Bois de Boulogne; but we have committed the blunder of placing therein a group of rocks and waterfalls; the artifice is discovered at a glance, and offends; English eyes would have felt it.

[A description of Regent's Park follows, with some words on the English love of out-door exercise. Piccadilly and Hyde Park are next mentioned.]

Hyde Park is the largest of them all, with its small rivulet, its wide greensward, its sheep, its shady walks, resembling a pleasure park suddenly transported to the centre of a capital. About two o'clock the principal alley is a riding-ground; there are ten times more gentlemen and twenty times more ladies on horseback than in the Bois de Boulogne on its most frequented days; little girls and boys of eight ride on ponies by the side of their father; I have seen ample and worthy matrons trolling along. This is one of the luxuries. Add to it that of having servants. For instance, a family of three persons which I visited keeps seven servants and three horses. The mother and daughter gallop in the park daily; they often pay visits on horseback; they economize in other things,—in theatre-going, for example; they go but seldom to the theatre, and when they do it is to a box which has been presented to them. This vigorous exercise appears indispensable for health; young girls and ladies come here even when it rains....

From five to seven o'clock is the review of ladies' dresses. Beauty and ornamentation abound, but taste is wanting. The colors are outrageously crude and the forms ungraceful; crinolines too distended and badly distended, in geometrical cones or bunched, green flounces, embroideries, flowered dresses, quantities of floating gauze, packets of falling or frizzed hair; crowning this display tiny embroidered and imperceptible bonnets. The bonnets are too much adorned; the hair, too shiny, presses closely on the temples; the small mantle or casaque falls formless to the lower part of the back, the petticoat expands prodigiously, and all the scaffolding badly joined, badly arranged, variegated and labored, cries and protests with all its gaudy and overdone colors. In the sunshine, especially, at Hampton Court the day before yesterday, among the shopkeepers' wives, the absurdity was at its height; there were many violet dresses, one being of a wild violet clasped round the waist with a golden band, which would have made a painter cry out. I said to a lady, "The toilette is more showy among you than in France." "But my dresses come from Paris!" I carefully refrained from replying, "But you selected them."

Excepting only the highest class, they apparel themselves as fancy dictates. One imagines healthy bodies, well-built, beautiful at times; but they must be imagined. The physiognomy is often pure, but also often sheepish. Many are simple babies, new waxen dolls, with glass eyes, which appear entirely empty of ideas. Other faces have become ruddy, and turned to raw beefsteak. There is a fund of folly or of brutality in this inert flesh,—too white, or too red. Some are ugly and grotesque in the extreme; with heron's feet, stork's necks, always having the large front of white teeth, the projecting jaws of carnivora. As compensation, others are beautiful in the extreme. They have angelic faces; their eyes, of pale periwinkle, are softly deep; their complexion is that of a flower, or an infant; their smile is divine. One of these days, about ten o'clock in the morning, near Hyde Park Corner, I was rooted to the spot motionless with admiration at the sight of two young ladies; the one was sixteen, the other eighteen years old. They were in rustling dresses of white tulle amid a cloud of muslin; tall, slender, agile, their shape as perfect as their face, of incomparable freshness, resembling those marvellous flowers seen in select exhibitions, the whiteness of the lily or orchis; in addition to all that, gayety, innocence, a superabundance of unalloyed sap and infantine expression, of laughter, and the mien of birds; the earth did not support them.

Many of the horsewomen are charming, so simple and so serious, without a trace of coquetry; they come here not to be seen, but to take the air; their manner is frank without pretension; their shake of the hand quite loyal, almost masculine; no frippery in their attire; the small black vest, tightened at the waist, moulds a fine shape and healthy form; to my mind, the first duty of a young lady is to be in good health. They manage their horses with complete ease and assurance.

Sometimes the father or brother stops and talks business or politics with a friend; the ladies listen and thus habituate themselves to serious topics. These fathers and brothers, too, are a pleasant sight; expressive and resolute faces, which bear, or have borne, the burden of life; less exhausted than among us, less ready to smile and to execute the tricks of politeness, but calmer and more staid, and who often excite in the onlooker a vague impression of respect, of esteem at least, and often of trust. Perhaps this is because I am instructed as to their condition; yet it seems to me that mistake is difficult; whether nobles, members of Parliament, landed proprietors, their manners and their physiognomies are those of men accustomed to authority, and who have wielded it.

WESTMINSTER ABBEY.

NATHANIEL HAWTHORNE.

[We do not class Hawthorne in usual lists of travellers, yet in his "Our Old Home: A Series of English Sketches," he gives us some thoughtful and interesting discussions of English scenes and institutions which are well worth reproducing. We accordingly select his description of London's great centre of pilgrimage to the devout antiquarian.]

On a Sunday afternoon, I passed through a side-entrance in the time-blackened wall of a place of worship, and found myself among a congregation assembled in one of the transepts and the immediately contiguous portion of the nave. It was a vast old edifice, spacious enough, within the extent covered by its pillared roof and overspread by its stone pavement, to accommodate the whole of church-going London, and with a far wider and loftier concave than any human power of lungs could fill with audible prayer. Oaken benches were arranged in the transept, on one of which I seated myself, and joined, as well as I knew how, in the sacred business that was going forward. But when it came to the sermon, the voice of the preacher was puny, and so were his thoughts, and both seemed impertinent at such a time and place, where he and all of us were bodily included within a sublime act of religion, which could be seen above and around us and felt beneath our feet.

The structure itself was the worship of the devout men of long ago, miraculously preserved in stone without losing an atom of its fragrance and fervor; it was a kind of anthem-strain that they had sung and poured out of the organ in centuries gone by; and being so grand and sweet, the Divine benevolence had willed it to be prolonged for the behoof of auditors unborn. I therefore came to the conclusion that, in my individual case, it would be better and more reverent to let my eyes wander about the edifice than to fasten them and my thoughts on the evidently uninspired mortal who was venturing—and felt it no venture at all—to speak here above his breath.

The interior of Westminster Abbey (for the reader recognized it, no doubt, the moment we entered) is built of rich brown stone; and the whole of it— the lofty roof, the tall, clustered pillars, and the pointed arches—appears to be in consummate repair. At all points where decay has laid its finger the structure is clamped with iron, or otherwise carefully protected; and being thus watched over,—whether as a place of ancient sanctity, a noble specimen of Gothic art, or an object of national interest and pride,—it may reasonably be expected to survive for as many ages as have passed over it already. It was sweet to feel its venerable quietude, its long-enduring peace, and yet to observe how kindly and even cheerfully it received the sunshine of to-day, which fell from the great windows into the fretted aisles and arches that laid aside somewhat of their aged gloom to welcome it. Sunshine always seems friendly to old abbeys, churches, and castles, kissing them, as it were, with a more affectionate, though still reverential, familiarity than it accords to edifices of later date. A square of golden light lay on the sombre pavement of the nave, afar off, falling through the grand western entrance, the folding leaves of which were wide open, and afforded glimpses of people passing to and fro in the outer world, while we sat dimly enveloped in the solemnity of antique devotion.

In the south transept, separated from us by the full breadth of the minster, there were painted glass windows, of which the uppermost appeared to be a great orb of many-colored radiance, being, indeed, a cluster of saints and angels whose glorified bodies formed the rays of an aureole emanating from a cross in the midst. These windows are modern, but combine softness with wonderful brilliancy of effect. Through the pillars and arches I saw that the walls in that distant region of the edifice were almost wholly incrusted with marble now grown yellow with time; no blank, unlettered slabs, but memorials of such men as these respective generations deemed wisest and bravest. Some of them were commemorated merely by inscriptions on mural tablets; others by sculptured bas-reliefs; others (once famous, but now forgotten, generals or admirals, these) by ponderous tombs that aspired towards the roof of the aisle, or partly curtained the immense arch of a window.

These mountains of marble were peopled with the sisterhood of Allegory, winged trumpeters, and classic figures in full-bottomed wigs; but it was strange to observe how the old Abbey melted all such absurdities into the breadth of its own grandeur, even magnifying itself by what would elsewhere have been ridiculous. Methinks it is the test of Gothic sublimity to overpower the ridiculous without deigning to hide it; and these grotesque monuments of the last century answer to a similar purpose with the grinning faces which the old architects scattered among their most solemn conceptions....

It is a characteristic of this grand edifice that it permits you to smile as freely under the roof of its central nave as if you stood beneath the yet grander canopy of heaven. Break into laughter, if you feel inclined, provided the vergers do not hear it echoing among the arches. In an ordinary church you would keep your countenance for fear of disturbing the sanctities or proprieties of the place; but you need leave no honest and decorous portion of your human nature outside of these benign and hospitable walls. Their mild awfulness will take care of itself. Thus it does no harm to the general impression, when you come to be sensible that many of the monuments are ridiculous, and commemorate a mob of people who are mostly forgotten in their graves, and few of whom ever deserved any better boon from posterity. You acknowledge the force of Sir Godfrey Kneller's objection to being buried in Westminster Abbey, because "they do bury fools there!"

Nevertheless, these grotesque carvings of marble, that break out in dingy-white blotches on the old freestone of the interior walls, have come there by as natural a process as might cause mosses and ivy to cluster about the external edifice; for they are the historical and biographical record of each successive age, written with its own hand, and all the truer for the inevitable mistakes, and none the less solemn for the occasional absurdity. Though you entered the Abbey expecting to see the tombs only of the illustrious, you are content at last to read many names, both in literature and history, that have now lost the reverence of mankind, if indeed they ever really possessed it. Let these men rest in peace. Even if you miss a name or two that you hoped to find there, they may well be spared. It matters little a few more or less, or whether Westminster Abbey contains or lacks any one man's grave, so long as the centuries, each with the crowd of personages that it deemed memorable, have chosen it as their place of honored sepulture, and laid themselves down under its pavement. The inscriptions and devices on the walls are rich with evidences of the fluctuating tastes, fashions, manners, opinions, prejudices, follies, wisdoms of the past; and thus they combine into a more truthful memorial of their dead times than any individual epitaph-maker ever meant to write.

When the services were over, many of the audience seemed inclined to linger in the nave or wander away among the mysterious aisles; for there is nothing in this world so fascinating as a Gothic minster, which always invites deeper and deeper into its heart both by vast revelations and shadowy concealments. Through the open-work screen that divides the nave from the chancel and choir we could discern the gleam of a marvellous window, but were debarred from entrance into that more sacred precinct of the Abbey by the vergers. These vigilant officials (doing their duty all the more strenuously because no fees could be exacted from Sunday visitors) flourished their staves and drove us towards the grand entrance like a flock of sheep. Lingering through one of the aisles, I happened to look down, and found my foot upon a stone inscribed with this familiar exclamation, "O rare Ben Jonson!" and remembered the story of stout old Ben's burial in that spot, standing upright,—not, I presume, on account of any unseemly reluctance on his part to lie down in the dust, like other men, but because standing-room was all that could reasonably be demanded for a poet among the slumberous notabilities of his age. It made me weary to think of it!—such a prodigious length of time to keep one's feet! Apart from the honor of the thing, it would certainly have been better for Ben to stretch himself at ease in some country church-yard.

To this day, however, I fancy that there is a contemptuous alloy mixed up with the admiration which the higher classes of English society profess for their literary men.

Another day—in truth, many other days—I sought out Poets' Corner, and found a sign-board and pointed finger, directing the visitor to it, on the corner house of a little lane leading towards the rear of the Abbey. The entrance is at the southeastern end of the south transept, and it is used, on ordinary occasions, as the only free mode of access to the building. It is no spacious arch, but a small, lowly door, passing through which, and pushing aside an inner screen that partly keeps out an exceedingly chill wind, you find yourself in a dim nook of the Abbey, with the busts of poets gazing at you from the otherwise bare stone-work of the walls. Great poets, too; for Ben Jonson is right behind the door, and Spenser's tablet is next, and Butler's on the same side of the transept, and Milton's (whose bust you know at once by its resemblance to one of his portraits, though older, more wrinkled, and sadder than that) is close by, and a profile-medallion of Gray beneath it. A window high aloft sheds down a dusky daylight on these and many other sculptured marbles, now as yellow as old parchment, that cover the three walls of the nook up to an elevation of about twenty feet above the pavement.

It seemed to me that I had always been familiar with the spot. Enjoying a humble intimacy—and how much of my life had else been a dreary solitude!— with many of its inhabitants, I could not feel myself a stranger there. It was delightful to be among them. There was a genial awe, mingled with a sense of kind and friendly presences about me; and I was glad, moreover, at finding so many of them there together, in fit companionship, mutually recognized and duly honored, all reconciled now, whatever distant generations, whatever personal hostility or other miserable impediment, had divided them far asunder while they lived.

I have never felt a similar interest in any other tombstones, nor have I ever been deeply moved by the imaginary presence of other famous dead people. A poet's ghost is the only one that survives for his fellow-mortals after his bones are in the dust,—and he not ghostly, but cherishing many hearts with his own warmth in the chillest atmosphere of life. What other fame is worth aspiring for? Or, let me speak it more boldly, what other long-enduring fame can exist? We neither remember nor care anything for the past, except as the poet has made it intelligibly noble and sublime to our comprehension. The shades of the mighty have no substance; they flit ineffectually about the darkened stage where they performed their momentary parts, save when the poet has thrown his own creative soul into them, and imparted a more vivid life than ever they were able to manifest to mankind while they dwelt in the body. And therefore—though he cunningly disguises himself in their armor, their robes of state, or kingly purple—it is not the statesman, the warrior, or the monarch that survives, but the despised poet, whom they may have fed with their crumbs, and to whom they owe all that they now are or have,—a name!

WESTMINSTER ABBEY AND VICTORIA TOWER

In the foregoing paragraph I seem to have been betrayed into a flight above or beyond the customary level that best agrees with me; but it represents fairly enough the emotions with which I passed from Poets' Corner into the chapels, which contain the sepulchres of kings and great people. They are magnificent even now, and must have been inconceivably so when the marble slabs and pillars wore their new polish, and the statues retained the brilliant colors with which they were originally painted, and the shrines their rich gilding, of which the sunlight still shows a glimmer or a streak, though the sunbeam itself looks tarnished with antique dust. Yet this recondite portion of the Abbey presents few memorials of personages whom we care to remember. The shrine of Edward the Confessor has a certain interest, because it was so long held in religious reverence, and because the very dust that settled upon it was formerly worth gold. The helmet and war-saddle of Henry V., worn at Agincourt, and now suspended above his tomb, are memorable objects, but more for Shakespeare's sake than the victor's own. Rank has been the general passport to admission here. Noble and regal dust is as cheap as dirt under the pavement.

I am glad to recollect, indeed (and it is too characteristic of the right English spirit not to be mentioned), one or two gigantic statues of great mechanicians, who contributed largely to the material welfare of England, sitting familiarly in their marble chairs among forgotten kings and queens. Otherwise the quaintness of the earlier monuments, and the antique beauty of some of them, are what chiefly gives them value. Nevertheless, Addison is buried among the men of rank; not on the plea of his literary fame, however, but because he was connected with nobility by marriage, and had been a secretary of state. His gravestone is inscribed with a resounding verse from Tickell's lines to his memory, the only lines by which Tickell himself is now remembered, and which (as I discovered a little while ago) he mainly filched from an obscure versifier of somewhat earlier date.

Returning to Poets' Corner, I looked again at the walls, and wondered how the requisite hospitality can be shown to poets of our own and the succeeding ages. There is hardly a foot of space left, although room has lately been found for a bust of Southey and a full-length statue of Campbell. At best, only a little portion of the Abbey is dedicated to poets, literary men, musical composers, and others of the gentle artist breed, and even into that small nook of sanctity men of other pursuits have thought it decent to intrude themselves. Methinks the tuneful throng, being at home here, should recollect how they were treated in their lifetime, and turn the cold shoulder, looking askance at nobles and official personages, however worthy of honorable interment elsewhere. Yet it shows aptly and truly enough what portion of the world's regard and honor has heretofore been awarded to literary eminence in comparison with other modes of greatness,——this dimly-lighted corner (nor even that quietly to themselves in the vast minster), the walls of which are sheathed and hidden under marble that has been wasted upon the illustrious obscure.

THE GARDENS AT KEW.

JULIAN HAWTHORNE.

[Kew Gardens stand pre-eminent among conservatories, and a description of the treasures of botany there gathered cannot fail to prove of interest to our readers. Julian Hawthorne, son of the celebrated novelist, and himself a writer of rich imaginative power, thus describes these famous gardens *con amore*.]

On the banks of the Thames, about a dozen miles from London in a southerly direction, lies the ancient town of Twickenham. In the seventeenth century, Alexander Pope had a villa there; somewhat later, Horace Walpole built his rococo castle at Strawberry Hill, a mile beyond the village; and close by, to the north, is Whitton, where Sir John Suckling lived. Within an easy hour's walk stands Hampton Court, built by Cardinal Wolsey of haughty and unhappy memory, and approached through the magnificent avenue of Bushey Park. Nearly as far in the opposite direction is Richmond, with its venerable bridge and famous hill, the latter commanding a view of rural English landscape which, as Thackeray says, looks as if it had its hair curled, like the waiters at the inn on its summit. A mile down the river from Richmond, and six miles from London, extend the renowned botanical gardens of Kew.

It will be seen, therefore, that Twickenham was not a bad place for a suburban residence: the roads were excellent, the scenery and associations delightful, and, by taking the train, one could be at Waterloo railway-station, in the heart of London, in half an hour. I lived there several years, and know something about it.

The most agreeable expedition of all, taking one month with another, was to Kew Gardens. In winter, it was a luxury to sit in the hot-houses; in summer it was lovely throughout. You could travel thither by train; but the best way was to go on foot. Passing through Twickenham town, and through the church-yard, with its gravestones centuries old, you came out upon the river banks. Here a broad, well-kept path followed the enchanting windings of the stream, and skirted the lawns of pretty villas on the left. On the right, soon appeared the green heights of the Hill, with clumps of mighty oaks, and the gleaming ramparts and windows of the hostelry over all. At its foot, on the river, were boat-houses and "hards," with slender rowing-craft drawn up, or lying afloat, or pushing off into the current with their freight of white-jerseyed oarsmen. And now came into view the quaint, hog-backed bridge, with its high stone parapet, and the eddies swirling against its piers; and Richmond itself, red with brick, white with stucco, green with trees; irregular and diversified in outline; resting snug against the base of the Hill, and clambering some distance up its long slope.

You crossed the bridge, lingering on the way to admire the railroad bridge a few hundred yards farther down, reflected in the river-mirror. Between the two bridges are a couple of islets, only a few yards in diameter, but with trees growing on them; and hereabouts are generally moored three or four fishing-punts, in which sit patiently, all day long, stout, middle-aged fishermen, watching their cork floats drift down the stream, and faithfully hoping that each new cast will bring the long-expected fish. Often have I watched them, but the fish never came. Probably, as Hood conjectured, "it was caught yesterday."

The river-side walk now continues along the Richmond side of the river. For half a mile it has the town on the right. Then the boundaries of Kew Gardens begin, and here is the most beautiful part of the walk. Immense trees stretch their ponderous boughs far across the path, and they droop so low that the pendent foliage almost sweeps the water. Through the fretted sun and shadow the path winds; every little way there is a hospitable bench, resting on which you gaze forth upon the quiet-moving river, with its passing wherries, its reflections of sky and cloud, and its battlemented residences far withdrawn beyond green meadows on the opposite side. The path is never overcrowded, even on holidays; but you may always see lovers wandering arm in arm along it; and occasionally there is a brisk exchange of "Thames chaff" between the occupants of the skimming boats and the loiterers on the shore. Meanwhile, the great domain of Kew keeps pace with you on the other hand. You are divided from it by a wide water-ditch, backed by a high stone embankment, in turn surmounted by an iron railing. But your eyes may stray whither feet cannot follow; and you note the lovely groves, the beautiful green glades and gracious vistas, the secluded paths weaving in and out, and now and then you catch the sparkle of lofty domes of glass rising above the trees, looking for all the world like gigantic soap-bubbles. It is a sort of fairy-land beyond there; and long before you arrive at the entrance your appetite for what lies within is sharp-set.

The feast in store for you more than fulfils expectation; but at this point, since we are journeying in imagination only, and miles count for nothing, we will turn back, and enter the gardens from the other end. By this route we approach its beauties gradually and in due order, and our pleasure has opportunity to grow from promising beginnings to complete content. The gate is small here, and the uniformed guardian simply gives us a glance, to assure himself that we are not toughs or pickpockets. Kew Gardens are free to the public in the afternoons, barring only the rowdy element. The public would like to have them free in the mornings, too; and, for aught I know, Sir Joseph Hooker may have yielded his assent by this time. But in the seventies, when I was there, he resisted, on the ground that it was necessary to close the gardens for half the day, in order to allow time for study, and for keeping the houses and plantations in order. The grounds are constantly visited by gardeners and botanists from all parts of the country, and from the world at large; and these persons require some measure of seclusion in order to prosecute their labors and investigations. Practical botany is not, as a rule, pursued at night; though, with the aid of electric lights, no doubt it might be.

However, we have by this time passed through some introductory shrubbery, and have emerged into a straight, open avenue, a third of a mile or more in length. Directly before us is an immensely high tower,—I should think nearly two hundred feet,—painted red, black, blue, and yellow, and fashioned to resemble a Chinese minaret or pagoda. The central shaft is circular, and, I believe, of masonry; but it is surrounded at short intervals by wooden balconies, and the roof is of a concave conical shape, like a mandarin's hat. I never saw any signs of life in this tower, and do not know what it is used for; but I have heard that the son-in-law of Lord Capel (who first laid out Kew Gardens some two hundred years ago) added to the importance of the place by making it the head-quarters of English astronomy; and this tower, which certainly would make an excellent observatory, may have had something to do with that.

Beyond the tower extends a broad, straight path, between well-kept lawns, on which are planted trees of both native and foreign growth. Towards the river, on the left, the grounds are irregular and diversified with clumps of trees, ponds, and grassy undulations. On the right, concealed by a hedge of foliage, is the highway between Richmond and London. Before us, at the end of the walk, is an iron fence, dividing the inner enclosure—the Botanical Gardens proper—from this outer region. We reach it in due time, and, having passed the gate, are in the immediate neighborhood of the palm-house, whose bulbous domes we saw just now from the river bank. It is as beautiful a piece of glass building as ever I saw, handsomely proportioned, and of noble outline. Its great size is somewhat concealed by its charming symmetry; but when we are within, the vast dimensions are realized. Beneath its central dome the tallest palms rise unimpeded. You peep through long vistas of broad green fronds and slender, bending stems: it broadens and reaches out on every side; the strange, exotic foliage rejoices the eye, and the warm embracing atmosphere makes you feel that you are in the tropics.

To one who, like myself, pretends to no scientific knowledge of botany, and who, during these temperate summers and fitful winters, often hankers after the equator, the atmosphere of a thorough-going conservatory has a profound fascination. At one step I pass from the latitude of "the roaring forties" to that of Martinique or the Galapagos Islands. I unbutton my coat, and inhale deep breaths of air laden with the fragrance of the sun-lands. The heat is not enervating, but stimulating; for it is redolent with the life-giving emanations of plants that riot in luxuriance all the year round,—that know neither spring, autumn, nor winter,—whose multitudinous boughs were made to be the haunt of paroquets and monkeys, and amidst whose fern-enwrapped roots lurk lizards and gliding serpents. Here thrive the dark-skinned races of the torrid zone, innocent of clothes and civilization, seeking excitement not in the mutations of the stock-exchange or the scandals of society, but in trapping the alligator and shooting the jaguar and the antelope with arrows deadly with *curari*. Into the intricate depths of these jungles the fierce sun scarcely penetrates; the unstinted energy of his own rays has erected a barrier against himself. Here, when the rain falls, it falls in rushing torrents; when the wind blows, it blows a shrieking hurricane; when the lightning flashes, the whole dome of heaven is ablaze with passionate splendor. Here the stars poise and smoulder close to the earth, and the moon is brighter than the sun of hyperborean England. Sitting on a rustic bench hedged round with tapering palm-stems, and screened by leaves two or three of which would carpet the floor of an ordinary drawing-room, I love to think of these things.

The enjoyment is perhaps enhanced by an occasional peep through the glass walls of the paradise, revealing the melancholy Britisher, close at hand in space, but thousands of miles distant in temperature, stalking rigidly about in overcoat and gloves. Then, too, the hot-house, while giving the charm and beauty of the tropics, dispenses with the inconveniences. Here are no coral-snakes to drop from the boughs down the back of your neck; no scorpions or tarantulas to crawl up your trousers; no apes to pelt you with cocoa-nuts; no rhinoceroses to toss you above the tree-tops; no tigers to disembowel you and bite your head off. On the contrary, everything is scrupulously neat and secure. The rich loam round the roots of the plants harbors nothing noxious; the asphalt walks that thread the thicket are clean and trustworthy. Ever and anon you come upon a native of the place,—not a savage, painted in red and black stripes and with his bow-string drawn to his ear, but—a quiet and sober gardener in his shirt-sleeves, pruning a dead leaf or bough, or raking the mould round the roots of a new importation, or wielding a watering-pot. The place is quite still; the huge leaves hang motionless; the noise of a pair of steps being dragged into position resounds through the building; and, if you listen, you will at all times hear the pleasant trickling of water in some reservoir or other. If the terrors of the jungle are still too much for your nerves, you may be comforted by observing that each plant wears a label, painted on wood or enamelled on tin, describing its scientific name and habitat. It cost money to bring them here, and the very leaves of their twigs are numbered.

But there are other places to be visited besides the palm-house. As we emerge from its luxurious warmth into the cool English air, we see in front of us a large, circular pool, with broad, shallow flights of stone steps leading down to it, and English willows bending over it. Water-fowl swim and quack here, and children elude their nurses and get their feet wet. If we pass round to the other side, and then look back to the palm-house, we behold it inverted in the smooth mirror of the water,—a delectable spectacle. It was like a fairy palace already; but this shadowy duplication of it quite removes it from the material sphere, and makes it a lovely dream. Kew Gardens are full of such felicitous devices.

To our right are acres of yet unexplored hot-houses. We stroll towards them along eccentric paths, amidst beds of purple rhododendrons, geraniums, tulips, narcissuses, hyacinths, according to the season; and everywhere is the matchless English turf, compact and flawless as velvet, and the leafy, overshadowing English trees. But let us seek the dwelling-place of the *Victoria Regia.* It grows, I believe, on the Amazon, which is as near the equator as one can well get; but latitudes are much mixed up in Kew Gardens, and this titanic water-lily is only a few rods distant. It basks on the surface of a pool, in an atmosphere of delicious warmth,—its leaves, each of the diameter of a dining-table, covering the water. Amidst these great green disks blossoms the flower, a nosegay of which would fill a farm-wagon. It is said that the native Brazilian savages and Guianians walk about on the green leaves, and use them as rafts or stepping-stones to cross the lagoons. As to the flowers, though it is difficult to imagine anything more beautiful than our own water-lilies, yet these blossoms fairly surpass them, not only because they are a foot across, but because of the richness of the innumerable petals, and the gorgeous cluster of purple stamens that form the centre. And they fill the air with a fragrance vital and voluptuous. One longs to verify in his own experience that story about walking on the leaves,—not to speak of lopping off a flower or two to furnish one's study withal. But the quiet gardener, in his shirt-sleeves, though he appears to be absorbed in his work, has his eye on you; and you can do nothing but stand and stare in admiration.

The hottest of the hot-houses, if my memory serves me, were the cactus-house and the fern-house. The cacti were not beautiful, but they were grotesque and curious. There were none that I should have cared to handle. Their uncouth shapes and awkward putting together seem characteristic of an epoch when Nature's handiwork was much less skilful and comely than it is now. They call up visions of forlorn wastes and desert solitudes. Their armature of thorns and prickles appears to indicate that they consider themselves very attractive and take unusual pains in the way of self-protection. Perhaps the donkeys of their time were unreasonably voracious. The modern thistle certainly indicates increased refinement of taste on the donkeys' part. Yet this ungainliness is occasionally redeemed by exquisite blossoms, of pale, pure hues, cropping out directly from the substance of the plant, without any pretence of a stem. One variety of cactus, in addition to its prickles, had provided itself with long white hair, which, surmounting its tall and rather meagre figure, gave it the aspect of an aged man of repulsive character. Among the cacti, though not of them, was a hideous plant (or it may have been a wax model of one) apparently of the fungus family. It grew on the bare sand or rock, and both flowers and leaves had a greasy, flesh-like surface, deeply tinted, and ornamented with poisonous-looking blotches. It was of immense size, the flowers being at least a foot in diameter; and if the Vale of Gehenna has any vegetation, I should expect it to be like this. A more depraved, diabolical plant it would be impossible to imagine. Its preposterous attempt to imitate the form and characteristics of ordinary vegetation made it still more revolting. The label described it as being very rare,—which is some comfort.

The fern-house, besides being hot, is dripping with moisture; and, the glass being tinged with green, the effect is somewhat like being submerged in a tropic ocean. The greenness of the ferns is vivid enough at any rate, but this artificial light adds such intensity to it that, after a few minutes, you are on the point of forgetting that there is any other color besides green in the world. The ferns are arranged in glass cases, or vivariums. There is nothing in nature to parallel their delicate and various beauty. I call it various; but it is chiefly beauty of form, and that, too, within comparatively narrow limitations. But the fineness, the subtilty, the changefulness of line, are endlessly charming; they may have other uses, but if they had been made for pure beauty it would be use enough. They must have been of great æsthetic value to artists, especially to architects, decorators, and chasers of metals. The mediæval illuminators certainly made capital out of them; reminiscences of their shapes render lovely the ornament of innumerable missals. As for the color, green seems to admit of more gradations than any other hue, as any one who has observed the woods in spring knows; and of all others it is the most grateful and wholesome to the eye. With the rough grays and browns of the rocks it makes enchanting combinations. But, really, this moist fern atmosphere is too languorous and enervating; we must escape into the outer world, which, for a time, will appear strangely red, like that which astronomers suppose to be characteristic of the planet Mars.

It would take too long, even in imagination, to go through all Kew Gardens at this leisurely rate. Only, for splendor of color and voluptuousness of perfume, there is nothing comparable to the Conservatory, in which roses and all other bright-hued flowers are grouped and massed in sumptuous magnificence. The rose is England's flower: she has taken possession of it, as of so many other good things, without troubling herself to prove any title to it; and there is nothing in her history or character to make her worthy of it. One can understand why Persia should claim the rose; and in our own Southern States the houses are smothered with roses, and the air that flows from them is sweeter than incense. I have, it is true, gathered English roses in December; and the houses of York and Lancaster wore roses which, red and white alike, were steeped in blood. But, if anything could justify England in her appropriation of the rose, it would be this rose-house at Kew, where criticism becomes impossible, and one can only gaze, and inhale, and love. Pink, white, crimson, golden, they cluster and triumph there: with their exquisite petals Venus and Mars might strew a couch worthy of an Olympian marriage. If love, romance, and beauty died out of human nature, this flower would bring them back; and so long as it stays with us, we may be sure that life will not lose the glory that entitles it to immortality.

While meditating these matters, we might take a turn in the wood-house,—by which I mean the building containing specimens, polished and in the rough, of all kinds of woods from all parts of the world. Their gamut of color embraces all the hues of the rainbow, and many others; and there are specimens of wood-mosaics that are inferior in beauty only to agate and marble. Or we may wander through the corridors and halls of the museum, which exhibits every sort of manufacture into which vegetable substances enter, including numberless fabrics of Indian or savage origin. One is surprised, after examining these things, that our little earth should be large enough to contain anything that is not more or less botanical.

CHATSWORTH CASTLE.

JOHN LEYLAND.

["The Peak of Derbyshire," concerning which Mr. Leyland has written a
highly interesting book, presents in its vicinity numerous points of attraction.
Here is the location of the castle of "Peveril of the Peak," the hero of one of
Scott's romances. Here are two much more famous residences of the nobility,
Haddon Hall and Chatsworth, the latter of which we have chosen as the
subject of our present selection.]

If some have burst into rhapsody in describing the glories of Chatsworth,
one can scarcely marvel at their extravagance, for there is in this "Palace of the
Peak" and its wooded valley such a rare conjuncture of the fascinating beauties
of nature with the finest expressions of art, that language can ill describe the
things that are indelibly impressed upon the memory. The placid Derwent,
here flowing gently between the meads on which the fallow deer are wont to
herd; the graceful slopes bestudded with many a noble tree, whose spreading
boughs cast down a wide expanse of shade; the hills on either hand rising in
varied height and contour, crowned with a rich woodland of oak, chestnut,
beech, and lime; a palace wherein every art finds most fitting expression, and
where the fruits of learning are plenteously upstored,—small wonder, indeed,
if here the imagination of many be stirred. As we approach the house from
Baslow, crossing the Barbrook, which rises in the heights of East Moor, we
enter the great park, and, passing the fruit and vegetable gardens on the
right, its varied beauties are gradually unfolded with entrancing effect until
Chatsworth itself is seen beyond the trees.

The House may be viewed in its majestic proportions from several points
in the valley and on the slopes. From across the classic bridge of three
arches, which Caius Gabriel Cibber (the father of Colley Cibber) adorned
with statues, the dignity of its many-pillared façade has an imposing effect.
More varied, however, is the view from the slope of the hill to the northward
on the right bank of the river, where the later wing, added by the sixth
Duke of Devonshire, lies prominently before the spectator, or again farther
southward, where the same wing recedes in the perspective. If one would

gain a fine prospect of the whole of this part of Derwent, and of the palatial edifice itself, there can be no better way than to climb to the old turreted hunting-tower, which is such a conspicuous object on the eastern hill.

There is nothing in the regular, classic lines of Chatsworth to remind us of that Chetel, the Saxon, who is believed to have given his name to the place in which he dwelt. His homestead and oxgangs of land fell, as Domesday records, to the Crown, and were given in custody to William Peveril, who had also the stronghold at Castleton, as we have seen, with Haddon by the Wye, and many a castle and manor besides. Nothing now remains of these times at Chatsworth, save, perhaps, the grove of venerable oaks, gnarled, shattered, and time-worn, upon the neighboring hill....

Sir William Cavendish and his wife built the first Chatsworth House of which we have any definite knowledge, for there is scanty record of any mediæval structure, and it was she who completed it some time after his death. The extraordinary lady—something of a vixen, we may believe—who was married to four husbands, and discomfited at any rate the last of them, was the builder also of Hardwick Hall, one of the most celebrated houses in England. The Chatsworth of her time was a quadrangular building of "surprising height," as Cotton says, with an embattled top, and massive angle, and lateral turrets strengthening its many-windowed walls, as may be seen by a painting of it which now hangs at Chatsworth. The third husband of "Bess of Hardwick" (Sir William St. Lo) being dead, she married that powerful nobleman, George, Earl of Shrewsbury; and it was during his lifetime that Chatsworth became the residence of Mary, Queen of Scots, when she was in captivity under his charge. The unhappy prisoner is said to have passed many of her lonesome hours in that moated garden, called Queen Mary's bower, which was laid out on the top of the low square tower or platform, seen by the visitor amid the trees as he approaches the house from the bridge; and certain rooms in the great quadrangle, though they were built long after her day, are still traditionally said to be hers. If the scandal of the Tudor court be true, the lovely queen and her imperious hostess did not well agree, and the story is not hard to believe. At any rate, the bickerings of the lady with her husband, the Earl, are matters of record, notwithstanding that Fuller has said she "was happy in her several marriages."...

Queen Mary was brought to Chatsworth in 1570, and was there long afterwards. In that year Cecil visited the house to conduct certain negotiations, and subsequently wrote that Elizabeth was willing her rival should "take ye ayre about your howss on horsbacke, so that your L. be in company, and not to pass from your howss above one or twoo myle except it be on ye moores." Several times during subsequent years she was permitted to visit Buxton, for its waters, in company with the Earl and Countess, and it will be remembered that so well did the Earl treat his charge at one time, that he thereby incurred suspicions of disloyalty to Elizabeth. During the Civil Wars the house was held by both parties. Sir John Gell occupied it for the Parliament in 1643, but, in the December of that year, the Earl of Newcastle captured it, and garrisoned it for the King, and Colonel Shalcross was besieged there in 1645 by the Parliamentary forces, but the leaguer was raised after fourteen days.

The descendants of Sir William Cavendish, and of his celebrated wife, were content, during these years, to preserve Chatsworth as it had been left to them. The present quadrangular building is the work of William, the fourth Earl and first Duke of Devonshire, who was one of those who brought about the Revolution of 1688, and placed the Prince of Orange on the throne. During the reign of James II., the Earl was committed to prison, as it is quaintly said, because he led Colonel Colepepper out of the royal presence-chamber by the nose, whereupon, after sundry difficulties, he betook himself to his estates, and, as a chronicler of the new order of things puts it, in order to prevent his patriotic mind from dwelling unduly upon the woes of his country, rebuilt the south side of Chatsworth....

Whatever the age possessed of skill and merit in every branch of art was employed for the beautification of the new Chatsworth. Caius Gabriel Cibber, the Laureate's father, with Geeraerslius, Augustine Harris, Nost, Davis, Lanseroon, Nadauld, and others, carved the friezes, adorned with rich foliage the door-cases, worked upon many vases and other objects in and about the mansion, and peopled the gardens with nymphs and goddesses. Cibber himself has left notes of some of the sums he received, and it appears that he executed two statues in the pediments, others, both in the round and in relief, heads of Roman emperors, figures of dogs, sphinxes, and such-like. "For two statues as big as life, I had 35*l.* apiece, and all charges borne, and at this rate I shall endeavor to serve a nobleman in freestone."

[Many others might be named who helped to give Chatsworth its wealth of carvings, but we shall omit the catalogue of their names.]

So completed, as a noble Palladian quadrangle, divided externally into sections by fluted Ionic pilasters, crested by a balustrade which is adorned with decorative vases, and having on its principal front a fine compartment with a sculptured pediment, Chatsworth remained, even then one of the noblest mansions of its kind in the kingdom, until the sixth Duke of Devonshire (ob. 1858) added to it the great northern wing, containing the magnificent dining-room, the sculpture-gallery, the orangery, and many other chambers, as well as a whole range of offices in the basement. Of this wing, which is three hundred and eighty-five feet in length, Sir Jeffrey Wyattville was the architect, and it will be observed that he has adopted a more broken style, and a somewhat more picturesque method, than that of Talmari, but there are many who think that his addition detracts from the classic character and fitting symmetry of the whole, to which, nevertheless, it must be admitted it gives a greater aspect of grandeur and magnificence.

We shall not here dwell at any very great length upon the many treasures of which Chatsworth is the storehouse, for they are described after the manner of a catalogue in several guide-books. Passing from the Porter's lodge, the visitor, having traversed the whole length of the new wing, arrives at the quadrangle, which is entered through the sub-hall, where the ceiling is painted with a copy of Guido's Aurora.

A corridor leads thence to the Great Hall, on the eastern side of the courtyard, which is a very impressive apartment, with its floor of black and white marble, laid down by the son of Watson, the wood-carver, the fine staircase at its farther end, its walls painted by Verrio and Laguerre with scenes from the life of Julius Cæsar,—among others the crossing of the Rubicon, the passage of the Adriatic, and the assassination by Brutus,—and the great scene of Cæsar's apotheosis on the ceiling, where he goes to join the Immortals. One very noteworthy object in it is the immense slab of Derbyshire encrinitic marble that forms the top of its table. It also contains a great Turkish canoe which the sultan gave to the sixth Duke.

The south corridor, hung with pictures, leads from this hall to the Chapel, one of the most interesting chambers in Chatsworth. Here everything that art could do to lend enchantment to the classic interior has been done. The lower walls are richly panelled with fragrant cedar; above, Verrio and Laguerre have depicted the miracles of our Lord; and on the ceiling is the "Ascension;" over the altar Verrio's "Incredulity of St. Thomas" is regarded as his masterpiece, though the work has been attributed to Laguerre; the baldacchino at the east end is of the choicest marbles and spars of Derbyshire, with figures of Faith and Hope by Gibber; and there are marvellous wood-carvings, probably by Samuel Watson and Thomas Young, but perhaps from the designs or with the assistance of Grinling Gibbons. Passing onward, the Gallery of Sketches is a place where not hours only, but days, might be spent with equal pleasure and profit, a treasure-chamber in which, as it were, the great masters of every school may be seen at their very work....

Entering the state apartments by the dressing-room, with its painted ceiling of the "Mission of Mercury to Paris," its carved marble door-cases, and its *tours de force* in wood, by Gibbons or Watson, as the case may be, we notice the great vista through the open doors of the suite and pass on into the state bedroom. Here Aurora chases Night on the ceiling; we notice the fine embossed leather on the walls, the canopy embroidered, it is said, by "Bess of Hardwick," the coronation chairs of George III. and Queen Charlotte, with their footstools, the wardrobe of Louis XVI., and much else. Next we come to the state music-room, which has similar decorations, and a strangely deceptive painting, attributed to Verrio, of a violin on its door. From this we enter the state drawing-room, where Phaeton drives the horses of the sun above us, where the walls are hung with Gobelin tapestry after the cartoons of Raffaelle, and where, in the malachite table and other fittings, there is much to attract the attention. In the state dining-room, which is the last of the suite, Verrio has depicted upon the ceiling, in his best manner, the "Fates cutting the Thread of Life." In this luxurious chamber it is hard to think the wood-carving can be by any other than Gibbons, if we regard his characteristic manner; but whoever he may have been, the skilful craftsman has surpassed himself in giving the very touch of nature to these marvellous representations of flowers, fruit, birds, and shells....

Passing into the new wing through the dining-room (rarely shown), which is a grand chamber, simple in its style, but having a coved ceiling of white and gold, and adorned with rare marbles and splendid furniture, including tables of hornblende, porphyritic syenite, and Siberian jasper, hung with family portraits, and having sculptures by Westmacott, and others, we enter the sculpture-gallery, which is so well known that we need in this article only say that it contains works by Canova, Thorwaldsen, Schadow, Gibson, Wyatt, Westmacott, and several foreign artists. Attention is here drawn to a magnificent vase of the Blue John spar, which is said to be the largest in existence. Having then passed through the orangery, which is filled with sweet-scented blossoms or rich in ripening fruit, we leave the house and enter the gardens.

These stand high among the attractions of Chatsworth, and with their varied character of the natural and the artificial, their terraces and walks, their gay parterres, their fine trees, their fountains and rocks, their great conservatory, and their many other houses stored with choicest exotics, they are certainly among the finest gardens in England.

Few things can be more pleasant, having passed through the luxurious chambers, than to linger in these sweet-scented pathways, which are bordered by rich clusterings of flowers, to listen to the music of the waterfalls, and to see the dark-green trees, and the white-limbed nymphs, reflected in the pellucid basins. We pass down a short flight of steps, between dancing-girls after Canova, and vases of Elfdalen porphyry, and then proceeding through the French gardens, where the pathways are separated from the bright flower-beds by delicate creepers turning about lofty pedestals supporting busts and vases, we reach the great cascade, which pours from a stone water-temple, and rolls foaming down its long flight of formal descents below, to where, amid the rugged rocks at the bottom, it disappears underground.

The waterworks, which are by Grillet, and belong chiefly to the old Chatsworth, include a magnificent jet d'eau, rising from a long sheet of water between lime-trees, to a height of about two hundred and sixty feet, and a strange "weeping willow" of copper, which mysteriously pours copious streams of water from every leaf and twig. This last curiosity is in a sequestered gorge, where the rocks, placed with great labor and ingenuity, lie about apparently in wild confusion, and reared in lofty piles overgrown with moss and creeping plants.

From hence we issue by a curious gate-way of rock, turning upon a pivot, and, passing lofty cliffs over which pour deliciously cool cascades,—being, with much more in the formal gardens, the work of Sir Joseph Paxton,—reach the great conservatory, one of the wonders of Chatsworth. This magnificent house is a parallelogram in form, two hundred and seventy-six feet in length by one hundred and twenty-three feet in breadth, which rises from its basement, by two segmental curves on every side, the apex of the first forming the base of the second, to a height of seventy-six feet. So great is the extent of this wonderful building that, from its portico, which is of Grecian character, a carriage road runs from one end to the other, on either side of which, flourishing, as it were, in the warm air of their native climes, are lofty pines and palms of various kinds, dragon-trees, bananas, and many such tropical growths, with papyrus, lotus, and other water plants in tanks, and gorgeous flowering shrubs, making the air heavy with the rare perfumes of the East. Before descending to the lower gardens, it is well to survey from the terraces near the conservatory, or the quaint old hunting-tower above, the wide prospect of Chatsworth Park, with the palatial house by the Derwent, the picturesque village of Edensor on the slope beyond, and the hills rising, covered with umbrageous groves of trees. Below, in the pleasure gardens, passing many bright parterres, we reach some very fine forest-trees, and notably a magnificent Spanish chestnut, and then, beyond the great Emperor Fountain, pass trees planted by Her Majesty (then Princess Victoria) in 1832, as well as by her mother, the Duchess of Kent, by Prince Albert in 1843, and by the Emperor of Russia and the Grand Duke Michael in 1816 and 1818. The Italian garden, with its trim flower-beds, edged with privet, its beautiful acacia and other trees, its wall-like hedges, its long still basin and lofty fountain, surrounded by sculptured vases, is, from its very characteristic features, among the most attractive and interesting of the formal portion of the Chatsworth grounds.

We have given a brief and altogether imperfect account of the celebrated gardens, but this is scarcely the place in which to dwell upon the rare varieties of plants that are successfully cultivated there, or upon the scientific skill which has enabled the finest growths of tropical climes to flourish in Derwent Dale. Certainly no visitor who has lingered in these enchanting places will fail to appreciate the graceful compliment that Marshal Tallard, who was taken prisoner by Marlborough in 1704, paid to the Duke of Devonshire on leaving the "Palace by the Peak." "My Lord Duke," he said, "when I compute the days of my captivity in England, I shall omit those I passed at Chatsworth."

KING ARTHUR'S LAND.

J. YOUNG.

[Cornwall, one of the last strongholds of the ancient Britons in their island realm, and famous as the scene of many of the adventures recorded of King Arthur and his Round Table Knights, has much in itself worthy of description, and we give in the following selection some appreciative Cornish notes.]

Large and merry was the party with which we sallied forth from Helstone on a beautiful September day to visit the Lizard and Kynance Cove. The drive itself is not especially interesting, but grand is the expanse of sea and coast which bursts upon you when you come in sight of the Lizard Point, which, be it remarked, is not considered to derive its name from any fancy resemblance between its shape and that of a lizard, or from the variegated color of the geological formation, but from the Cornish word *Liazherd*, a headland.

This is in every way a remarkable piece of coast,—to geologists especially so,—as it is the *one* district in all Great Britain in which the serpentine formation is to be met with, whereas most of the Cornish coast is either granite or slate. Of the peculiar beauty of the serpentine marble one has no occasion to speak, almost every one having seen a specimen of it in one shape or another, either as forming part of the internal decoration of a church, or as worked up into some trinket, as a brooch, bracelet, cross, sleeve-link, or other nicknack. It is of two kinds, the red and the green,—they are, indeed, frequently found intermixed,—the former somewhat resembling porphyry, and the latter verd antique. Frequently a vein of steatite, or soapstone, introduces a lustrous white streak into the serpentine, and occasionally it is crossed by a beautiful purple or lilac band.

The beauty of the serpentine district, especially at the Lizard and Kynance Cove, can scarce be imagined by those who have not visited it, as the perpetual friction of the waves has worn the rocks to such a degree of smoothness as makes crag and cavern appear as if they had been subjected to a high polish. The serpentine formation is said to begin at the Manacles, a chain of rocks near Falmouth; but the marble of the Manacles is not true serpentine, being a much duller green, unrelieved by the bright red and purple tints. Serpentine is extensively employed in the interior decorations of churches, particularly in the West of England. It is also used for ornamental work in some of the London shops; but any one desirous of seeing it without the trouble of a journey to Cornwall may do so by going to the Geological Museum, Jermyn Street, which contains beautiful specimens of serpentine both in the architectural decorations and among the minerals collected for exhibition.

Among other objects of interest in the neighborhood of the Lizard is Llandewednack Church, famed as being the last edifice in which divine service was ever performed in Cornish. This latter fact is interesting to the philologist, but the naturalist and the epicure may care more to know that Asparagus Island, close to Kynance Cove, is the habitat of that vegetable which we deservedly reckon among the choicest of our spring delicacies. The Lizard Lighthouse and the curious piece of coast about Cadgwith are also worth a visit.

Our head-quarters at the time of making this excursion were at Helstone, rather an interesting old town. One ancient custom still exists there, in the observance of "Furry Day," supposed to be the corruption of "Flora's Day," which festival is annually held on March 9, and is celebrated by the principal inhabitants dancing and carrying flowers up and down the High Street. The entertainment concludes with a ball in the evening at the town hall or one of the inns. Harvest is gathered in with great rejoicings in this part of the country, as in the whole West of England. When the last sheaf is gathered in, the farmer or the principal "hand" cries out, cutting off at the same time a handful of the corn and holding it by the *neck,—i.e.*, stalk,—

"I hab 'im! I hab 'im! I hab 'im!"

The answer is,—

"What hab ye? What hab ye? What hab ye?"

And the rejoinder,—

"A neck! A neck! A neck!"

A handful, called collectively "the neck," is preserved, decorated with flowers and ribbons, in farm-kitchen or hall of manor-house, as it may be, until the next harvest. There can be little doubt that we see in these old customs the traces of some long forgotten heathen observances.

Near Helstone is the Looe Pool, the largest lake of Southwestern England, and believed by some to be the lake described by Tennyson in the "Morte d'Arthur," though the Rev. Mr. Hawker, in his "Footprints of Former Men in Old Cornwall," claims the honor for the Dozmere or Dermary Pool in North Cornwall. If the mysterious mere into which the magic sword Excalibur was thrown by Sir Bedivere at the dying king's command, and caught by the wondrous arm

"Clothed in white samite, mystic, wonderful,"

was but a creature of the poet's own brain, we fancy Dozmere Pool must have been the spot intended, the laureate being, we believe, better acquainted with northern than with western Cornwall. But if Tennyson founded his descriptions of the passing away of Arthur on old chronicles or romances partly handed down by tradition, we give our vote in favor of the Looe, which, like the lake in the idyll, has on its bank the remains of an ancient chapel, and in which the poet's description of

"The long wave lapping on the shingly beach,"

is completely realized.

It is also comparatively near to Land's End; and "the land of Lyonnesse," so often alluded to in the legends of King Arthur, is said to be a district now submerged by the sea, but formerly lying between Land's End and Scilly. All these are but conjectures, however. More reliable records of the past are to be found in the traces of charcoal-burning in the woods round the Looe, which bear evidence of the sacrifice of their trees made by the then owners of the property to the royal cause during the civil wars. The Cornishmen were mostly Royalists. Though the Looe is always spoken of as a *lake*, it is, in fact, only divided from the sea by a narrow neck of land called the Bar, which once in about every three years is cut through with a great amount of ceremony, the mayor of Helstone asking permission of the lord of the manor, and presenting him, as immemorial custom enjoins, with three half-pence.

Porthleven, the little port or watering-place of Helstone, may be interesting to Londoners as the shipping-place of much of the granite used in building the Thames embankment.

Between the Lizard and Mount's Bay is a fine rugged piece of scenery, the grandest headland of which is called Trewarvas Point. From it can be seen the three noble capes of Mullion, Helzephron, and the Lizard; and at Trewarvas itself are some romantic fantastic-shaped rocks, one of which, from some fancied resemblance to an ecclesiastic in his robes, has obtained the name of the "Bishop."

From Helstone we went to Falmouth, the enchanting beauty of the scenery round which place is little known to those who have merely paid a flying visit to that dirty seaport, and perhaps inspected the harbor. Falmouth itself, as we suppose most persons know, is not a particularly ancient town. Sir Walter Raleigh was the first to discover its great advantages of situation, and it was at his recommendation that Queen Elizabeth had the town and harbor built. But, comparatively modern as is Falmouth itself, its neighborhood abounds in the associations of antiquity. A gentleman's seat on the shore of the beautiful creek known as Helford River still bears the name of Gyllindune,—*i.e.*, "William's grave," from being a traditional burial-place of Prince William, son of Henry I., and lost in the wreck of "The White Ship." This tradition goes far to contradict a statement we met with in a number of a popular magazine, to the effect that while the French popular mind retains many legends of the highest antiquity, in England popular tradition does not stretch back to a period more remote than the civil wars of the seventeenth century....

The scenery in the neighborhood of Falmouth, especially on the banks of Helford River, is beautiful in the extreme. Rugged wildness contrasted with fertility, tropical foliage, and an endless succession of romantic creeks and headlands, combine to form an earthly paradise. After several delightful weeks in this picturesque region, we proceeded northwards to the little town of Liskeard, in East Cornwall, in which we had been recommended to pass a couple of days, on account of its extreme quietude and seclusion. Our surprise may be easily imagined, therefore, when we found, on reaching this tranquil spot, that we were in the midst of Vanity Fair. We had not known, previously to our arrival, that the second and third of October were the grand saturnalia of the inhabitants of Liskeard and neighborhood, the annual honey fair, or St. Matthew's Fair.

St. Matthew's Day, indeed, takes place a fortnight previously, but doubtless the fair dates from a period antecedent to the alteration of the style. The sale of honey, cattle, etc., only occupies the morning of the first day; the afternoon, and, indeed, the night until a late hour, and the whole of the second day, being devoted to pleasuring. Sweetmeats of various kinds, particularly a sticky-looking kind of taffy, called, we believe, "clidgy," seem the staple commodity of the pleasure fair. Some of the little baskets and other ornaments made out of these appetizing comestibles are really very elegant. Another great feature is the "Cheap Jack," or rather "Cheap Jill," a young lady who, with untiring lungs, sells by auction the whole day long fancy articles, of which bead fly-traps seem by far the most numerous. Could not this branch of female employment be suggested to those interested in enlarging the sphere of women's occupations, as one especially appropriate to the fair sex? The two qualifications most necessary for a "Cheap Jack," volubility and mercantile smartness, are usually considered, even by her detractors, as especial *fortes* of woman.

From the windows of our hotel we saw, as from a stage-box, the humors of the fair, and especially did we obtain an excellent view of "The Enchanted Temple of Science and Mystery," and similar enlivening exhibitions. The wrestling booth was, as might be expected in this muscularly Christian country, a favorite resort. A peep within this gladiatorial arena, however, only revealed very mild-looking athletes, and spectators as grave as judges, looking much more as if they were at meeting than at a fair. It must be stated, to the credit of the Liskeard revellers, that everything went on with the utmost decorum and order. It shows the primitive simplicity of these west country folks that they can still find so much pleasure in these unsophisticated amusements, but it must be borne in mind that Liskeard is a town usually so quiet, not to say sleepy, that it has been declared by a resident that he could fire a gun down the street without hitting any one!...

The Cornish folk are, as a rule, earnest in their religious convictions, though, like other Kelts, occasionally inclined to fanaticism. All traces of the savagery which distinguished them in the rough days of the wreckers, have, of course, entirely passed away under the light of advancing civilization. The Cornishmen are extremely hospitable, and the county dainties of cider, clotted cream, potato cake, griddle or girdle cakes (baked upon the hearth), and fish or squab pies, are luxuries not to be despised any more than the *figgadowdy* (Anglicé, plum-puddings). Like all the inhabitants of remote districts, the Cornish folk are extremely clannish, and think much of the ties of kindred, the proverbial expression "A Cornish Jack" showing how every individual endeavors to prove himself everybody else's "Cousin John." They are very superstitious, though whether they yet retain the old beliefs mentioned by Polwhele, such as that of the ghost of a ship-wrecked mariner announcing his fate by calling his own name on the rock, and that when the wind roars boisterously it is the wicked giant Tregeagle roaring, we cannot, of course, say.

Many names of places bear witness to the widely scattered traditions connected with King Arthur. One group of rocks of various sizes goes by the name of "King Arthur's cups and saucers," a name involving a bold anachronism, for one hardly imagines saucers to have been much used before the introduction of tea and coffee, beverages, as every one knows, not brought into use in this country for more than a thousand years after the supposed period of King Arthur.

The belief in fairies has not yet gone out in this remote shire, and we have been in an old house said to be haunted by the ghost of a cow.

The fauna and flora of Cornwall are much the same as in other parts of Western England, except, of course, that some shrubs and other plants usually found only in warm climates or in greenhouses grow here freely out of doors. The Cornish chough among birds, and among plants the Cornish heath, are, as the names show, indigenous here. It is strange that the little harebell, so universal in Scotland and in most parts of England, should be here a great rarity. We recollect how, on our excursion to the Lizard, a lady of the neighborhood of Helstone had been entreated by a friend unable to accompany her to bring home a harebell, if she found any, as none grew near her own residence.

Those travelling in a country new to them are often more struck by some feature of the landscape different to what they have been accustomed to, than by the grander outlines of the scenery. Who, for instance, that has ever travelled in Western Cornwall, can fail to recollect the milestones in the shapes of obelisks, or the substitutes for stiles formed by narrow openings in the hedges with stepping-stones placed at equal distances, like the ploughshares in the ordeal by fire, for foot passengers to pass across? The little cabbage-plantation or mound of *débris* in the centre of a field is another characteristically Cornish institution. Any account of Cornwall would be incomplete without some allusion to the pilchard fishery, next to mining, the great industry of the county. Innumerable quantities of this fish are annually salted and exported to the Roman Catholic countries of Southern Europe to be eaten during Lent. The popular Cornish name of the pilchard, "Fair Maid," is said to be from the Spanish *fumado,—i.e.,* "smoked fish."

THE ENGLISH LAKE DISTRICT.

AMELIA BARR.

[The lakes of Cumberland and Westmoreland, England, possess a double attraction to the tourist, the one being for their intrinsic beauty and charm, the other for their fame as the loved haunts of Wordsworth, Coleridge, Southey, and other famed writers. They have become a place of pilgrimage to the devotees of poetry, and we give their story in the words of one who saw in them this double charm.]

While dinner was being prepared, we strolled to the bridge which spans the Leven,—at this point a swift, shallow stream, with an inconceivable sparkle, scarcely deep enough to float the light skiff in whose shadow a great trout was posing himself against the crystal water. In half an hour we had a couple of his fellows in a napkin, deliciously browned. It is worth while mentioning that Loch Lomond in Scotland and Lake Windermere in England discharge by rivers of the same length and name; but the Scotch Leven passes through a bleak, uninteresting country, while the English Leven ripples and dances through a vale of sylvan beauty, full of the music of many cascades.

We hired a row-boat to take us up Windermere to the Ferry Inn; and here, as an old Laker, I may say, have nothing to do with a *sail*; take a row-boat, and you are safe; but all these mountain-locked waters are subject to what is known in the district as a "bottom-wind;" and the sail-boat caught in that passionate gust will need the most skilful handling.

As we neared Storrs Hall, all the bright loveliness of the lake broke upon us, as it did upon Scott in 1825, on that memorable day when Southey, Wilson, Wordsworth, and Canning met him here, and Windermere glittered with all her sails in honor of the great Northern minstrel. The Bailie had the whole passage from Lockhart's Life of Scott by heart,—the brilliant cavalcades through the woods, the boatings on the lake by moonlight, the music and sunshine, the flags and streamers, the gay dresses and beautiful women, the hum of voices, the cheers of the multitude, and the splash of innumerable oars: he recalled for us the whole scene of the flotilla, as it wound among the beautiful isles of the loveliest lake in the world, half a century ago.

We had sent our luggage on to the Salutation Inn at Ambleside, for we had determined to stay one night at the Ferry Inn, nearly opposite Bowness, and about half-way up the lake. I had wonderful memories of this charming old hostelry, and many a time, when thousands of miles away, I had heard the pleasure-skiffs fret their cut-waters against the pebbly shore, many a time in dreams dripped silver from my oars in the moonlight, or wandered in the groves of laurel and lilacs and laburnums behind it.

Then it was a perfect old English inn, with a kitchen whose Homeric breadth and bright cheerfulness made it a constant picture. Then there was on one side of it a curiously carved and twisted oaken dresser, extending from the floor to the ceiling, black with age and bright with labor. Mugs and tankards of bright pewter stood out against this dark background; huge hams and sad-colored herbs descended from the rafters. A great wood-fire always blazed on the hearth. Lasses in snow-white jackets and linsey-woolsey petticoats went in and out about their duties. The handsome, motherly landlady looked after every guest; and Arnold, the jolliest landlord that ever lived, sat smoking in the ingle, chatting with some traveller, or listening to the yarn of a lake fisherman.

As we approached the little bay, I saw that the Ferry Inn had gone; a grand modern hotel stood upon its site. I refused to be disenchanted. Perhaps Arnold was dead also. Nothing could be as it had been, and I asked to cross over at once to Bowness. But, while I am speaking of Arnold, I may tell again a story he was very fond of telling about Wordsworth.

"Knaw'd Wadswuth?" he would say, with a merry twinkle. "I did, a few. This wuz the way I comed to knaw him, so as I shan't forget 'n again in a hurry. When I wuz guard of the Whitehaven mail, as we wuz a-slapping along, and just coming to a sharpish turn,—the carner near the bridge, this side Keswick,—what should we see but sumthin' uncommon tall and grand, tooling along a little pony-shay!

"'Oh, Lord! here's a smash,' said I, and afore the words wuz out of my mouth, crash went the shay all to smitherins, and slap went the driver over a wall into a plantation, arms out and great-coat a-flying. We thought fur sure 'twas all over with 'n; but presently he picked hisself up uncommon tall again, and sez he, 'I'll have this matter thoroughly investigated.' With that he walked off towards the public.

"'Bill,' said coachee to I, very down like, 'who de think that is?'

"'Well, who be 't, Jem?' sez I.

"'Why, who but the powit Wadswuth.'"

Then he would add, "If you goes to Keswick, just by the bridge you'll see the place *where we spilt the powit*! Ay, often and often since that, when I've a-seen the grand fowks draw up to the Mount, I've a-said sly like to myself, 'Ah, gentlemen, you be going to see the powit, but you never had him to call upon you, unexpected like, on a flying visit over a wall.'"

Windermere at Bowness is like what the Thames is at Richmond. Bowness is the pleasure-village of the lake country. There yachtsmen flourish and beauties linger. The band makes music in the grounds of the Royal Hotel, and the crowds promenade or float gracefully past in the dreamy waltz. Every window is open, the balconies are full of life and color, lovely faces peep out from among the clustering clematis, twinkling lights and soft strains are on the lake until midnight, and flowers, flowers, flowers touch you everywhere.

Two men, as dissimilar as possible, I can always see in the streets of Bowness—the handsome Professor Wilson, poet and athlete, whom the Westmoreland people so aptly described as "strang as a lion, lish as a trout, *wi' sich antics as niver*," and the little, plain-faced, serious Wilberforce,—Wilson joyous and strong, and settling all things "wi' the waff o' his hand," Wilberforce sauntering along, as he tells us in his diary, comforting himself by repeating the one hundred and nineteenth Psalm. Wilson lived at Elleray, now close to Windermere railway-station, and Wilberforce had a residence among the stately woods of Rayrigg, just outside Bowness.

The next morning we started for Ambleside, taking on the way the village of Troutbeck. Troutbeck is a funny misnomer for the rivulet so named, for not a trout has ever been found in it. But for a typically exquisite village, no dream of painter or poet can rival it. The cottages, with their numerous gables, seem to have been built on some model conceived by the rarest poetical genius. They are of the stone and slate of the country; age has given them "a green radiance" and bathed them in the lustre of lichens. The porches are of meeting tree-stems or reclining cliffs, and are dripping with roses and matted with virgin bower. Nowhere else in the world is there "a mile-long congregation of such rural dwellings, dropped down just where a painter or poet would wish them, and bound together by old groves of ash, oak, and sycamores, by flower-gardens and fruit-orchards rich as those of the Hesperides."...

There are places we visit and forget, but this is never the case with Ambleside; walk through its streets, and they become forever a part of the spirit's still domains. John Ruskin, in his "Characteristics of Nature," has referred to the peculiar influence which is exerted upon people who live in a neighborhood where granite is abundant; and Wordsworth tells us that

"One impulse from a vernal wood

May teach us more of man,

Of moral evil, and of good,

Than all the sages can."

If this be true, then what influence must be morally exerted over those who dwell in such a bower of Paradise as Ambleside!

The vale of Windermere is watered by two little rivers, the Rothay and Brathay. They unite a few yards above the head of the lake, and enter it together. In the spawning season a singular sight may be witnessed at this spot: the trout and char, for which Windermere is famous, separate where the rivers meet; the char go up Brathay to spawn, the trout all go up Rothay.

The most charming way to see the vale of Ambleside is to saunter about it; to walk to Stock Ghyll Force and look at the old mill made famous by the painting of Birket Foster; to lean over Rothay Bridge and Pelter Bridge and dream away the hours on the shores of the wildly-sylvan Rydalmere; or to go into Rydal Park and lose ourselves among the cooing of cushats and the shrill cries of blackbirds. Stock Ghyll Force is worth seeing. The word "force" is one of the few words of the past still lingering in secluded places: it signifies to "rush thoroughly:" the waters fall from a height of seventy feet, and make a terrific noise as they rush in two channels down the rocky gorge.

The slopes are covered with the rarest ferns, probably most of them indigenous to the soil, for we were told that few of them lived if transplanted from it. The path leading to the falls now belongs to the town of Ambleside, but a year or two ago it was in the possession of a gentleman who purchased the property at an auction. It had always been free and open to the public, but this speculative individual bought up the waterfall and hemmed it in with a fence. He then made a charge for admission. The townspeople were indignant; a sum of a thousand pounds was raised, and the man bought out at double the amount. The toll for the present is charged, but it will be abolished as soon as the other thousand has been collected,—a consummation fully expected during the present year.

The spirits of the great and good walk the lovely lanes and climb the hills with us, for all around Ambleside is haunted ground. Just outside is the ivy-covered house so long the home of Harriet Martineau, one of the bravest and hardest-working women that ever lived.

"Day by day our memory fades
From out the circle of the hills,"

but the memory of the invalid deaf lady, so loving, so simple, so neighborly, so old in years, so young in heart, is one that will not soon be forgotten, even in the land of Wordsworth and Southey and Arnold.

A little farther, Fox How nestles at the foot of a craggy height. This was for many years the home of Dr. Arnold; and not far away is Fox Ghyll, a beautiful villa belonging to the Right Honorable W. E. Forster, who, it will be remembered, married a daughter of Dr. Arnold's. Mr. Forster spends a great deal of his time here, glad to escape the "madding crowd" and the bickering and fever of political life.

A lovely drive through "a spot made for nature by herself" brought us to Rydal Mount, so long the home of Wordsworth. He went there in 1813, and at that time the lakes were hardly known. The poet Gray was the only eminent Englishman who visited them before the present century, and he complained that "the great forests and the total want of communication was a barrier he could not surmount." Upon Goldsmith they made no impression; and Tickell, born within a mile of Derwentwater, has not a line in their praise, though he wrote a long poem on Kensington Gardens. But in 1813 Englishmen were compelled to travel in their own country, for Napoleon had closed the continent of Europe to them, or, as a Westmoreland woman expressed it, "there was sic a deal of uneasiness i' France."

And here I may notice, in passing, the peculiar habit of *understating* everything, so characteristic of Westmoreland people. Where a Yorkshire man would say unequivocally, "The fellow is a scoundrel," the Westmoreland man would remark, "There were a deal o' folks more particler about doin' reet nor him." A bad man is a bad man all the world over, except in Westmoreland: there he is "a varra moderate chap." All over the world, when it rains as hard as it can, people do not scruple to say, "It rains hard;" but a Westmoreland man only admits, "It's softish."...

At Rydal Mount, Wordsworth lived nearly forty years, roaming over the mountains or sitting down by some lonely tarn to write his "solemn-thoughted idylls;" for he seldom wrote in-doors. A visitor once asked to see his study, and a servant showed her a room containing a number of books. "This is the master's library," she said: "his study is out o' doors and up on t'hill-tops." The house is a lovely spot now, but it owes much to Wordsworth. I have a drawing of it, made soon after he removed there, which represents only a very plain stone house, standing on a natural terrace of turf. The interior has been often described, for no visitor with a respectable claim on the poet's attention was ever turned away. But it is now in the possession of a man who suffers no one to approach it. In fact, he has taken care to post conspicuously the following notice: "No person is allowed in these grounds under any circumstances." In 1850, Wordsworth died at Rydal Mount,—a sweetly-solemn death, which gave to his mourning heart the glad assurance that he was "going to Dora," his dearly beloved daughter, whose death on the threshold of a beautiful and happy womanhood he had never ceased to mourn.

On the road which skirts Rydal Water is Nab Cottage, forever associated with De Quincey and poor Hartley Coleridge. Standing before it, how easy it was to imagine the small, fragile Opium-Eater, with his wrinkled face and arched brows loaded with thought, and those haunted eyes peering out from their dark rings! How vividly we could see him in the small parlor, with its five thousand books and bright fire and decanter of laudanum, or imagine him rambling through the summer nights upon the hills, in solitary possession of the whole sleeping country, when that fine expression he applied to Coleridge in similar situations might so well designate himself,—"an insulated son of revery"!

[The travellers next set out for a tramp to the top of Helvellyn, the loftiest mountain of the lake district. On their way thither they came upon an interesting pastoral scene.]

The farm-yard went straight up the hill, but was surrounded by buildings of every kind. What a busy, merry, picturesque gathering was in it! The old men, in clean, white shirt-sleeves, with long clay pipes in their mouths, were wandering about the yard, watching the shearers, who were working with a silent rapidity that showed a very keen contest. For these "shearings" are a kind of rural Olympics; and proud is the young farmer who has finished his sixscore sheep in a day.

There were seven shearers present, wonderfully handsome, stalwart fellows. Each sat upon a bench, their pillar-like throats uncovered, their arms bare to the shoulder; and, as the sheep were brought to them, they lifted them on to the bench, turned them with the greatest ease, and cut off the wool with amazing rapidity, rarely allowing the shears to injure the animal. If such an accident occurred, it was a blemish on the shearer's fame.

At a long impromptu table women were just as rapidly folding the fleeces ready for market. Some were handsome matrons, some were young lasses, but all wore the snow-white kirtle and the short, striped linsey petticoat that showed their slender ankles and trimly-shod feet. Peals of merry laughter and shafts of harmless satire flew from them to the shearers, who were far too busy to answer just then, but who doubtless promised themselves future opportunities. In a small enclosure at the extreme end there was perhaps the merriest group of all,—about a dozen school-lads, whose duty it was to bring the sheep to the shearers. How the heated air quivered above the panting creatures, and how the lads laughed and shouted and tugged and pulled and pushed and dragged, their brown faces glowing to crimson, their parted scarlet lips and intense blue eyes making them perfect pictures of splendidly healthy, happy boyhood!

And with what indulgent tolerance the sheep-dogs watched them! I am sure the good-natured ones laughed quietly to themselves at all the unnecessary fuss, while others lay with their heads between their paws and opened their eyes sarcastically at the whole affair. They would have taken a sheep by the ear and walked it up to the bench without a bark. It was a perfect idyllic picture, in which every age of manhood and womanhood blended.

At sundown over six hundred sheep had been sheared, and a number of visitors arrived. Then a feast was spread for more than fifty people, and after it the fiddlers took the place of honor, and dancing began. No one could resist the mirthful infection, and, after a slight hesitation, Christina drew on her gloves and allowed herself to be persuaded to open the ball with "the master." She was just stepping daintily down the middle, with a smile on her face, when the Bailie looked in at the open door. He professed to be "vera weary;" but in half an hour he was taking his part in "Moneymusk" with a lively agility that won him much admiration. "Such hours dinna come every day," he said. And so we stayed until the dancing ceased and the company scattered at the fell foot into parties of twos and threes.

[From Grasmere they made their way to Keswick, the capital town of the lake district, and the home of Southey and Coleridge.]

When Southey came to Greta Hall, in 1803, Coleridge, the "noticeable man with large gray eyes," was living there, delighting the reading world with his vast and luminous intellect and his Miltonic conceptions, reaching "the caverns measureless to man." Here that marvellous boy Hartley ran about, and so charmed Coleridge's landlord that he could scarcely be persuaded to take the rent for Greta Hall, considering the joy of the child's company a full equivalent. For three years Coleridge and Southey occupied the Hall together; then Coleridge became the slave of that opium-habit which made his comings and goings more uncertain than a comet's. He flitted about between Southey and Wordsworth; and never since Shakespeare's time have three men of equal genius lived on such terms. Landor called them "three towers of one castle." Very soon De Quincey made a fourth in this remarkable group. And two of them were wise, and two of them were stranded on the same poppy-covered coast, the land of the Lotos-Eaters.

We wandered about Keswick, but wherever we went the shades of these great men followed us, and half a mile out of it, on the Penrith road, we were suddenly met by another wraith of genius, for there stood the pretty cottage to which Shelley brought his first wife, the lovely woman of humble birth whom he offended society by marrying. Here they were visited by the Southeys and De Quincey, and the latter in his "Sketches" has a very charming picture of the girl-wife playing gravity before her visitors and running about the garden with Percy when they were tired of the house. Shelley was then nineteen and Southey thirty-seven; and Southey says, "Shelley acts upon me as my own ghost might do; he has all my old dreams and enthusiasms: the only difference is the difference of age."

Many bitter things were said of the handsome, gifted Shelley in his day; but, as Dr. Arnold in his quaint, Luther-like phraseology observes, "Doubtless it is good for a man to have to do with Mr. Posterity," for that impartial judge has done Shelley justice. We bought his "Alastor" as we went back to the hotel, and in the evening twilight read it, remembering the while that it was written "in the contemplation of death, which he felt to be certain and near."...

The next day we went around Derwentwater in a boat,—certainly the best way to see it, for the bays and islands and points of interest on this lovely sheet of water can thus be leisurely visited. Soon after leaving Keswick, Skiddaw appears to rise from within a stone's cast of the shore, and continues a magnificent object during most of the way. At the head of the lake the mountains rise, height above height, from the Lodore crags to the lofty summits of Scawfell Pike and Scawfell, the latter the highest mountain in England. Southey had told us how "the water comes down at Lodore," but we wished to see it for ourselves: so we landed at the long wooden pier belonging to the Lodore Hotel, and, guided by the tremendous roar, scrambled a short distance among the crags and boulders, and saw the wild waters

"Retreating and beating, and meeting and sheeting,

Delaying and straying, and playing and spraying,
Advancing and prancing, and glancing and dancing,
Recoiling, turmoiling, and toiling and boiling,
And gleaming and streaming, and steaming and beaming,
And rushing and flushing, and brushing and gushing,
And curling and whirling, and purling and twirling,
And flapping and rapping, and clapping and slapping,
And dashing and flashing, and splashing and crashing,
And so never ending, but always descending,
Sounds and motions for ever and ever are blending,
All at once and all over, with mighty uproar,
And this way the water comes down at Lodore."

THE ROMAN WALL OF CUMBERLAND.

ROSE G. KINGSLEY.

[On the borders of Cumberland, at the northern boundary of Roman occupation of England, a wall of defence against the barbarians of Scotland was built, and manned by sturdy legions. This wall still exists, and its present condition is described below.]

Half an hour's drive brought us to the farm-house at Birdoswald, and here the real interest of our expedition began. We were now on the Roman Wall; and, except Borcovicus or Housteads, near the Northumberland lakes, Birdoswald is the most perfect station along its line. It is supposed to be the Roman Ambloganna, which was garrisoned by a strong force of Dacians from Wallachia and Moldavia. The camp is five and a half acres in extent. The eastern gate-way is in very perfect preservation, the large blocks on each side of the double portal being in their original position and still containing the pivot-holes. The arch above the gate-way is gone; but some of the stones which formed it lie strewn about. Close to the gate are the ruins of a guard-house, and a portion of the boundary-wall, six feet in breadth. The western and southern gate-ways and walls are all well preserved, the walls having five or six courses of facing-stones, and being seven to eight feet thick.

In the farm-house the buxom farmer's wife showed us an ancient arch in the wall of the passage, under which lay a collection of curiosities found from time to time about the camp,—a beautiful stone figure with flowing drapery, small stone altars, such as the soldiers used in their private devotions, and so forth. Outside, pinks, lilies, and roses were filling the air with their perfume, as we made our way through the little garden to the green field where stood the camp. We wandered about round the low stone walls, through the gate-way, where we saw the actual marks of the chariot-wheels on the pavement,—two ruts in the stone. We looked into the remains of the guard-house, where the sweet thyme and delicate clover now creep over stones against which Dacian warriors rested their heavy heads. We tried to trace out the course of streets, temples, and barracks among the grass-grown heaps in front of the farm-garden; and then I went out to the brow of the hill to see what was there.

What a surprise! The green field fell away abruptly in a great cliff, and down below the Irthing foamed over its stony bed, twisting and winding in sinuous curves of silver along the narrow valley, among wooded slopes and rocky crags. Green ridge and brown fell in endless succession led the eye away into the far distance, where Skiddaw loomed up in the south.

The late Lord Carlisle, in his "Diary in Turkish and Greek Waters," compares this view to the first sight of Troy after crossing the tame low plain of the Troad. It was certainly a grand point of vantage which, with their usual wisdom, the Romans pitched upon. The one thing one does not see at first is, where they got their water; and this was always one of the first points they considered in choosing a site. The river is too far off, and no spring now appears inside the camp. Last year my friends showed Birdoswald to the learned head-master of one of our most famous public schools. The absence of water puzzled the wise man not a little, and he asked one of the farm maidens who was showing the party round if she knew where the spring had been. She professed entire ignorance; but another lassie standing by reminded her in broad Cumbrian, "It's where t' goose laid her eggs last soummer." We soon found it out to our cost, as, thanks to the rainy season, the ancient Roman well had formed a little quagmire hidden in long grass, into which we plunged unwittingly and came out with wet boots.

The Roman Wall adapts itself to the northern rampart of the camp, or fort, and runs close to the road for some five hundred yards westward from the farm-house. This wall—seventy-five miles long—has been the subject of many antiquarian discussions, with which we need not meddle. Those, however, who have gone most thoroughly into the subject now agree that it was erected by the renowned emperor Hadrian, when he came to Britain, in the year 119. The inscribed slabs and altars found at the stations and castles on the line of the wall are undoubtedly of his reign; so are most of the coins that are found with them; and from this fact it appears that the Roman legions received their pay at the wall in his reign.

The conception of this stupendous barrier is singularly simple and effective. The wall, though varying a little in width, according to the nature of the ground it traversed, was about eight feet broad and fourteen feet high. The north side was further crowned by a parapet of four feet, making the total height eighteen feet. The outside stones were regularly-shaped and well-dressed freestone, fifteen to twenty inches long, ten inches broad, and eight inches thick. So well were they cut that one can detect them in an instant in any cottage-wall, from their smooth, finely-chiselled face as compared with the coarser dressing of modern stones. Most of them have a wedge shape, tapering towards the end which is set into the wall. Dr. Bruce thinks that stones of this shape would have been conveniently carried on the backs of "the poor enslaved Britons." The present dwellers along the wall say that they were all brought in an old woman's apron and the wall built in one night. Mr. Jenkinson, on the contrary, in his charming and learned guide-book to Carlisle and the Roman Wall, thinks "both these modes of conveyance are too romantic for the practical Romans, who were not unacquainted with horses and carts."

The inside part of the wall consists of rubble-stone, like that found in the massive walls of Cæsar's Tower at Kenilworth and many other old castles. The stones, evidently picked up on the spot, while the dressed stone for the wall was brought in many instances from a great distance, were cemented together as hard as a rock by pouring fresh lime mixed with sand and gravel upon them.

Every four miles along the wall there was a fortified camp or station, like that at Birdoswald, each capable of containing from six hundred to one thousand foot- or horse-soldiers, as the case might be. "They were generally," says Mr. Jenkinson, "close to the wall, on the southern side, and appear from the remains existing to have formed almost a square, containing three to six acres, surrounded by high thick walls, provided with four gate-ways, and laid out in streets, barracks, temples, baths, etc., some of the buildings having massive and occasionally beautifully-sculptured stones. Outside these stations are heaps of grass-grown rubbish, from which it is inferred that there also existed suburbs, where dwelt natives and camp-followers."

Between the stations were *castella*, or mile-castles, about a mile apart. These were sixty feet square, built also on the south side, of solid masonry, about the same height and thickness as the wall itself. In each of these were stationed a company of some twenty men, who were yet further distributed singly in stone turrets, or watch-towers, used as sentry-boxes, of which there were four between each mile-castle, about three hundred and fifty yards apart. The sentries, being within call of each other, could thus keep up a complete system of communication along the line, and, as soon as danger threatened, troops could be concentrated at once on any spot from the stations or camps. Unluckily, none of these turrets remain, though Hodgson says that he saw one opened so lately as 1833, about three hundred yards west of Birdoswald.

Along the northern face of the wall the Romans still further strengthened it by making a ditch below, thirty-six feet wide and fifteen feet deep. It was evidently a dry ditch, as it follows the line of the wall up hill and down dale. In some places the solid rock has been excavated to make it, and occasionally the earth dug from it has been thrown up into a bank on its farther side, thus making a third line of defence. To the south of the stone wall, at a distance perpetually varying from a few yards to half a mile, runs the vallum, or earthwork, consisting, where most perfect, of three ramparts and a fosse. The origin and use of the *vallum* has also been a moot point among antiquaries. But now there seems little doubt that the vallum was the ancient Roman road running inside the wall. Pavements have been found upon it in various places. At Gilsland, exactly on the spot where the vallum would have to cross the Poltross Burn, the abutment of a Roman bridge has been lately discovered; and the highest authorities are now agreed, from these and many other indications, that this dispute may at last be laid to rest.

Climbing once more into our "heaven chariot," we bade farewell to Birdoswald and its many memories and drove due west along the line of the wall. For five hundred yards it ran close beside us on the left, about seven feet high and seven feet broad,—the stones in some places untouched since the day the Roman legions laid them one on another, clear cut as when they came out of the quarry. The short turf had clothed the top of the ancient barrier with a fragrant carpet, and in crevices where the cement had weathered away, the honeysuckle found root-hold; a tall purple foxglove reared its proud head as if it were acting sentry to the Border, and the fresh green lady-fern brushed the rugged stones lightly with waving plumes.

After a time the wall grew lower, and finally disappeared. Our road, which had been running straight as a bee-line, rose and swerved a few feet to the left, and we found that we were actually driving along the top of the wall. For nearly five miles we followed it. There it ran as straight as an arrow over every obstacle, with the great green ditch to our right and the great earth-bank beyond it, a type of the resistless determination of the great people who made it. High moorland pastures, reclaimed from the Waste, lay on either side. In some, the sweet hay was being cut, and the buzz of an American mowing-machine brought our wits with a sudden shock out of the by-gone ages where they had been wandering. In others, herds of polled Galloways, the sleek black cattle of the Border, were grazing peacefully, without fear of moss-troopers or cattle-thieves. Here stood a mile-castle,—four rude grass-grown banks marking its outline,—its stones being used to build a little cottage crouching in one corner. There an old lime-kiln, like some troll's dwelling, broke the endless swell of green and brown. The few cottages at the hamlet of Banks Head looked forlorn and dreary, as if they had been dropped by mistake on the desolate wild. They are all built of stone from the wall, which has proved an invaluable quarry to the whole neighborhood, and, in consequence, has been ruthlessly destroyed. A hideous fashion prevails about here. Most of the houses are whitewashed, the stones round the doors and windows are painted black, and, with their cold gray slate roofs or dilapidated thatch, they but add to the dreary look of this district. It is a dismal land up there on the Waste,—a sad, hard country, with its stone walls and boggy uplands, that must have bred a sad, hard race, one would think. But if one looks beyond the dreariness close at hand, what a wondrous view stretches away all round! East, are the greenish swells and conical crests of the Northumberland Fells; south, lie Tindale, Talkin, and Castle Carrock Fells across the valley of the Irthing, which is marked by a line of wood, and beyond them rise the noble group of Lake mountains. Helvellyn and the two giants Saddleback and Skiddaw, looming up veiled in mystery and golden haze; northward, the line of the Cheviot Hills shows that we are looking right into Scotland; westward, across the fertile plain, where park and pasture, river and forest, are bathed in sunshine, Criffel rears his head above Melrose Abbey; and there, right under the western sun, gleams a line of silver in the flat, extremest distance,—the Solway Firth.

It was with the feeling of parting from a friend that we bade adieu to the Roman Wall and turned downward from the bleak moorland into the rich vegetation of the valley. The glamour of the Roman period had laid hold upon us. We longed to follow up the course of this great barrier, to know more of its builders, of their lives, their works, their history, than we had ever done before. This monument of their almost superhuman power must awaken some kind of enthusiasm in the dullest mind, and one can echo Sir Walter Scott's words in "Guy Mannering:" "And this, then, is the Roman Wall. What a people, whose labors even at this extremity of their empire comprehended such space, and were executed upon a scale of such grandeur! In future ages, when the science of war shall have changed, how few traces will exist of the labors of Vauban and Coehorn, while this wonderful people's remains will even then continue to interest and astonish posterity! Their fortifications, their aqueducts, their theatres, their fountains, all their public works, bear the grave, solid, and majestic character of their language; while our modern labors, like our modern tongues, seem but constructed out of their fragments."

ENGLISH RURAL SCENERY.

SARAH B. WISTER.

[For a country rich in its verdant beauty and perfect in its grooming, England is unsurpassed. While containing little of the grand, it has much of the charming, and is abundantly calculated to rest the eyes of the sight-weary traveller. We append an enthusiastic description of this garden-land from an American visitor.]

When we got into the country we grudged the time we had spent in London. The true English landscape has a great and peculiar charm until the stranger learns its secret and wearies of its sameness. Never shall I forget the journey from Southampton to London on the day we landed. Something must be allowed for the delight of eyes that had been looking over endless ridges of sea-waves to the blank horizon for so long; but what a blushing, smiling land it was that greeted them! The verdure was the first thing that struck us,—very different from ours. There is more blue and less yellow in it, resting and refreshing the eyes with a cooler, deeper tone; the trees are denser in foliage too, and fuller in form; the whole scene had a boskiness and boweriness due to innumerable hedges, orchards, shrubberies, and plantations. Woodland, strictly speaking, there was none,—only here and there little triangular bits, not an acre in extent, for game-covers, or lines of tall feathery elms with bushy heads along the hedgerows, clipped close that they might not shut out the scanty sunshine from the farmer's field. The hawthorn was covered with its pink-and-white blossoms, May as they call it; acres of the gently-rolling country were crimson with Dutch clover; the laburnum, a small, graceful tree, was full of drooping strings of delicate yellow flowers; the banks were ablaze with scarlet poppies and golden broom.

Low-arched stone bridges spanned small brimming streams; quaint old gate-ways opened into shady avenues; thatched cottages, beautiful ancient parish churches with gray towers, pretty, quiet hamlets peeped out from the luxuriant leafiness; comfortable, solid, old-fashioned farmhouses reigned among their outbuildings and orchards; in the distance were grand country-places, scarcely visible in the depths of their stately parks; and, what raised our enthusiasm to the utmost, we passed a beautiful Gothic ruin half hidden in ivy. Everything looked trim and orderly; not an inch of ground wasted; all turned to account for use or beauty; little vegetable-gardens on the slopes of the railway-embankments and along the edges of the track; little flower-gardens on both sides the station-houses, and roses and honeysuckle trained over their porches.

This is the genuine, characteristic English scenery, and it is found in perfection in Warwickshire. About Leamington, thanks to the contiguity of several large estates, parts of the country are heavily wooded, and a deep rural seclusion pervades the whole neighborhood. We were there in July: the earlier flowers were gone, but in the green embowered lanes the banks were rich with purple foxgloves; pale, shadowy bramble-roses were blossoming in the hedges, over which climbed woodbine and a pure white convolvulus; the gaudy poppies still held their own, as they do, though with thinner ranks, to the end of the season; and the splendid gorse spread over the uncultivated hill-sides like yellow flame. Many birds make their home here. We came too late for the nightingales, and it was elsewhere that we heard a cuckoo once or twice in a distant thicket, for it is silent after June; but larks warbled in mid-air, and thrushes filled the lanes with their liquid notes, besides a host of little unknown birds who sang their simple song very sweetly all day.

One of the finest country-seats in the county was originally a Cistercian abbey, founded in the reign of Henry II.: a noble gate-way of that period, half shrouded in ivy, still remains, but nothing more except fragments of the cloisters embedded in the main building, which is partly Elizabethan, but chiefly in Queen Anne's style. Uninteresting and tasteless as the latter is, it produces more effect by its solid mass and unbroken façade than Tudor gables or castellated towers. Within are great lofty square rooms, a fine hall and staircase,—all on a scale which with us would be seen only in a public building,—and a whole series of family portraits, priests, knights, courtiers, and dames, by all the famous painters from Henry VIII.'s time to Queen Victoria's.

CANTERBURY CATHEDRAL FROM THE NORTHWEST

The gardens of this place are beautiful, but most artificial-looking, the shorn grass and geometrical flower-beds producing the effect of a worsted pattern; stone steps, balustrades, fountains, statues, urns, vases, and clipped hedges and shrubbery giving them a formal and stately air in keeping with the house itself: not a blade of grass, not a leaf, not a pebble, is out of place. From these one passes into the park, where for miles the undulations of the land form a succession of lovely knolls and dells shaded by magnificent oaks, imperial trees, and groves of lindens and chestnuts hardly less grand, while underfoot all is fern and soft turf. Herds of dappled deer browse beneath these lordly trees or come down to drink at the Avon, a slow little stream which winds through the sylvan glades. Since then I have seen a number of great places, some of them finer than this, but with its legends and associations it is not a bad type of them all. It was the first I saw, and will always be first in my recollection.

Besides the beauty of that region, it is full of interest. There are the romantic ruins of Kenilworth; there are Warwick Castle (partly burnt) and Warwick town, with Leicester's Hospital, and St. Mary's Church, and the Beauchamp Chapel, one of the gems of ecclesiology, with stained-glass windows five hundred years old, and splendid tombs with effigies in brass and alabaster. There is Coventry with all its traditions, from the Lady Godiva to Mary Queen of Scots. The procession of the Lady Godiva still takes place every few years. Last summer there was a celebration: the lady engaged to perform the part of "the woman of a thousand summers old" was not forthcoming in time, and some other eligible female was caught up, clapped on horseback and sent forth: at the same moment the first one arrived, and the consequence was a lawsuit.

Stratford-on-Avon, too, belongs to this part of the country,—a little old-world town, where the bust of Shakespeare looks down upon you from every coign of vantage. Mysterious being! who sprang from impenetrable obscurity in that quiet village to light the beacon of an immortal fame, and sink back into the uncertain shades of his native place until he rests definitely in the beautiful parish church, so still among its trees, with the Avon laving the wall of the church-yard.

Anne Hathaway's cottage remains in good preservation, a picturesque object among the fields; Lucys still live at Charlecote; but too many people have written of these things,—nobody better than Geoffrey Crayon, whose sketch I read over as we waited for luncheon at the Red Horse Inn in the little room called Washington Irving's parlor. Something ought to be said about that luncheon, which, when good, is the best of English meals, dinner as a rule being too heavy and monotonous. On a table-cloth of the traditional whiteness of all napery which is written about, were set out a lordly cold round of beef, a jug of home-brewed ale, a substantial loaf of home-made bread, a smaller one of simple cake, a currant-pie, a rich country cheese, and a pitcher of thick cream. There were three of us: we ate as much as we liked, and paid seven shillings, less than two dollars, but I do not give either the bill of fare or the bill of costs as a sample of ordinary luck.

We saw nothing in England proper prettier than the shady lanes and green foot-paths of Warwickshire. The view from Harrow Hill and the country around Malvern are greatly admired, but they are exceedingly tame, merely an extent of rather flat land seen from an insignificant height, without water, too patchy to have breadth, which is the strong point of flat scenery; there are no stretches of field or forest-land; it is all broken up like a checkerboard by hedgerows and high-roads. We thought the Fen country roads more striking: it has been reclaimed, and is now a fine agricultural district. The eye ranges over wide expanses of cultivation: great plains of pale green bean-vines and yellow grain, alternating with the rich brown of the peat soil, whose pungent odor fills the air, stretch away to the horizon, unbroken save by now and then a row of Lombardy poplars or a line of low willows; the ditches by which the land is drained and divided are marked by long lines of brighter green, and full of graceful waving marsh-grass; and at long intervals a broad, straight, shining path of water takes its way to the sea. Here and there a solitary windmill reminds one of Holland, but it is altogether finer than Holland. With all the teeming fertility there is something which recalls the original desolation: it is very sparsely settled; one seldom sees a house, and then it is not clustered about with outbuildings, but stands up alone against the horizon, and makes one think of Mariana's moated grange. In the midst of these flats rises the majestic tower of Ely, seen for many a mile.

We passed from this into a wild waste in Norfolk, whose sandy hillocks were clad in purple heath and green fern, with an occasional pine wood, dark and mysterious-looking, for in England even the pine is not the scrubby, scraggy tree of our barrens. This country has a picturesque, original character of its own, and is somewhat thinly settled too, but among the heaths and pines we saw more beautiful ruined churches than in any district south of the Tweed. The unfailing ivy is there, but it does not grow with over-luxuriance, as it does elsewhere in England, making a lovely covering for an ugly building or an unsightly stump, but sometimes muffling and hiding the beauties of finer architecture, and disguising delicate Gothic outlines like a thick hood.

[Our traveller follows this description of scenery with an account of what she saw in the great cathedrals of England, including Westminster, Winchester, Worcester, and Gloucester. Her description of these is too extended for our space.]

Besides these, we saw Chester, Peterboro', York Minster, Wells, Ely, Canterbury: for the first three I cared less than for the others, though Peterboro' is very fine, especially the west front, which is a miracle of richness and proportion; and York is grand from its size and the harmony which reigns throughout, all the additions and restorations having been made in such perfect accordance with the original design that it looks as if it were the work of the same century. Besides the fine monuments, there are superb stained-glass windows, one very old, and called the "Five Sisters," said to have been the gift of five maiden ladies, each of whom bestowed a compartment designed from her own embroidery; for which *vide* "Nicholas Nickleby." We went down into the crypt to see the remains of the old Norman church and some fragments of a Saxon one, most ancient of all: there, among those venerable, those sacred stones, was a steam-engine, contrived to blow the huge bellows of the organ; and there were the gas-pipes by which the cathedral is now lighted: a number of jets were flaring in the vaults; the steam-engine blew and heaved in a horrible manner; there were heaps of coal lying between the grand broken Norman pillars; the light and smell of gas pervaded the whole place. It was like the cellar of a manufactory, and we went up-stairs with outraged sensibilities. Ely is glorious within and without; Wells is the loveliest of cathedrals; Canterbury is Canterbury.

Besides cathedrals, almost every parish in England has at least one beautiful church. The most interesting of them to us was the Holy Sepulchre at Cambridge. It belonged to the Knights Templars, and is circular, like most of their churches, in imitation of our Saviour's tomb at Jerusalem. It is very small, very low, very massive, with short round pillars, round arches, decorated only with the simple, effective zigzag moulding peculiar to the early Norman style; corbels running down from the domical vaulted roof (still recalling Moslem architecture), and ending in strange faces, military yet melancholy in expression,—probably portraits of the knights by whom it was founded in the year of our Lord 1101. The Temple Church in London is much larger and handsomer, but not nearly so curious and striking.

Almost all the old churches in England suffer exceedingly either from the defect of the stone of which they are built or the action of the atmosphere upon it: they look honeycombed, worm-eaten; their tracery is obliterated, their mullions are wasted as if by wear and tear. The interiors, protected from the weather, fare best, but even the cloisters, which are open on one side, are often in a ruinous condition, and the stone peels and crumbles under the touch like rusty iron. Chester Cathedral is an extreme instance: its dilapidation amounts to disfigurement. It is one of the least imposing and interesting, yet for an American just landed it is a profound revelation; and as Chester is close to Liverpool, one cannot do better than stop there for a day.

The old city is full of quaint characteristics, too well known to need description here. One of the gates is called by the odd title of the Pepper-gate. In the sixteenth century there was a mayor named Pepper, who had a young daughter in her middle teens. One evening, as she was playing ball with her companions near this gate, an impetuous youth rushed in, snatched her up, and carried her off through it. The mayor caused the gate to be closed, which gave rise to the saying, "When the daughter is stolen shut the Pepper-gate." Chester is the only city in England which has preserved the entire circuit of its walls: the town has spread far beyond them in every direction, except where they are washed by the Dee, but they form an unbroken round, and are used as a public walk, from which one looks into many a queer corner. Following its course, one comes upon a small turret rising from the battlements, on which is the inscription, "From this tower, on September 27, 1645, King Charles saw his army defeated at Rowton Moor." How much of anguish and doom lies in those few words! No doubt Sir Walter Scott is much to blame, but he can hardly be held answerable for all the sentiment with which we trace the footsteps of the Stuarts, dogged by fanatical hatred and murderous revenge, upheld by adventurous, daring, romantic loyalty and chivalrous self-devotion.

THE "OLD TOWN" OF EDINBURGH.

ROBERT LOUIS STEVENSON.

[From one of the most notable of Scotland's literary sons we extract the following attractive description of the famous capital city of that land, the source of our selection being Stevenson's "Edinburgh: Picturesque Notes." The "Old Town" section of the city is particularly limned for us in the selection here given.]

The ancient and famous metropolis of the North sits overlooking a windy estuary from the slope and summit of three hills. No situation could be more commanding for the head city of a kingdom, none better chosen for noble prospects. From her tall precipice and terraced gardens she looks far and wide on the sea and broad champaigns. To the east you may catch at sunset the spark of the May light-house, where the Firth expands into the German Ocean; and away to the west, over all the carse of Stirling, you can see the first snows upon Ben Ledi.

But Edinburgh pays cruelly for her high seat in one of the vilest climates under heaven. She is liable to be beaten upon by all the winds that blow, to be drenched with rain, to be buried in cold sea fogs out of the east, and powdered with snow as it comes flying southward from the Highland hills. The weather is raw and boisterous in winter, shifty and ungenial in summer, and a downright meteorological purgatory in the spring. The delicate die early, and I, as a survivor, among bleak winds and plumping rain, have been sometimes tempted to envy them their fate. For all who love shelter and the blessings of the sun, who hate dark weather and perpetual tilting against squalls, there could scarcely be found a more unhomely and harassing place of residence. Many such aspire angrily after that Somewhere-else of the imagination, where all troubles are supposed to end. They lean over the great bridge which joins the New Town with the Old——that windiest spot or high altar in this northern temple of the winds——and watch the trains smoking out from under them and vanishing into the tunnel on a voyage to brighter skies. Happy the passengers who shake off the dust of Edinburgh, and have heard for the last time the cry of the east wind among her chimney-tops! And yet the place establishes an interest in people's hearts; go where they will, they find no city of the same distinction; go where they will, they take a pride in their old home.

Venice, it has been said, differs from all other cities in the sentiment which she inspires. The rest may have admirers; she only, a famous fair one, counts lovers in her train. And, indeed, even by her kindest friends, Edinburgh is not considered in a similar sense. These like her for many reasons, not any one of which is satisfactory in itself. They like her whimsically, if you will, and somewhat as a virtuoso dotes upon his cabinet. Her attraction is romantic in the narrowest meaning of the term. Beautiful as she is, she is not so much beautiful as interesting. She is pre-eminently Gothic, and all the more so since she has set herself off with some Greek airs, and erected classic temples on her crags.

In a word, and above all, she is a curiosity. The Palace of Holyrood has been left aside in the growth of Edinburgh, and stands gray and silent in a workmen's quarter and among breweries and gas-works. It is a house of many memories. Great people of yore, kings and queens, buffoons and grave ambassadors, played their stately farce for centuries in Holyrood. Wars have been plotted, dancing has lasted deep into the night, murder has been done, in its chambers. There Prince Charlie held his phantom levées, and in a very gallant manner represented a fallen dynasty for some hours. Now, all these things of clay are mingled with the dust; the king's crown itself is shown for sixpence to the vulgar; but the stone palace has outlived these changes.

For fifty weeks together it is no more than a show for tourists and a museum of old furniture; but on the fifty-first, behold the palace reawakening and mimicking its past. The Lord Commissioner, a kind of stage sovereign, sits among stage courtiers; a coach and six and clattering escort come and go before the gate; at night the windows are lighted up, and its near neighbors, the workmen, may dance in their own houses to the palace music. And in this the palace is typical. There is a spark among the embers; from time to time the old volcano smokes. Edinburgh has but partly abdicated, and still wears, in parody, her metropolitan trappings. Half a capital and half a country town, the whole city leads a double existence; it has long trances of the one and flashes of the other; like the king of the Black Isles, it is half alive and half a monumental marble. There are armed men and cannon in the citadel overhead; you may see the troops marshalled on the high parade; and at night, after the early winter even-fall, and in the morning, before the laggard winter dawn, the wind carries abroad over Edinburgh the sound of drums and bugles. Grave judges sit bewigged in what was once the scene of imperial deliberations.

PRINCES STREET AND SIR WALTER SCOTT'S MONUMENT, EDINBURGH

Close by in the High Street perhaps the trumpets may sound about the stroke of noon; and you see a troop of citizens in tawdry masquerade, tabard above, heather-mixture trouser below, and the men themselves trudging in the mud among unsympathetic by-standers. The grooms of a well-appointed circus tread the streets with a better presence, and yet these are the Heralds and Pursuivants of Scotland, who are about to proclaim a new law of the United Kingdom before twoscore boys, and thieves, and hackney-coachmen. Meanwhile, every hour, the bell of the University rings out over the hum of the streets, and every hour a double tide of students, coming and going, fills the deep archways.

And lastly, one night in the spring time—or say one morning rather, at the peep of day—late folk may hear the voices of many men singing a psalm in unison from a church on one side of the old High Street, and a little after or perhaps a little before, the sound of many men singing a psalm in unison from another church on the opposite side of the way. There will be something in the words about the dew of Hermon, and how goodly it is to see brethren dwelling together in unity. And the late folk will tell themselves that all this singing denotes the conclusion of two yearly ecclesiastical parliaments,—the parliaments of churches which are brothers in many admirable virtues, but not specially like brothers in this particular of a tolerant and peaceful life.

Again, meditative people will find a charm in a certain consonancy between the aspect of the city and its odd and stirring history. Few places, if any, offer a more barbaric display of contrasts to the eye. In the very midst stands one of the most satisfactory crags in nature,—a Bass Rock upon dry land, rooted in a garden, shaken by passing trains, carrying a crown of battlements and turrets, and describing its warlike shadow over the liveliest and brightest thoroughfare of the new town. From their smoky beehives, ten stories high, the unwashed look down upon the open squares and gardens of the wealthy; and gay people sunning themselves along Prince's Street, with its mile of commercial palaces all beflagged upon some great occasion, see, across a gardened valley set with statues, where the washings of the old town flutter in the breeze at its high windows.

And then, upon all sides, what a clashing of architecture! In this one valley, where the life of the town goes most busily forward, there may be seen, shown one above and behind another by the accidents of the ground, buildings in almost every style upon the globe. Egyptian and Greek temples, Venetian palaces and Gothic spires, are huddled one over another in most admired disorder, while, above all, the brute mass of the Castle and the summit of Arthur's Seat look down upon these imitations with a becoming dignity, as the works of Nature may look down upon the monuments of Art.

But Nature is a more indiscriminate patroness than we imagine, and in no way frightened of a strong effect. The birds roost as willingly among the Corinthian capitals as in the crannies of the crag; the same atmosphere and daylight clothe the eternal rock and yesterday's imitation portico; and as the soft northern sunshine throws out everything into a glorified distinctness,—or easterly mists, coming up with the blue evening, fuse all these incongruous features into one, and the lamps begin to glitter along the street, and faint lights to burn in the high windows across the valley,—the feeling grows upon you that this also is a piece of nature in the most intimate sense; that this profusion of eccentricities, this dream in masonry and living rock, is not a drop-scene in a theatre, but a city in the world of every-day reality, connected by railway and telegraph-wire with all the capitals of Europe, and inhabited by citizens of the familiar type, who keep ledgers, and attend church, and have sold their immortal portion to a daily paper. By all the canons of romance, the place demands to be half deserted and leaning towards decay; birds we might admit in profusion, the play of the sun and winds, and a few gypsies encamped in the chief thoroughfare; but these citizens, with their cabs and tramways, their trains and posters, are altogether out of key. Chartered tourists, they make free with historical localities, and rear their young among the most picturesque sites with a grand human indifference. To see them thronging by, in their neat clothes and conscious moral rectitude, and with a little air of possession that verges on the absurd, is not the least striking feature of the place.

And the story of the town is as eccentric as its appearance. For centuries it was a capital thatched with heather, and more than once, in the evil days of English invasion, it has gone up in flame to heaven, a beacon to ships at sea. It was the jousting-ground of jealous nobles, not only on Greenside or by the king's stables, where set tournaments were fought to the sound of trumpets and under the authority of the royal presence, but in every alley where there was room to cross swords, and in the main street, where popular tumult under the Blue Blanket alternated with the brawls of outlandish clansmen and retainers.

Down in the palace John Knox reproved his queen in the accents of modern democracy. In the town, in one of those little shops plastered like so many swallows' nests among the buttresses of the old Cathedral, that familiar autocrat, James VI., would gladly share a bottle of wine with George Heriot the goldsmith. Up on the Pentland Hills, that so quietly look down on the Castle with the city lying in waves around it, those mad and dismal fanatics, the Sweet Singers, haggard from long exposure on the moors, sat day and night with tearful psalms to see Edinburgh consumed with fire from heaven, like another Sodom or Gomorrah. There, in the Grass-market, stiff-necked, covenanting heroes offered up the often unnecessary, but not less honorable, sacrifice of their lives, and bade eloquent farewell to sun, moon, and stars, and earthly friendships, or died silent to the roll of drums. Down by yon outlet rode Grahame of Claverhouse and his thirty dragoons, with the town beating to arms behind their horses' tails,—a sorry handful thus riding for their lives, but with a man at the head who was to return in a different temper, make a dash that staggered Scotland to the heart, and die happily in the thick of fight. There Aikenhead was hanged for a piece of boyish incredulity; there a few years afterwards, David Hume ruined Philosophy and Faith, an undisturbed and well-reputed citizen; and thither, in yet a few years more, Burns came from the plough-tail, as to an academy of gilt unbelief and artificial letters...

The Old Town occupies a sloping ridge or tail of diluvial matter, protected, in some subsidence of the waters, by the Castle cliffs which fortify it to the west. On the one side of it and the other the new towns of the south and of the north occupy their lower, broader, and more gentle hilltops. Thus, the quarter of the Castle overtops the whole city and keeps an open view to sea and land. It dominates for miles on every side; and people on the decks of ships, or ploughing in quiet country places over in Fife, can see the banner on the Castle battlements, and the smoke of the old town blowing abroad over the subjacent country. A city that is set upon a hill. It was, I suppose, from this distant aspect that she got her nickname of *Auld Reekie*. Perhaps it was given her by people who had never crossed her doors: day after day, from their various rustic Pisgahs, they had seen the pile of building on the hill-top, and the long plume of smoke over the plain; so it appeared to them; so it had appeared to their fathers tilling the same field; and as that was all they knew of the place, it could be all expressed in these two words.

Indeed, even on a nearer view, the Old Town is properly smoked; and though it is well washed with rain all the year round, it has a grim and sooty aspect among its younger suburbs. It grew, under the law that regulates the growth of walled cities in precarious situations, not in extent, but in height and density. Public buildings were forced, wherever there was room for them, into the midst of thoroughfares; thoroughfares were diminished into lanes; houses sprang up story after story, neighbor mounting upon neighbor's shoulder, as in some Black Hole of Calcutta, until the population slept fourteen or fifteen feet deep in a vertical direction.

The tallest of these *lands*, as they are locally termed, have long since been burnt out; but to this day it is not uncommon to see eight or ten windows at a flight; and the cliff of building which hangs imminent over Waverley Bridge would still put many natural precipices to shame. The cellars are already high above the gazer's head, planted on the steep hill-side; as for the garret, all the furniture may be in the pawn-shop, but it commands a famous prospect to the Highland hills. The poor man may roost up there in the centre of Edinburgh, and yet have a peep of the green country from his window; he shall see the quarters of the well-to-do fathoms underneath, with their broad squares and gardens; he shall have nothing overhead but a few spires, the stone top-gallants of the city; and perhaps the wind may reach him with a rustic pureness, and bring a smack of the sea, or of flowering lilacs in the spring....

One night I went along the Cowgate after every one was abed but the policeman, and stopped by hazard before a tall *land.* The moon touched upon its chimneys, and shone blankly on the upper windows; there was no light anywhere in the great bulk of the building; but as I stood there it seemed to me that I could hear quite a body of quiet sounds from the interior; doubtless there were many clocks ticking, and people snoring on their backs. And thus, as I fancied, the dense life within made itself faintly audible in my ears, family after family contributing its quota to the general hum, and the whole pile beating in tune to its time-pieces, like a great disordered heart. Perhaps it was little more than a fancy altogether, but it was strangely impressive at the time, and gave me an imaginative measure of the disproportion between the quantity of living flesh and the trifling walls that separated and contained it.

There was nothing fanciful, at least, but every circumstance of terror and reality, in the fall of the *land* in High Street. The building had grown rotten to the core; the entry underneath had suddenly closed up, so that the scavenger's barrow could not pass; cracks and reverberations sounded through the house at night; the inhabitants of the huge old human bee-hive discussed their peril when they encountered on the stair; some had even left their dwellings in a panic of fear, and returned to them again in a fit of economy or self-respect; when, in the black hours of a Sunday morning, the whole structure ran together with a hideous uproar and tumbled story upon story to the ground. The physical shock was felt far and near, and the moral shock travelled with the morning milkmaid into all the suburbs.

The church-bells never sounded more dismally over Edinburgh than that gray forenoon. Death had made a brave harvest, and, like Samson, by pulling down one roof destroyed many a home. None who saw it can have forgotten the aspect of the gable: here it was plastered, there papered, according to the rooms; here the kettle still stood on the hob, high overhead; and there a cheap picture of the Queen was pasted over the chimney. So, by this disaster, you had a glimpse into the life of thirty families, all suddenly cut off from the revolving years. The *land* had fallen; and with the *land* how much! Far in the country, people saw a gap in the city ranks, and the sun looked through between the chimneys in an unwonted place. And all over the world, in London, in Canada, in New Zealand, fancy what a multitude of people could exclaim with truth, "The house that I was born in fell last night!"

IN THE LAND OF ROB ROY.

NATHANIEL P. WILLIS.

[From Willis's "Famous Persons and Places" we select an interesting description of some Scottish scenes which the works of Scott have rendered famous, including the home of Rob Roy and the lakes Lomond and Katrine, the latter the scene of the "Lady of the Lake." Passing many famous places on his way north, the traveller at length reached the "far-famed and much-boasted valley of Glencoe," which he describes in the chapter following.]

We passed the head of the valley near Tyndrum, where McDougal of Lorn defeated the Bruce, and were half-way up the wild pass that makes its southern outlet, when our Highland driver, with a shout of delight, pointed out to us a red deer, standing on the very summit of the highest mountain above us. It was an incredible distance to see any living thing, but he stood clear against the sky, in a relief as strong as if he had been suspended in the air, and with his head up, and his chest towards us, seemed the true monarch of the wild.

At Invarenden, Donald McPhee begged for the discharge of himself and his horse and cart from our service. He had come with us eighty miles, and was afraid to venture farther on his travels, having never before been twenty miles from the Highland village where he lived. It was amusing to see the curiosity with which he looked about him, and the caution with which he suffered the hostler at the inn to take the black mare out of his sight. The responsibility of the horse and cart weighed heavily on his mind, and he expressed his hope to "get her back safe," with an apprehensive resolution that would have become a knight-errant girding himself for his most perilous encounter. Poor Donald! how little he knew how wide is the world, and how very like one part of it is to another!

Our host of Invarenden supplied us with another cart to take us down to Tarbot, and having dined with a waterfall looking in at each of our two opposite windows (the inn stands in a valley between two mountains), we were committed to the care of his eldest boy, and jolted off for the head of Loch Lomond.

I have never happened to see a traveller who had seen Loch Lomond in perfectly good weather. My companion had been there every summer for several years, and believes it always rained under Ben Lomond. As we came in sight of the lake, however, the water looked like one sheet of gold leaf, trembling, as if by the motion of fish below, but unruffled by wind; and if paradise were made so fair, and had such waters in its midst, I could better conceive than before the unhappiness of Adam when driven forth. The sun was just setting, and the road descended immediately to the shore, and kept along under precipitous rocks, and slopes of alternate cultivation and heather, to the place of our destination. And a lovely place it is! Send me to Tarbot when I would retreat from the world. It is an inn buried in a grove at the foot of hills, and set in a bend of the lake-shore, like a diamond upon an "orbed brow;" and the light in its kitchen, as we approached in the twilight, was as interesting as a ray of the "first water" from the same. We had now reached the route of the cockney tourists, and while we perceived it agreeably in the excellence of the hotel, we perceived it disagreeably in the price of the wines, and the presence of what my friend called "unmitigated vulgarisms" in the coffee-room. That is the worst of England. The people are vulgar, but not vulgar enough. One dances with the lazzaroni at Naples, when he would scarce think of handing the newspaper to the "person" on a tour at Tarbot. Condescension is the only agreeable virtue, I have made up my mind.

Well—it was moonlight. The wind was south and affectionate, and the road in front of the hotel "fleck'd with silver," and my friend's wife, and the corresponding object of interest to myself, being on the other side of Ben Lomond and the Tweed, we had nothing for it after supper but to walk up and down with one another, and talk of the past. In the course of our ramble we walked through an open gate, and, ascending a gravel walk, found a beautiful cottage, built between two mountain streams, and ornamented with every device of taste and contrivance. The mild pure torrents were led over falls and brought to the threshold of bowers, and seats, and bridges, and winding paths were distributed up the steep channels in a way that might make it a haunt for Titania. It is the property, we found afterwards, of a Scotch gentleman, and a great summer retreat of the celebrated Jeffrey, his friend. It was one more place to which my heart clung in parting.

Loch Lomond sat still for its picture in the morning, and after an early breakfast we took a row-boat, with a couple of Highlanders, for Inversnade, and pulled across the lake with a kind of drowsy delightfulness in the scene and air which I had never before found out of Italy. We overshot our destination a little to look into Rob Roy's cave, a dark den in the face of the rock, which has the look of his vocation; and then pulling back along the shore, we were landed, in the spray of a waterfall, at a cottage occupied by the boatman of this Highland ferry. From this point across to Loch Katrine is some five miles, and the scene of Scott's novel of Rob Roy. It has been "done" so often by tourists that I leave all particular description of the localities and the scenery to the well-hammered remembrance of readers of magazines, and confine myself to my own private adventures.

The distance between the lakes is usually performed by ladies on donkeys, and by gentlemen on foot, but being myself rather tender-toed with the gout, my companion started off alone, and I lay down on the grass at Inversnade to wait the return of the long-eared troop, who were gone across with an earlier party. The waterfall and the cottage just above the edge of the lake, a sharp hill behind, closely wooded with beech and fir, and, on a greensward platform in the rear of the house, two Highland lassies, and a laddie, treading down a stack of new hay, were not bad circumstances in which to be left alone with the witcheries of the great enchanter.

I must narrate here an adventure in which my own part was rather a discomfiture, but which will show somewhat the manners of the people. My companion had been gone half an hour, and I was lying at the foot of a tree, listening to the waterfall and looking off on the lake, and watching by fits the lad and lassies I have spoken of, who were building a haystack between them, and chattering away most unceasingly in Gaelic. The eldest of the girls was a tall, ill-favored damsel, merry as an Oread, but as ugly as Donald Bean; and after a while I began to suspect, by the looks of the boy below, that I had furnished her with a new theme. She addressed some remark to me presently, and a skirmish of banter ensued, which ended in a challenge to me to climb upon the stack. It was about ten feet high, and shelving outward from the bottom, and my Armida had drawn up the ladder. The stack was built, however, under a high tree, and I was soon up the trunk, and, swinging off from a low branch, dropped in the middle of the stack.

In the same instant I was raised in a grasp to which I could offer no resistance, and, with a fling to which I should have believed the strength of few men equal, thrown clear of the stack to the ground. I alighted on my back, with a fall of perhaps twelve feet, and felt seriously hurt. The next moment, however, my gentle friend had me in her arms (I am six feet high in my stockings), and I was carried into the cottage, and laid on a flock bed, before I could well decide whether my back was broken or no. Whiskey was applied externally and internally, and the old crone, who was the only inhabitant of the hovel, commenced a lecture in Gaelic, as I stood once more sound upon my legs, which seemed to take effect upon the penitent, though her victim was no wiser for it. I took the opportunity to look at the frame which had proved itself of such vigorous power, but, except arms of extraordinary length, she was like any other equally ugly, middle-sized woman. In the remaining half-hour before the donkeys arrived we became the best of friends, and she set me off for Loch Katrine with a caution to the ass-driver to take care of me, which that sandy-haired Highlander took as an excellent joke, and no wonder!

The long mountain glen between these two lakes was the home of Rob Roy, and the Highlanders point out various localities, all commemorated in Scott's incomparable story. The house where Helen McGregor was born lies a stone's throw off the road to the left, and Rob Roy's gun is shown by an old woman who lives near by. He must have been rich in arms by the same token, for, besides the well-authenticated one at Abbotsford, I have seen some dozen guns and twice as many daggers and shot-pouches which lay claim to the same honor. I paid my shilling to the old woman not the less. She owed it to the pleasure I had received from Sir Walter's novel.

The view of Loch Lomond back from the highest point of the pass is incomparably fine; at least when I saw it, for sunshine and temperature and the effect of the light vapors on the hills were at their loveliest and most favorable. It looks more like the haunt of a robber and his caterans, probably, in its more common garb of Scotch mist, but, to my eye, it was a scene of the most Arcadian peace and serenity. I dawdled along the five miles upon my donkey, with something of an ache in my back, but a very healthful and sunny freedom from pain and impatience at my heart. And so did *not* Baillie Nicol Jarvie make the same memorable journey.

The cottage inn at the head of Loch Katrine was tenanted by a woman, who might have been a horse-guardsman in petticoats, and who kept her smiles for other cattle than the Sassenach. We bought her whiskey and milk, praised her butter, and were civil to the little Highlandman at her breast; but neither mother nor child were to be mollified. The rocks were bare around, we were too tired for a pull in the boat, and three mortal hours lay between us and the nearest event in our history. I first penetrated, in the absence of our Hecate, to the inner room of the sheiling. On the wall hung a broadsword, two guns, a trophy or two of deer's horns, and a Sunday suit of plaid, philibeg and short red coat, surmounted by a gallant bonnet and feather. Four cribs, like the berths in a ship, occupied the farther side of the chamber, each large enough to contain two persons; a snow-white table stood between the windows; a sixpenny glass, with an eagle's feather stuck in the frame, hung at such a height that, "though tall of my hands," I could just see my nose; and just under the ceiling on the left was a broad and capacious shelf, on which reposed apparently the old clothes of a century,—a sort of place where the gude-wife would have hidden Prince Charlie, or might rummage for her grandmother's baby linen.

The heavy steps of the dame came over the threshold, and I began to doubt from the look in her eyes whether I should get a blow of her hairy arm or a "persuader" from the butt of a gun for my intrusion. "What are ye wantin' here?" she *speered* at me, with a Helen-McGregor-to-Baillie-Nicol-Jarvie sort of an expression.

"I was looking for a potato to roast, my good woman."

"Is that a'? Ye'll find it ayont, then!" And pointing to a bag in the corner, she stood while I subtracted the largest, and then followed me to the general kitchen and receiving-room, where I buried my *improvista* dinner in the remains of a peat-fire, and congratulated myself on my ready apology.

What to do while the potato was roasting! My English friend had already cleaned his gun for amusement, and I had looked on. We had stoned the pony till he had got beyond us in the morass (small thanks to us if the dame knew it). We had tried to make a chicken swim ashore from the boat, we had fired away all my friend's percussion-caps, and there was nothing for it but to converse *à rigueur*. We lay on our backs till the dame brought us the hot potato on a shovel, with oatcake and butter, and with this Highland dinner the last hour came decently to its death.

An Englishman with his wife and lady's maid came over the hills with a boat's crew, and a lassie who was not very pretty, but who lived on the lake, and had found the means to get "Captain Rob" and his men pretty well under her thumb. We were all embarked, the lassie in the stern-sheets with the captain, and ourselves, though we "paid the scot," of no more consideration than our portmanteaus. I was amused, for it was the first instance I had seen in any country (my own not excepted) of thorough emancipation from the distinction of superiors. Luckily, the girl was bent on showing the captain to advantage, and by ingenious prompting and catechism she induced him to do what probably was his custom when he could not better amuse himself, point out the localities as the boat sped on, and quote the Lady of the Lake with an accent which made it a piece of good fortune to have "crammed" the poem beforehand.

THE FORTH BRIDGE FROM THE NORTH

The shores of the lake are flat and uninteresting at the head, but towards the scene of Scott's romance they rise into bold precipices, and gradually become worthy of their celebrity. The Trosachs are a cluster of small, green mountains, strewn, or rather piled, with shrubs and mossy verdure, and from a distance you would think only a bird, or Ranald of the Mist, could penetrate their labyrinthine recesses. Captain Rob showed us successively the Braes of Balquidder, Rob Roy's birth- and burial-place, Benledi, and the crag from which hung, by the well-woven skirts of braid cloth, the worthy bailie of Glasgow; and, beneath a precipice of remarkable wildness, the half-intoxicated steersman raised his arm, and began to repeat, in the most unmitigated gutturals,—

"High *o'er* the south hung Ben*venue,*
Down *to* the lakes *his* masses threw,
Crags, knowls, and mounds *confusedly* hurl'd
The frag*ments* of an earlier *wurruld.*"

I have underlined it according to the captain's judicious emphasis, and in the last word have endeavored to spell after his remarkable pronunciation. Probably to a Frenchman, however, it would have seemed all very fine,— for Captain Rob (I must do him justice, though he broke the strap of my portmanteau) was as good-looking a ruffian as you would sketch on a summer's tour.

Some of the loveliest water I have ever seen in my life (and I am rather an amateur at that element to look at) lies deep down at the bases of these divine Trosachs. The usual approaches from lake to mountain (beach or sloping shore) are here dispensed with; and straight up from the deep water rise the green precipices and bold and ragged rocks, overshadowing the glassy mirror below with tints like a cool corner in a landscape of Ruysdael's. It is something (indeed, on a second thought, exceedingly) like Lake George; only that the islands in this extremity of Loch Katrine lie closer together, and permit the sun no entrance except by a ray almost perpendicular. A painter will easily understand the effect of this,—the loss of all that *makes a surface* to the water, and the consequent far depth to the eye, as if the boat in which you shot over it brought with it its own water and sent its ripple through the transparent air. I write *currente calamo,* and have no time to clear up my meaning, but it will be evident to all lovers of nature.

Captain Rob put up his helm for a little fairy green island, lying like a lapful of green moss on the water, and, rounding a point, we ran suddenly into a cove sheltered by a tree, and in a moment the boat grated on the pebbles of a natural beach perhaps ten feet in length. A flight of winding steps, made roughly of roots and stones, ascended from the water's edge.

"Gentlemen and ladies!" said the captain, with a hiccup, "this is Ellen's Isle. This is the gnarled oak" (catching at a branch of a tree as the boat swung astern), "and—you'll please to go up them steps, an' I'll tell you the rest in Ellen's bower."

The Highland lassie sprang on shore, and we followed up the steep ascent, arriving breathless at last at the door of a fanciful bower, built by Lord

Willoughby d'Eresby, the owner of the island, exactly after the description in the Lady of the Lake. The chairs were made of crooked branches of trees and covered with deer-skins, the tables were laden with armor and every variety of weapon, and the rough beams of the building were hung with antlers and other spoils of the chase.

"Here's where she lived!" said the captain, with the gravity of a cicerone at the Forum, "and *noo*, if ye'll come out, I'll *show* you the echo!"

We followed to the highest point of the island, and the Highlandman gave a scream that showed considerable practice, but I thought he would have burst his throat in the effort. The awful echo went round, "as mentioned in the bill of performance," every separate mountain screaming back the discord till you would have thought the Trosachs a crew of mocking giants. It was a wonderful echo, but, like most wonders, I could have been content to have had less for my money.

There was a "small silver beach" on the mainland opposite, and above it a high mass of mountain.

"There," said the captain, "gentlemen and ladies, is where Fitz-James *blew'd* his bugle, and waited for the 'light shallop' of Ellen Douglas; and here, where you landed and came up *them* steps, is where she brought him to the bower, and the very tree's still there,—as you see'd me tak' hold of it,—and over the hill, yonder, is where the gallant gray giv' out, and breathed *his* last, and (will you turn round, if you please, them that likes?) yonder's where Fitz-James met Red Murdoch that killed Blanche of Devon, and right across this water *swum* young Greme that disdained the regular boat, and I s'pose on that lower step set the old Harper and Ellen many a time a-watching for Douglas,—and now, if you'd like to hear the echo once more———"

"Heaven forbid!" was the universal cry; and, in fear of our ears, we put the bower between us and Captain Rob's lungs, and followed the Highland girl back to the boat.

From Ellen's Isle to the head of the small creek, so beautifully described in the "Lady of the Lake," the scenery has the same air of lavish and graceful vegetation, and the same features of mingled boldness and beauty. It is a spot altogether that one is sure to live much in with memory. I see it as clearly now as then.

The whiskey had circulated pretty freely among the crew, and all were more or less intoxicated. Captain Rob's first feat on his legs was to drop my friend's gun-case and break it to pieces, for which he instantly got a cuff between the eyes from the boxing dandy that would have done the business for a softer head. The Scot was a powerful fellow, and I anticipated a row; but the tremendous power of the blow and the skill with which it was planted quite subdued him. He rose from the grass as white as a sheet, but quietly shouldered the portmanteau with which he had fallen, and trudged on with sobered steps to the inn.

We took a post-chaise immediately for Callender, and it was not till we were five miles from the foot of the lake that I lost my apprehensions of an apparition of the Highlander from the darkening woods. We arrived at Callender at nine, and the next morning at sunrise were on our way to breakfast at Stirling.

THE ISLAND OF STAFFA AND FINGAL'S CAVE.

BERIAH BOTFIELD.

[The islands adjoining the Scottish Highlands have much in them to interest the traveller, both in the character and habits of the people and the aspects of nature. As respects natural phenomena, the scenery of the island of Staffa and Fingal's Cave is of especial interest, the development of columnar basalt rocks here being unequalled in extent and perfection. From Botfield's "Journal of a Tour through the Highlands of Scotland during the Summer of 1829" we select the following description of Staffa and the adjacent coast and islands.]

The full moon shone in cloudless splendor upon the tranquil waters of the bay and the dark shore of Morven. Lights were occasionally seen to gleam from the motionless vessels, and, in the stillness of the night, the distant waterfalls were heard to pour amidst the woody recesses of Drumfin, the romantic residence of McLean, the laird of Coll, on the opposite side of the bay. Beyond the mouth of the harbor, across the Sound of Mull, appeared the rugged coast and wild hills of Morven, so celebrated in the heroic strains of Ossian, upon which, whatever may be the opinion of the spectator as to the authenticity of these celebrated poems, it is impossible to look, at such a time as this, without the deepest emotion. Indeed, the celebrated traveller, Dr. Clarke, who ever regarded them as an ingenious fiction, blended with a very scanty portion of traditional information, confessed that he could not, nevertheless, avoid feeling some degree of local enthusiasm as he passed the shores upon which so vast a superstructure of amazing but visionary fable had been erected....

At daybreak we were summoned on board the steamboat, whence we enjoyed a pleasing prospect of the woods and waterfalls surrounding the handsome modern mansion of Drumfin, the residence of McLean, "the chief of the sandy Coll," situated under a range of woody cliffs, upon the margin of a lovely lake, at the eastern point of the Bay of Tobermory. Upon emerging from this harbor, the opening of Loch Sunart, an arm of the sea which deeply indents the rugged coast of Morven, and separates it from the still more wild and rugged district of Ardnamurchan, appeared on our right....

Upon the wild mountain-shore of Ardnamurchan, immediately upon the edge of the sea, the castle of Mingarry appeared, "sternly placed," being surrounded by a polygonal wall, whose edges coincide with those of the ledge of rocks on which it stands; and though it can no longer be said "to overawe the woodland and the waste," yet it is an object of striking interest both from its situation and ancient history. The cliffs which bind this rude shore scarcely rise beyond sixty or one hundred feet in height, but are of a peculiarly savage character, which, combined with the prevailing swell of the mighty Western Ocean, renders any attempt at landing both difficult and dangerous.

[As they proceeded, a long chain of islands was passed, while on the coast at length appeared Cailleach Head, so called from the extremely close resemblance of a portion of the rock to the human head. Thence they gained a magnificent view of the coast of Canna, and saw, beautiful in the distance, the dark-blue mountains of the island of Skye, while other islands gemmed the waters nearer at hand.]

Upon this beautiful view of these islands we longed for winged feet to leap from isle to isle; and though the number of the Western Islands exceeds two hundred, our flight of fancy would not

"pause till perched on Kilda's steep,
The last fair daughter of the Western deep."

On emerging from the Sound of Mull, and passing the stormy cape of Cailleach Head, we observed the bold rocks of the western coast of Mull, veined with trap, and frequented by flocks of sea-fowl. As we proceeded down the strait, between the islands of Coll and of Mull, the little archipelago of the Treshanish Islands came in sight. As we drew near these singular islands, consisting of Fladda, Linga, Bach, and the two Cairnburgs, we gradually discerned their columnar structure, which, though not so decided as that of Staffa, yet appeared sufficiently evident to warrant the supposition that these are similar rocks of basalt emerging from the deep, and just sufficiently clothed with verdure to merit the appellation of islands. Upon the larger of the Cairnburgs we saw, upon our right, as we approached its shore, a ruined fortalice, used as a place of refuge by the warlike and turbulent McLeans of Duart. This was a place of strength in the Norwegian times, but is now only tenanted by a few wandering sheep, as are also Fladda and Bach, which last, from its singularly oval shape, has obtained from mariners the name of the Dutchman's Cap.

This little chain of islets, with their treble summits and varied forms, appeared under a thousand different aspects as we advanced between them and the coast of Mull. Engaged as our attention had been by these interesting objects, it was effectually diverted when we beheld, for the first time, the celebrated island of Staffa, so justly esteemed one of the greatest natural curiosities the world can boast, and well worth all the perils of the voyage; since no description, however eloquent, no picture, however vivid, can portray this admirable demonstration of nature's power as it is seen and felt by the beholder.

Beyond Staffa we discerned, as yet indistinctly, the tower of the cathedral upon the Isle of Iona; and, more distantly to the extreme west, the island of Tiree; while close upon our left appeared the range of rocky precipices which render the coast of Mull so interesting.... In the distance rose proudly to heaven the lofty summit of Ben More, and the lesser mountain of Mamclachaig, in Mull.

Little islets, some of them bearing vestiges of ancient forts, are scattered over the face of the deep, between Ulva and Staffa, to which island, as we approached, our gaze was eagerly directed; and as we beheld its unrivalled columnar structure more distinctly, we were enabled to appreciate more justly the far-famed wonders of this precious gem of the sea. Having stayed our course underneath its most precipitous and attractive side, fronting the southwest, we instantly got into the boat, and rowed off for Fingal's Cave, over unusually quiescent water.

As the tide was ebbing fast, we landed at the entrance of the cave underneath the most magnificent arch it is possible to conceive; the mouth of the cave being seventy feet high and about forty-two broad. We scrambled on without difficulty along its eastern side, over the flat tops of the broken yet upright pillars, which form an excellent causeway, into the interior of the cave, and there contemplated, with infinite awe and admiration, this magnificent temple of the God of Nature....

This celebrated cave is entirely composed of basaltic pillars, having from five to six sides in general, but varying to seven or eight, the ends of which are generally about two feet in diameter, accurately corresponding with each other at the roof and bottom of the cavern, which has been formed, it may be conjectured, by the action of the sea undermining the jointed columns, and thus producing the excavation, which gradually diminishes in breadth to its termination, two hundred and twenty-seven feet from its entrance. This majestic vault is poetically termed in Gaelic, Uiamh Binn—the Musical Cave—from the echo of the waves within its mighty recesses, and somewhat unaccountably has obtained the name of Fingal, though tradition has not connected it in any way with the illustrious exploits of that Ossianic hero.

As the tide never entirely leaves the cave, the only floor it has is the beautifully translucent green wave of the sea, reflecting from its bosom those tints which vary and harmonize the darker hues of the rock, and often throwing on the basaltic columns the flickering lights which its undulating surface receives from the rays of the sun without.

The roof of the cave is extremely curious and beautiful, the interstices between the pillars being filled up by stalactites of varied hue, whose beautiful tints have the fine effect of greatly enriching this natural mosaic work. The murmur of the swelling tide, mingling with the deep-toned echoes of the vault, which grandly reverberated to the repeated reports of our double-barrelled pistol, added to the stupendous magnificence of the columns, and the splendid singularity of the scene, produced emotions in the mind which defy description, and which future impressions will never be able to obliterate.

Reluctantly quitting the Cave of Fingal, we proceeded in our boat under the highest part of the magnificent colonnade of basaltic pillars, which rise to the height of one hundred and twelve feet above high-water mark, between Fingal's Cave and a square dark aperture in the lowest stratum of the rock called the Boat Cave, because it is accessible by that mode alone, and runs in the rock one hundred and forty feet, like the gallery of a mine. The columnar structure of the trap rock is extremely evident above and around this cave, and continues equally so as far as the Cormorant's or McKinnon's Cave to the west, which derives its former name from the feathered race that inhabit it, and of which a fine specimen flew over our heads as we approached the spacious entrance of the cave.

This singular aperture is peculiarly striking from the simplicity and regularity of its form. The columns are extremely perfect, and rise immediately from a black amorphous mass of indurated matter, through which are dispersed nodules and fragments of a still darker rock, altogether closely resembling the scoriæ of a volcano, strongly corroborative of the igneous origin of basaltic rocks. The height of this cave is fifty feet, its breadth forty-eight, and its length two hundred and twenty-four feet. The range of columns over its front is extremely beautiful, being hollowed or bent into a concave recess, while the upper part presents a curious and regular geometric ceiling of a striking and unusual appearance.

Repassing the Boat Cave and the range of columns above it, we landed below the echoing arch of the great cave, and availing ourselves of the natural steps afforded by the gigantic causeway, which rises step by step up to the base of the grand colonnade, walked to the detached rock called Buachaille (B   ), or the Herdsman. This noted rock rises about thirty feet above the waves, consisting of an agglomeration of columns resting against each other, and meeting, until they form a conical body, which appears to lie upon a bed of singularly curved horizontal columns visible only at low water,—an advantage which we fortunately enjoyed, and found several sea anemones in the hollows of the rocks.

Passing a rugged point where the causeway projects considerably, we came suddenly upon the Scallop or Clamshell Cave, so justly esteemed one of the most wonderful features of this famous island. This cave is a large rent or fissure in the rock, one hundred and thirty feet long, thirty in height, and eighteen in breadth at its entrance, where it presents on one side the singular phenomenon of the curved and contorted, yet as usual polygonal, columns of basalt, bent so as to form a series of ribs, each forty or fifty feet long, without a joint, their ends standing up and terminating abruptly, not unlike the inside view of the timbers of a ship. On the opposite side of the cave the broken ends of the pillars are so disposed as to bear a general resemblance to the surface of a honeycomb. The lateral dimensions of this cave gradually contract until they terminate in a long, narrow fissure in the rock. By the continued basaltic causeway on the northern side access is obtained to the table-summit of the island, upon which black cattle find good pasturage, though a ruined hut and an extensive prospect are all that can be expected in requital of the fatigue of the ascent.

This celebrated island, it may be remarked, lies in the same longitude with the Giant's Causeway on the northern coast of Ireland.

Returning from the Clamshell Cave round the point of the causeway, we regained the Buachaille rock, under which, in the narrow channel between it and the causeway, just sufficient to allow it to swim, we found our boat, and were conveyed in it back to the steamboat, whence we surveyed, with unsated curiosity, the wonderful island we had just explored, and had ample opportunity of appreciating the truth of its Norwegian derivation from *staff*, a stave, to which those barbarians likened its columns. The grand southern façade of the island is formed of three beds of trap-rock of unequal thickness; the lowest being a conglomerate tufaceous trap, about fifty feet thick on the western side, but, in consequence of its inclination, disappearing under the sea a little to the westward of the great cave. The middle bed is composed of basaltic columns, placed vertically on the plane of their bed, and of unequal depth, varying from thirty-six to fifty-four feet. The upper stratum consists of amorphous and tufaceous trap, intermixed with small basaltic veins and columns, and by its inequality and depth forms the contour of the island, whose surface is covered with turf, and presents nothing remarkable. The cliffs upon the northern shore of the island are very rugged and irregular, and contain about five caves of lesser note, being remarkable only for the resounding of the waves upon breaking into them, resembling much "the cannon's opening roar."

[Not far removed from Staffa is the famous isle of Iona, celebrated as the place where Columba, an Irish sixth century saint, founded a monastery and converted the inhabitants from Druidism to Christianity. The establishment founded by him flourished for centuries, and the ruins of the cathedral and other antique buildings still remain. One of these, "the Reilig Ouran, to the south of St. Oran's Chapel, was for centuries the ordinary burial-place of the Scottish kings, whose tombs, to the number of forty-eight, form a long and continuous series of oblong narrow stones, laid flat side by side, and bearing scrolls and effigies, but no inscriptions."]

Tradition has recorded Fergus the Second as the earliest monarch of the line, having been entombed about 420 A.D., and included among the number his successors down to Macbeth; though Macculloch conjectures, from the circumstance of the body of Alexander II., who died at Kerrera, having been conveyed to Melrose for burial, that Iona did not enjoy so great a reputation as the burial-place of kings as it is commonly said to have done in the earlier ages of the Scottish monarchy. However, our conductor, parallel to the royal tombs of Scotland, pointed out to us a similar line, containing eight Norwegian princes or viceroys of the island, during the remote period when that barbarous people exercised sovereignty over the Isles of the Gael. These tombs are chiefly distinguished by the Runic knots and curious representations of vessels rudely sculptured upon the oblong pieces of primitive rock which cover their graves. Adjoining these, a row of four similar stones indicate the graves of as many Irish kings, near to which is said to lie one king of France. Altogether they constitute perhaps the most extensive association of crowned heads in the habitable globe.

[The latter "kings" were perhaps but chiefs, and here, near the royal tombs, are buried most of the insular Highland chieftains, the Macdonalds, the Macleans, and others of ancient days.]

IRELAND AND ITS CAPITAL.

MATTHEW WOODS, M. D.

[Among recent books of travel few have attained more immediate and flattering success than Dr. Woods's "Rambles of a Physician," the racy story of a run through Ireland, Britain, and the continent of Europe. The author has keen powers of observation and fluency in description, and has put on record much that other travellers fail to mention. We give his *résumé* of his run through Ireland and his telling description of what he saw in the people's quarter of Dublin.]

I have been strolling at leisure through the streets, and find myself at the end of the long twilight perplexed instead of pleased by what I have seen. Why is it so difficult to get at the truth about Ireland? Why is it that, when a man begins to talk about even its beauty, he exaggerates it beyond recognition, and that the very few who do give the plain facts are not believed? Why do I read in a little book that I have just found on the parlor table, and which explains the origin of the name "Emerald Isle," the following words, paraphrased from a popular history: "The name Emerald Isle is generally supposed to have been derived from the *evergreen appearance of her shores*, whereas it really originated from the ring which was set with the words 'Optimo Smaragdo,' and which Pope Adrian sent to King Henry IV. as the instrument of his investiture with the dominion of the land." Now, the truth is, Ireland's shores are not "evergreen;" not green at all, but brown and barren, with occasional patches of bright yellow when the *prussach's* in bloom, and bronze when the blossoms fall.

From Queenstown to Cork there is, I admit, a refreshing verdure, especially attractive because of the monotony of the recently-crossed sea, and the houses, too, in this strip, are enveloped in flowers; but this is not because they are in Ireland, but is rather due to their being occupied by English or Scotch or their descendants, who sing thus "the Lord's song in a strange land." Yet from Cork to Killarney, by the Prince of Wales route, you rarely see a bit of verdure; not a flower by the roadside, nor in a window, nor the slightest attempt at the beautification of a home, or to make the best of little. For part of the way not a green field, nor a tree, nor a shrub, nor a weed, nor a blade of grass, nor the song of a bird, nor the hum of an insect,——nothing, absolutely, but brown, barren desolation, associated with a sort of solitude that but intensifies the gloom. Occasionally a narrow belt of potatoes encircling a cabin, always built without mortar, as there is no sand in Ireland, is the only relief from the depressing waste until you reach Glengariff, where you find the English idea again, which has covered the barren rocks with flowers and fruit, comfortable homes and waving grain, the contrast, indeed, making the most taciturn eloquent in praise. From Glengariff to Killarney the same sterile desolation. Miles and miles without a bit of pleasant vegetation to rest the weary eyes. The district suggesting rather some of the dismal places described by Dante or Virgil, Ariosto, Tasso, or Milton, as the abode of souls condemned, rather than districts occupied by living men.

CUSTOM-HOUSE, DUBLIN, IRELAND

After passing through these regions of perpetual misery and despair, these birdless and treeless wastes, you get to regard any little bit of green as a godsend. You have, perhaps, closed your eyes to shut out the depressing melancholy of the apparently anathematized place; you cannot shut out all thoughts of the wretched and benighted men that relentless fate seems to have anchored on these more relentless shores. You have for some time past been ascending the side of a whin-spangled mountain; having reached the summit, the vehicle stops,——you look abroad, and behold the Islands of the Blest, Civitas Solis, Utopia, the New Atlantis, Paradise, what you will; otherwise, Killarney is at your feet, and you feel

"Like stout Cortez when, with eagle eyes,
He stared at the Pacific,—and all his men
Looked at each other with a wild surmise,—
Silent, upon a peak in Darien."

It was here that, when we sought O'Holleron [an enthusiastic Irish patriot of the party], who had suddenly disappeared, we found him with bent head, tears running down his cheeks, and sobbing. You descend from this Pisgah to the lakes, and remain for a few days, until you have exhausted your collection of exclamations, and have repeated them again in writing to your friends, when you proceed.

From here to the Liffey the country is not so brown as the region through which you have passed, but still unattractive in the extreme. It is not green, but greenish, with most of the small fields, as is the mode here, enclosed within thick walls of stone, built without mortar, and void of vegetation. Farms small (average size about six acres), tumble-down houses, no inspiring legends nor traditions, intellects dead, no past, present, nor future, nothing but the same dreary lament, in which everything participates,—the emigrant, landlord, tenant; the very clouds weep over it; hardly ever cease. At every cluster of houses, at a crossroad, the number of bare-limbed women, wearing but two garments, one of them a petticoat, coming only below the knees, makes you think of Gros's remark, that "Irishwomen have a dispensation from the pope to wear the thick end of their legs downward."...

Visitors here find the country so ludicrously, or rather so mournfully, different from what they have been taught to expect—the Isle of Saints; the Emerald Isle; "the land of chaste women and brave men;" the hospitable land; "a kind-hearted people;" "a people of sobriety and industry," are some of the epithets used—that, unless sickened into silence by the humiliating reality, they think of what they have read and heard as a joke, and, to keep the tears back, joke too; and this I believe is the origin of many of the hilarious things written about Ireland.

You might think the birth of the Duke of Wellington and Oliver Goldsmith here would have raised this part of the island above the commonplace, as that of Burns did Ayr; of Shakespeare, Stratford; of Gray and Penn, Stoke Poges; of Goethe, Frankfort; or of Emerson, a few white houses upon a New England plain; but no, there are no memorials in this district at all, except the scant fragments left by the old pagan and semi-christianized natives before the land was the home of thriftlessness and whiskey. The picture is the saddest of all the sad pictures of modern retrogression, with no prospect of the advent of a mind capable of suggesting the proper remedy.

[Certainly one cannot but say, after this depressing picture by one "to the manner born," that Ireland needs regenerating. We give next his impressions of Dublin, which are no more enlivening in tone.]

But about Dublin. What of it? It is certainly a place of handsome municipal buildings, and others, too, built in an imposing manner, and yet all there is architecturally great in the whole city you see at a glance, the moment you cross O'Connell's Bridge. The first view, therefore, is impressive in the extreme; the buildings magnificent, splendidly proportioned, symmetrical. You can see them all at once, and are delighted; but penetrate those vistas, and behold them,—a suit of sixteenth-century mail for man and horse on Sancho Panza and his mule, or a gracefully painted window that shuts off an ugly view,—all that you see at the first glance is all that there is.

To be sure, there are many churches,—perhaps one hundred,—including Methodists, Moravians, Friends, Baptists, Unitarians, Presbyterians, Jews, besides those belonging to the two religious bodies most numerous here,—the Churches of Ireland and Rome; some of them of great beauty; ostentatious, to be sure, as if they were competing with each other in display; and yet with all this the city has none of those pleasant surprises that you expect in old towns, and that you find even with us [in America], and more so, I judge, in towns on the Continent; that is to say, narrow, clean streets opening into wide courts, having buildings with carved fronts and pillars, and the like, or sudden bends in a street, where the commonplace becomes magnificence. There is nothing of this in Dublin,—no curious doors or windows, no "jutty frieze" nor "coign of vantage." Very often an attempt at grandeur, but marred by defective details. The interiors, too, as far as I could penetrate, indicating more the desire for elegance than the capacity,—gay-colored window-shades, but torn; door- and window-curtains, but faded; window-boxes, broken and hanging askew, with flowers withering, either from the smoky atmosphere or neglect; everything black from coal-dust, and no flowers at all. No wonder Moore wrote so touchingly about the last rose of summer.

Plants, to my sorrow, were not in abundance. I searched the grounds of Trinity and everywhere else in vain for a rose or anything else that bloomed, and feel, therefore, as if Tom Moore's rose must have been the last of its race; but what Dublin lacks in flowers it makes up in taverns. Myriads—to quote again from Adam Clarke—of groggeries and distilleries; one of these so large that it looks as if the muddy river that runs through the city was dug there merely to carry its barges of stout to people at the other end. It appears also here, like home, as if these same gentry, who become rich on the drunkenness of the people, were rather important factors in municipal affairs. One of these, Guinness,—I feel, though, like apologizing for mentioning his name in connection with liquor-dealers, as his commodity is stout,—however, is the philanthropist of Dublin, the restorer of St. Patrick's, the supporter of missionaries, the insurer of all his employés' lives, etc., and not only has a monument here by Foley, but was also knighted during the present reign. You remember Dickens,—"The nobility can brew, but they can't bake."

The streets are ornamented with many good statues, including Goldsmith, Moore, Burke, Grattan, Stokes, Lords Carlisle, Corrigan, Eglinton, Smith O'Brien, and others; but the University, the gift of that friend of learning, Queen Elizabeth, is perhaps the chief glory of the town; while "the Liberties," a portion of which I explored to-day, is probably her greatest disgrace. From the lanes and alleys that penetrate this malodorous district emerge the most curious race, I would judge, that has ever been found in a civilized town. Here you find illustrations in abundance, not only of the "philosophy of clothes," but of the comedy and tragedy as well; this tendency to wear other people's garments being one of the characteristics of the tribe, and the city being very liberal in the matter of supplying them with shops where they may procure their wares.

In Cork the chief articles of *petit* commerce are cast-off clothing and "bits of mate," especially tails of things piled up on stalls, the clothing spread on the streets; while in Dublin it is second-hand clothing and bones, sold in mouldy dens,—"bone warehouses,"—twelve feet wide, yawning like Elijah's cave after the ravens had been doing the generous thing by him for months. In turning a corner, a fellow, standing on his knees (stumps) near one of these, accosted me, asking for money to help pay for a pair of cork legs, his own blown off in a dynamite "experiment." Why not Dublin legs? I thought. "He needed but five shillings more," he said; "they were already made, but the thief of a maker would not let him have them until he had paid every penny." Looking up into my face in a sort of confidential aside, he added, "True enough, sir; he's giving them to me at cost."

In the act of contributing to the needed balance, a young lady of perhaps thirty-five autumns, and dressed in a crape hat, linen duster, split down the back, and who had heard the pitiful story of the descendant of Simon Tappertit, approached and said, "Don't give him a ha'penny, sir; he has one pair of legs in pawn already; and he has two wives and nine children that beg for him besides. If you have anything to spare, give it to me, sir; I'm an orphan."

What could not Herr Diogenes Teufelsdröckh say about such a pandemonium of rags as are to be found here? "Happy he who can look through the clothes of man into the man." No difficulty here in being happy, if holes can help you. You are among a colony of savages, as much in conceit with their parti-colored wardrobe as a Mohawk with his beads. Everything, from the "goodly Babylonish garments—the mantles of Shinar, from Assyrian looms," down to the cast-off tarpaulin of discharged or disgraced tars, are on the backs of the denizens of the Liberties. No one is wearing the clothes made for him. The unexpected is the most common. One fellow had on the cast-off coat of a policeman, too small to reach across his naked body, with a pair of trousers with scarlet stripes, billowing down to the uppers of his soleless shoes. Another bare-footed man had nothing on but an ulster; another, daintily picking his way across the street to one of the rag and bone shops that are as thick here as leaves in Vallombrosa, and between his trousers and short-waisted coat, with long tails, was a yawning gulf of dark flesh, that a crimson sash tried in vain to conceal. Another had on an overcoat with but one sleeve; a hole in the back large enough for him to thrust his head through; fastened down the front by having bits of the coat pulled through the buttonholes, and kept from slipping back by butchers' skewers.

Knee-breeches, red coats, cocked and battered stove-pipe hats, swallow-tailed coats, costumes of every clime, together with the official garments of the army in rags, are found here on the backs of scoundrels that look as if they would run from a bit of soap as if it were the plague,—if, indeed, they would *run* from anything. The women, like the men, indescribable. The saddest part of it, the children; scores of half-naked little souls, swarming around and looking as if all they ever had to eat they picked up in the streets; have nothing of childhood about them but its seriousness; children that have never been combed or washed; boys having nothing on but the trousers of men, the waistband tied about their necks, their arms thrust through the pocket-holes, and the legs rolled up like the coat-sleeves of "the Artful Dodger." One little fellow wore a swallow-tailed coat and stockings, nothing else; the strange thing about it, they are not aware how curious they look; but the ladies! the very exuberance of grotesque finery they exhibit silences my modest pen....

P.S.—You know that it is a custom among the subjects of England to conclude all public meetings, especially of a secular nature, by singing "God save the Queen." The only exception to this rule, I believe, are the Irish Nationalists; they don't want God to do anything of the sort, and have consequently substituted for the National Anthem a song entitled "God save Ireland," which they sing in season and out of season. You can always tell the politics of a district by the number of fiddlers, *prima donnas*, tin whistle and jews-harp performers that play this new vent for patriotism.

À propos of this, in coming home this evening I read on a great sign, at the door of a dingy little drug-shop near the Liberties, the following combination of enterprise and patriotism (which struck me as being odd, and which, for your amusement, I transcribed, punctuation points and all):

"Prepared Castor Oil a penny a dose!

God Save Ireland?

Epsom salts 4 doses for a half-penny!

God Save Ireland?

Seidlitz Powder 6 pence a box!

God Save Ireland?"

and so on, all the way to the bottom, until God had saved Ireland, I think, some fifteen or sixteen times, but always after a powerful physic; the last line of the placard was,—

"Home Rule Forever!

God Save Ireland?"

FROM CORK TO KILLARNEY.

SARAH J. LIPPINCOTT.

[Mrs. Lippincott, the favorite "Grace Greenwood" of former American readers, was the author of several works of European travel. The following selection is from her "Haps and Mishaps of a Tour in Europe," and includes her interesting description of Blarney Castle, Killarney, and the country between.]

The passage from Holyhead to Kingstown was accomplished in four hours; but throughout the trip I felt that I would sooner cross the Styx to the Plutonian shores than attempt it again. I thought that I had sounded the lowest depths of mortal suffering in the way of sea-sickness, but I found that my Atlantic experiences were but a faint prelude to a mild suggestion of this.

A gentleman at Cork told me an anecdote of a company of emigrants who were observed passing back and forth on one of the ferry-boats during an entire day, and when questioned in regard to their strange movements, answered, they were bound to America in the next ship, and were "practising at say-sickness, just." So the tourist in the utmost he may endure on an Atlantic voyage, before crossing the Irish Channel, may have the consolation of knowing that he is but "practising at say-sickness."

At Kingstown we were treated to a taste of nationality in the shape of a bit of a row between two carmen. At the Dublin station we took that peculiar and distinctive Irish vehicle, an outside jaunting-car, which has the merit of giving you a variety in the way of exercise,—joltings, backward, forward, and sidewise,—a vigilant and vigorous endeavor to keep yourself and your luggage on, and an alert watchfulness to keep other vehicles off. There are two kinds of jaunting-cars, which are thus distinguished by the Irish carmen: "The outside car, yer honor, has the wheels inside, and the inside car has the wheels outside."...

The route from Dublin to Cork leads mostly through a barren, boggy, miserable country, with here and there an oasis of waving green and gold, telling of careful cultivation and wise husbandry. There are some fine old ruins along the way, among which I best remember those of Kilmallock, Kildare, where the pious nuns once kept the holy fires burning "through long ages of darkness and storm," Loughman Castle, and the Rocks of Dunamore and Cashel. But all along the line the ruins are almost countless. You grow mortally weary of crumbling turrets, tumble-down gate-ways, battered arches, and staggering towers, all standing out boldly in the sun and storm, for the absence of trees and shrubbery is a marked feature in the agricultural districts of Ireland. Indeed, the larger part of this ill-fated isle seems, in contrast with fruitful, prosperous, beautiful England, a wild, weary, shadowless waste, scathed, peeled, desolated, and abandoned.

On the following morning [after a night spent at Cork], amid golden sunshine and silvery showers, we drove to Blarney Castle, and wandered through those umbrageous grounds immortalized by the poet in the famous song of the "Groves of Blarney." The castle itself is a noble old ruin, and its situation and surroundings are remarkably picturesque and curious. There are natural subterranean passages leading down to the lake, and a black dungeon, where, according to our guide, "Cromwell, the bloody nagur," confined his prisoners. The lake is small, but, according to the above-mentioned authority, quite bottomless. He told us, with a grave face, that the late "Lady Jeffers," having taken a whim into her head to draw it off, had a drain dug full three feet below the surface, but not a drop would run out,—a sturdy, conservative old lake.

We ascended the great tower, at the top of which we all kissed the new Blarney stone,—it being morally and physically impossible for ladies to salute the real Simon Pure, which is outside the wall some feet from the summit. The gentlemen who accomplish this feat must be held by the feet over the wall, one hundred and twenty feet from the ground, by a stout guide, who is liable to be seized with a sudden weakness, and to call out that he must stop "to spit on his hands,"—that he can *howld* on no longer, unless his fee is double; and the unhappy dog in suspense pledges himself to a treat. Our guide assured me that the new Blarney stone was quite as good as the "rale,"—that a certain "widdy lady" made a pilgrimage all the way from the north of England, kissed the spurious stone most rapturously, and made a great match soon after. The question arises, Lay the virtue in the stone, or in the pilgrim's faith?

Our return drive was very charming,—the rain was past and sunlight and fresh breezes poured beauty and gladness on our way. I cannot remember to have seen anywhere within so short a distance so many wild flowers. The shrubbery was more luxuriant, the trees finer and more abundant, than we had ever seen,—everything on our path was beautiful and gracious save the *humanity*, which was wretched and poverty-stricken in the extreme. From the miserable little mud huts along the road ran scores of children, of all sizes, bare-headed, bare-footed, and bare-legged, with rags of all imaginable hues and textures fluttering in the wind, and attached to their bodies by some unknown and mysterious law of attraction, certainly by no visible bond or support. With faces begrimed by smoke, and wild eyes overhung with wilder locks, they stretched out their dirty beseeching palms, and assailed us on all sides of our outside car,—most assailable of vehicles,—fit contrivance for a beggared land.

Irish carmen are a race of Jehus,—driving with eccentric flourishes of the whip, and when more than usually excited, with strange barbaric whoops and hellos, making their odd little vehicles jump along at an astonishing rate. They are commonly communicative and amusing, though by no means the quaint, cunning, delightful, inimitable wags and wits your Lovers and Levers, your Edgeworths and Halls, have pictured. It is a singular thing that, though they are from the first free and easy in word and manner, they are never offensively so. Native tact, good humor, and warmth of heart take from their advances all appearance of boldness or impertinence. Our driver on this occasion was disposed to be particularly sociable, though not in the jocular way. He was a man of much intelligence for his station, of a serious, even sad expression of face, and he talked powerfully and with intense bitterness of the wrongs and sorrows of the Irish peasantry. I was struck by hearing him ascribe most of their sufferings not to the English government but to the *native Irish proprietors*, who, he averred, had revelled in heartless, wasteful extravagance, while the people starved, until, since the failure of the potato, many of them have been reduced to absolute want. It was almost fearful to mark the wild gleam in the man's eye as he spoke his fierce joy in this retributive justice....

On the morning of August 16 we left Cork for Killarney, by way of Bantry and Glengariff. After a short run on the rail we took a stage-coach, choosing outside seats, like enthusiastic tourists as we are, though the day was dark and showery. There was little in the scenery, and less in the condition of the country and people, to repay us for our exposure to wind and weather till we reached Bantry. I can never forget the forlorn unmitigated wretchedness of the people who thronged around us at the little town of Dunmanway. Among the crowd appealing to us, in all possible variations of the whine mendicious and mendacious, we saw not one man or woman in the national costume and cover-all,—the double cape great-coat and the hooded cloak; all was squalor and tatters soul-sickening and disgusting. Here was infancy, nude and needy, reaching out its dirty little hands; and second childhood bent and tottering, with palsied palm extended, eying you with all the mute wistfulness of a starved spaniel. There was a full assortment of the halt, the hump-backed, and the crippled,—all degrees of sightlessness and unsightliness. I turned away from the miserable creatures with a heart heavy with hopeless sympathy and vain pity, and with a conscience stricken for all my own sins of unthankfulness and discontent.

And here I may as well pause to remark briefly on the condition and appearance of the peasants in the south of Ireland. Knowing that I could not fairly judge of this class by the idle and ragged crowd who gather round the coach or car in the towns and hamlets, I took occasion, during my stay at Cork, to visit several of the country cottages of the working peasants in company with one of the landed proprietors. In but one out of six did I find a regular fireplace and chimney; in but one was there a window of glass, and that consisted of a single pane. The others had—with the exception of the door, and a hole in the roof, from which the smoke, after wandering at its own sweet will through the cabin, found its way out—no opening whatever for light or ventilation. But I forget—we did remark a sort of improvised window in one other. In a low, miserable hovel, belonging to a carman, we found a horse occupying full a third of the scanty room; and above his manger a small hole had been made through the mud wall, the good man having found that the health of the animal required what himself and family lived without,—air.

To the mistress of this unique habitation, whose one apartment served for kitchen, sleeping-room, *stable*, and hall, I said, in horrified amazement, "How is it possible you can live with that horse?" "Sure, miss, he's no throuble," she replied; "and it's little room he takes, after all; for the childer can sleep on the straw under him, just, and creep between his legs, and he never harming them at all, the sensible cratur." It is a common thing to see hens drying their feathers by the genial peat glow, and pigs enjoying the pleasures of the domestic hearth. In another cabin we found two curious old crones, living together on apparently nothing, who loaded us with blessings in the original tongue, and actually went on their knees to offer up thanksgiving for a few half-pence, which we gave as a consideration for intruding on their retirement.

Yet, though living in low, smoky, ill-ventilated cabins,—often with mouldering thatches, and always with damp earth floors, with a pool of stagnant water or a dung-hill before the door,—though themselves ill fed and but half clad, it is a singular fact that the peasants of southern Ireland are apparently a healthful and hardy race. You occasionally see fine specimens of manly and childish beauty among them; but a pretty Irish peasant girl we found the rarest of *rara avises.* There are some families of Spanish origin about Bantry, and of these we encountered one or two dark-eyed, olive-cheeked beggar boys, who seemed to have leaped out of one of Murillo's pictures. The policemen everywhere are a particularly fine-looking set of fellows; indeed, none but well-made, tall, and powerful men have any chance of enrolment in this honorable terror-inspiring, omnipresent corps.

The professional beggars of Ireland seem a peculiarly hopeless and irredeemable class,—not because of the poverty of the country alone, but from their own inherent and inherited idleness and viciousness. They are persistent, pertinacious, sometimes impudent, and often quick-witted and amusing. A friend of ours was waylaid by a certain "widdy" woman, with an unlimited amount of ragged responsibilities at her heels. On hearing her doleful story, our friend advised the fair mendicant to take refuge in the poor-house. "The poor-house!" she exclaimed; "sure it's meself that keeps the poorest house in all Cork, yer honor." I was amused by an appeal made by an elderly dame to one of our fellow-passengers: "Here's a fine fat gentleman, sure; sure he'll give a sixpence to a poor bony body that hasn't broken her fast at all the day."

If you wish to take a meditative walk among the hills, the chances are that you will return with a considerable ragged retinue; but the larger detachment of this ignoble army of alms-seekers are stationed along the public roads. They make their startling sorties from the most lonely, wild, and inaccessible places; like Roderick Dhu's men, they leap up from "copse and heath." Every rock hides a waiting mendicant, and every tuft of broom stirs as we approach with a lurking tatterdemalion. They leap on your way from behind walls, and drop down upon you from overhanging trees,—small footpads, or rather *paddies*, who present palms instead of pistols, and blarney and worry you alike out of pence and patience.

After a day of wet and weary travel through a melancholy country, we enjoyed to the utmost the beautiful approach to Bantry, under a clear and sunny sky, and welcomed with enthusiasm the sight of its lovely and famous bay. But even this bright vision was soon eclipsed by Glengariff, where we spent the night. Thus far on my tour I have seen nothing to compare with the glorious beauty of that place. In all the solemn shadows of its wild loneliness, the dark deeps and frowning heights of its grandeur, in all the sweet lights of its loveliness, it lives, and must ever live, in my charmed memory; but I will not attempt to picture it in words.

After dinner, though a light rain was falling, we took a row around the bay, and remained on the water until the night set in. I think we shall none of us soon forget that row over the smooth and silent bay, in the rain and deepening twilight, under the shadows of mountain and rock. The scene would have been too wild, solemn, and awfully lonely but for the peculiar wit and story-telling talent of "Jerry," our guide and helmsman. He entertained us with some wonderful legends of a certain Father Shannon, a priest, and a famous character in this region about half a century ago.

QUEENSTOWN HARBOR

One anecdote illustrative of the holy man's quick-wittedness impressed me as an instance of "cuteness" passing the cuteness of Yankees. "The good father," says Jerry, "was one day fishing, in his boat, on the bay, when he heard a swarm of bees buzzing about him. Then he begins to rattle with a knife, or spoon, in an iron kettle he had with him in the boat, till he feels that all the bees have settled on his shoulders. Then he slyly reaches back, and takes hold of the tail of his shirt (begging your pardon, ladies!) and he suddenly turns it over his head, bees and all, and puts it into the kettle, which he covers over in a second just; and so he takes the whole swarm to Lord Bantry, and sells them for three pounds, and gets his shirt back, too, yer honor."...

The mountain road from Glengariff to Killarney is a splendid specimen of engineering, and leads through scenery wild and beautiful in the extreme. On the sunny morning of our leaving Glengariff, landscape and air were fresh and delicious after the night's abundant rain, and with thrills and palpitations of inexpressible joy my heart responded to the gladness of nature. I shall never forget the childish ecstasy of delight with which I gazed around me, and drank in the fragrant air of the morning.

The three lakes of Killarney descended upon by this road are likely to disappoint the tourist, especially if he be an American, more especially if he be a reader of, and a devout believer in, Mrs. Hall's beautiful and most poetical book, "A Week in Killarney." In truth, such fairy sheets of water seem little to deserve the name of lakes at first, but they grow on your respect rapidly as you approach; their beauty is, near or afar, quite exquisite and undeniable, and the mountains which surround them are really very respectable elevations. Our first visit was to the Tore Waterfall, by far the most beautiful cascade I have seen since coming abroad. The fall is between sixty and seventy feet; the glen into which the water comes leaping, and foaming, and flashing is wild and rocky, and overhung with richest foliage....

Our first expedition was to the Gap of Dunloe, a wild and gloomy mountain-pass, especially interesting to the reader of Gerald Griffin's fine novel of "The Collegians" as the scene of poor Eily Connor's happy honeymoon and tragic taking off. Our guide furnished myself and a pleasant English friend with ponies; the remainder of the party took a car.

Though tolerably well mounted, and able to abruptly cut the company of the old, crippled, and blind of the begging fraternity, we found that we had small advantage over the boys; the fleet-footed little rascals kept up with us for miles,—one juvenile Celt, literally *sans culotte*, but in a shirt of elder-brotherly dimensions, giving us a sort of Tam O'Shanter chase. A pretty, dark-eyed boy, running by my side, held up a bunch of purple heather and wild honeysuckle, saying, with an insinuating smile, "Plase, my lady, buy these ilegant bright flowers, so like yer honor's self, this beautiful summer morning." What woman could resist such an appeal?

At the entrance of the Gap we were met by a detachment of volunteer guides, and a company of "mountain-dew" girls,——maidens with cans of goats' milk and flasks of "potheen," with which they are happy to treat the traveller, for a consideration. After listening to some grand echoes, called forth by the rich bugle-notes of our guide, we proceeded through the pass. This, by itself, did not equal our expectation; its finest feature is the "Purple Mountain," which in the glorious sunlight of that morning was beautiful beyond conception.

From Lord Brandon's demesne we embarked upon the upper lake, rowed among its fairy islands, and ran down "the long range" to the middle lake, pausing for a little gossip with the echoes of "Eagle Nest," and shooting "Old Wier Bridge" on our way. The bay and mountain of Glena are the gems of Killarney. Even now, looking back upon the scene through the sobered light of recollection, it is all enchantment,——the shore gorgeous with magnificent foliage, the waters flashing with silver gleams, the sky golden with sunset light; and it is difficult for me to believe that there is under the broad heaven a lovelier spot. Even the echoes from this beautiful green mountain seemed clearer, yet softer and more melodious, than any we had heard before.

We took dinner on shore, in a delicious little nook shadowed by arbutus-trees, dining off a large rock, some seated *à la Turc*, some reclining in the ancient Oriental style. Oh, we had merry times! And what with toasts and songs and legends, and joyous laughter ringing out, peal on peal, over the still water, the wonder is we failed to rouse the great O'Donoghue, who, according to popular tradition, dwells in a princely palace under the lake, and only comes to the surface to take an airing on horseback every May morning. Our row homeward, through the soft lingering sunset light, with the plash and murmur of the blue waves, rising with the rising wind, heard in the intervals between the sweet songs of our guide, was a fitting close to a day of shadowless pleasure.

NORTH OF IRELAND SCENES.

W. GEORGE BEERS.

[We have described a run through the south of Ireland, which to the traveller seemed but a brown and barren commentary on the so-called Emerald Island. The traveller from whom we now quote found the aspect of nature verdant enough fully to justify this title. But the poverty and shiftlessness which appeared so patent to Dr. Woods proved equally evident to Mr. Beers, to whom the lack of snakes in Green Erin seemed more than replaced by the multitude of beggars.]

Up in the forecastle of an ocean steamer a group of sea-tired souls look away to starboard, where a faint shape lies on the horizon like an early-morning cloud. "It's only a bit of old-country fog," mutters the Grumbler, and goes back to his bed. A thrush had been playing for over an hour on the spars and rigging, and we fancied we could smell the land from which it had flown to greet us. And by and by the dim line took a more solid shape, and soon we could see the rough rocks of the northern coast. We were nearing Innistrahull light-house and Malin Head, and the ship's engines stopped, for the first time since leaving the New World, to take on a pilot. A short sail along the rocky coast, passing the ivy-covered ruins of an ancient castle, the green refreshing grass, the hedges, and the white houses, and the beautiful panorama of Moville, at the mouth of the Foyle, was unfolded, and Nature tinged the sea and sky with a masterpiece of sunset. Suddenly a few jaunting-cars came flying down the hill like highway comets, and the Grumbler came up again, in time to find that we were only a hundred yards from shore. "That's Ireland," said he. We felt enlightened. It was not long before we were ashore at Moville, a quiet watering-place for the people of Derry, Tyrone, and Donegal counties.

Our first reception was from a sturdy beggar, who apologized for the absence of the mayor and corporation. I had heard of this genius of Moville before. He is a character of the place, and one of the most original hypocrites among the begging fraternity. When I was in Queenstown, a few weeks afterwards, I saw a perfect shoal of his kind, of all degrees of dirt, disease, and disaster,—a sort of ragged resurrection through which passengers from an American steamer had to pass. There were beggars with strong lungs and stout legs; beggars with scarce a lung and but one leg; paupers in all the traditional heraldry of rags and wretchedness,—blind, crippled, crooked, and crazy; with bags and babies, sticks and dogs, canes and crutches, all colors of hair and all sorts of disease, real or feigned; some funny, some furious, some bold, some blushing, nearly all overwhelming in benediction.

One sore-eyed veteran, whose apostolical succession from blind Bartimeus I should have been easily disposed to accept, stuck to my heels, and in a tone that would have melted the Blarney stone implored me, "A pinny, yer honor." With New-World innocence of Old-World wickedness, I gave my Irish Moses a sixpence, upon which the crowd came upon me in a ring of blessing, until I pushed through it with some rough epithet. In the twinkling of an eye the circle of sickly saints fell into a close column of renovated sinners, and yelled after me the characteristic south-of-Ireland curses, from the mild "Bad luck to ye!" to the more historical "The curse of Cromwell upon ye!" One crooked old lady had got close to my ear: "Shure, yer honor, I've been bint up like this these twinty year wid the rheumatiz, and me back's bruk and one of me lungs is gone;" but when I shook her off she straightened up like a giantess and swore at me with as hearty a pair of respiratory organs as any Glasgow fish-wife might boast. I felt as if I had performed a miracle upon the old lady's spine. But I nearly collapsed with laughter when I saw one mild-looking fellow, who had been limping near me with his right leg held up in a wooden crutch and his right hand apparently shrivelled beyond the power of use, holding the crutch, which he had unhitched, under his left arm and shaking the game leg and the lame fist at my back.

Our arrival at the north, however, was less ceremonious. I do not know whether our Moville beggar was the last of the mendicant Mohicans of the coast or had simply stolen a march upon the rest of his fraternity, but there he stood, a monopolist of the art: "Good luck to ye, jintlemen! Ye're welcome to Ireland. Ye'll give me a few pennies for luck, yer honors, won't ye? Jist whativer ye like, jintlemen. Be good to the motherless and sivin small childer, and niver a bite to ate since yesterday mornin'. Jist whativer ye like, jintlemen." Our first Old-World beggar had caught us in the tide of good nature, and the pennies soon grew to shillings. It was our first experience, and we were on the "Green Isle." We learned to be wiser before we had gone much farther, and by the time we left the island we felt as if we could throttle every beggar we met.

"How long have you been begging?" I asked the Moville suppliant.

"I began wid me mother, sir, soon after I was born."

"And do you never work?"

"Work, is it? Shure, sir, I was niver educated to it. And there's too many people working already, sir."

"How long is it since you used soap and water?" said I.

"Now, yer honor, where'd *I* get soap, when I can't get bread? Me childer would ate it if there was any in the house."

"Well, I'd like to see what you look like when you're clean. There's another sixpence for you,—half for your stomach and half for your skin. If you'll get some soap and go down to the sea there and wash yourself well while we're away, I'll give you sixpence more when we come back."

"Shure," quickly replied the Moville wit, "doesn't yer honor know that ye can't use soap in salt water? But I'll go to the pump, so I will."

It was quite a disappointment afterwards to learn that, like Montaigne's page, our beggar was never guilty of telling the truth, that the "sivin small childer" had yet to be born, and that he considered our party the best fools he had met that season.

We were to drive down to Green-Castle, in the vicinity of which the jarvies said we should be sure to hear the cuckoo. Our first experience of a jaunting-car was pleasant, though precarious. It had the dash of danger which spices adventure. A sober foreigner can seldom keep his seat at first; an Irishman may be so drunk that he walks zigzag on the sidewalk, but he never falls off a car—unless he's sober. At first blush, especially in the cities, the jaunting-car seems an ingenious device to furnish Irish surgeons with amputations. As you go tearing along the streets and flying around corners, your legs hanging over the sides in close proximity to other "highway comets" tearing along the opposite way, you have a choice of death by being dashed to "smithereens" on your face by a jerk or dying in desperate collision with a street-car. Our jarvie was a genuine Paddy, full to the brim of wit and song. Between the stretches of his imagination in tale-telling (all his native geese were royal swans, and for the one ruin we were approaching he built a score of castles in the air) he made the road lively with local Irish airs. During the winter these jarvies have little or nothing to do, and one of them, being asked how they spent that season, replied, "Making up stories, sir, to tell the travellers in summer."

However much we were imposed upon in the matter of tale and tradition, there was no deception in the interest of the drive. The sea lay to the right. Along the highway and in many of the fields, though much of the country to the left was barren and hilly, the daisy was peeping up for our first recognition; the primroses lay in rich golden clumps upon the banks; violets, blue, red, and white, little purple bluebells, day-nettles, which the bees and boys love to suck, and many other new and old wild flowers, were pointed out to us as we jogged along. Sometimes we jumped down to pick them, gathering whole handfuls of the faintly-perfumed primroses and burying our noses in their exquisite blossoms in a way to make an emigrant homesick. On we jolted, and soon came within sight of the romantic hamlet, its picturesque castle and fort facing the sea. With a final quick trot and a jerk our driver pulled up at the Green-Castle Hotel, with the artless hint that its champagne for jintlemen and its whiskey for jarvies had no rival from Malin Head to Cape Clear.

[After giving his readers the legendary history of Green-Castle our author proceeds to describe its present appearance.]

The old castle is now a roofless wreck of time and siege, but enough is left of its walls—eight feet thick—and its deep dungeons to show that it was in its time a strong fortress. We walked over the space between the walls, about eighty yards by forty, upon which the sun and the rains descend and where the grass grew knee-deep. Detached bits of wall were covered with splendid ivy. On the walls here and there we saw the little whitlow-grass, and in the crevices of the rocks the lilac flowers of the toad-flax, which one sees in all such sea-side ruins in Ireland. We climbed the steep crag of the highest portion facing the sea. Many of the stones were loose and slipped out from under our feet. We mounted to the very top of the old battlement,—a glorious spot from which to watch a storm when the great waves roll up in close column and break over the rocks. Creeping from the base of the perpendicular rock a hundred feet below, thick ivy had grown to the very summit, its rootlets and tendrils turning and twisting into and upon each other, binding the stones better than mortar, sucking out the moisture of the wall, and keeping it as dry as punk. Everywhere in Ireland one is struck by the wonderful tenacity of ivy, which creeps along the ground or crawls up and clings to the barest flint. If you lift one of the young shoots, it clings to the earth like a hungry leech to human skin. If you turn it up, you see rootlets, like the legs of a caterpillar, by which it attaches itself to the ground, and which it seems to lose when transplanted to America.

We leaned over on the thick leaves and tendrils to pull the pungent berries, when out flew two scared jackdaws just below. We rustled the tendrils, and away scudded a score or more of birds to tell the sea-gulls of this invasion of their ancient nest. Down near the shore white daisies speckled the green grass like a first snow-fall.

But hark! Is that the mystic cry of the cuckoo we are hearing for the first time? How plaintive and lonely its monotone!—"Cuckoo! cuckoo! cuckoo!" We have never heard that sound in America except from wretched Swiss clocks. What a world of delightful associations thrills through our veins! How the old familiar stories told us of our parents' romps in the green lanes of the old country come to our memories, and the wonder with which in their childhood days they stopped to listen to this classic bird. There it is again, over in the woodland. Hark! "Cuckoo! cuckoo! cuckoo!" One of our company, born in the old land, and now returned for the first time in thirty years, began to reach the melting-point, when, looking in the direction of the cry, we caught sight of an incautious Irish boy peeping from behind a tree, with one hand to his mouth, just in the act of repeating this old Green-Castle trick of "fooling the people from America who want to hear the cuckoo."

When we came down from the battlement we were told that a drunken sailor of H. M. "Vanguard" had fallen asleep on top of the wall a few weeks before and had rolled off to the bottom, a distance of a hundred feet, but had not been hurt enough to prevent his marriage the day before our arrival. Our informant added that it was the "potheen" that had saved him: "If he'd been sober, sir, shure he'd have wakened up a dead man."

We had a rattling drive back to Moville. The first sight we met on reaching the wharf was our jolly beggar, transformed almost past recognition by soap and water, sneezing and coughing and claiming the promised sixpence: "Shure, yer honor, ye might make it a shillin', for in the washin' I've caught the divil of a cowld." When we came back a few months afterwards we missed him. I made up my mind that he had never recovered from that cleansing; but a more recent visitor tells me that he is still alive, as witty and as dirty as ever.

[The traveller next made his way, *via* Londonderry, to Antrim, where stands a celebrated round tower.]

There is perhaps nothing of more puzzling interest to the Irish antiquary than the round towers, of which there are about eighty in the island. Their origin and purpose have been variously guessed at, some maintaining that they were erected by the Danes as watch-towers and afterwards changed by the Christian Irish into clock- or bell-towers. But why should the Danes confine these structures to Ireland, and not build them in England, Scotland, and other regions where they had a much firmer foothold? Others regard them as fire-temples, where the Druids lit the sacred flame and kept it safe from pollution. This view was accepted for a long time as a settlement of the question, on account of the resemblance of these towers to similar structures found in India and thought to have been used in an extinct form of worship. The Irish Druids followed many Eastern customs in their religious rites, but these may have been mere coincidences. The turrets in the vicinity of Turkish mosques, from the summits of which approaching festivals were proclaimed, suggested the hypothesis that the Irish towers were intended for the same purpose. Others held the theory that they were built by the ancient bishops as strongholds for the sacred articles belonging to the churches. In the neighborhood of many of these towers churches still exist. A very picturesque one forms part of a church in Castle-Dermot, in the county Down. At Drumbo, a few miles from Belfast, the ruin of one stands in the church-yard of a Presbyterian chapel.

The Antrim tower is in fine preservation to the very summit, but no trace has been found to indicate that a church existed in its vicinity. It is ninety-three feet high, and about fifty-three feet in circumference at its base, is built of rough stone, and has a stone flooring, underneath which it is supposed a sepulchre, as at Ardmore, exists. Above the door-way is a bas-relief like a Maltese cross. I climbed into the tower through the entrance, two feet by four. Its width inside is about eight feet, but narrows gradually to the top. The ivy which clung affectionately to its outside had grown into several of the windows and lay in decayed brambles inside. Up at the very top the jackdaws had a gloriously independent life of it all to themselves. The grass outside was as level as a century's care and rolling could make it. And hark! "Cuckoo! cuckoo! cuckoo!" "No, you don't, my dear fellow!" I replied. "You are a relative of our cuckoo of Green-Castle." "Cuckoo!" he replied in denial; and I found out that it was a live cuckoo coaxing me to play at hide-and-seek. I started to accept the challenge,—when "Trespassers will be Prosecuted" stared me in the face as I mounted an innocent stile. Forty jackdaws—the Forty Thieves—got together on the topmost boughs of trees near by and discussed my intentions: Was I loading a gun, or only making a sketch? Was I painter or poacher? I followed the cuckoo's cry in spite of the trespass, but caught no second glimpse of him.

Coming back and crossing a picturesque stream, a short walk brought me to the famous Lough Neagh, the fourth largest lake in Europe, twenty miles in length and fifteen in breadth. In size it seemed a mere pond, compared to the great inland seas of America; but the legend of its buried glories, and the belief of the fishermen that when the water is clear they can see round towers and high steeples and churches of the land below, would waken any one's interest. Wonderful petrifactions are found along its margins, referable to some remote geological era, and no doubt these fossil woods gave rise to the fishermen's superstition. On the borders of the lake you see the ruins of the seat of Lord O'Neill, "Shane's Castle," which is surrounded by as much superstition as the lake. The banshee of the O'Neills was a firm article of faith of mine host in Antrim, who told me that his father had heard its wail.

As I came back to the town I saw a characteristic scene which reminded me of Father Prout's remark, that "the pig is as essential an inmate of the Irish cabin as the Arab steed of the shepherd's tent on the plains of Mesopotamia." At the door of a thatched mud hut there was a fierce tooth-and-nail contest between two pigs. Out sallied the good woman of the house and belabored the nearest one gently with stick, roughly with tongue: "Whist wid ye! Take that, now! *Come into the house wid ye!*" With well-trained docility Piggy obeyed. A short distance away I saw a crowd gathered about a cart covered with a pure white sheet. The look of delight upon the faces of those who had peeped under the cover tempted my curiosity, and I lifted the linen. It was a young pig, as white as snow and as fresh as a daisy.

But I intended only to take a peep at the northern coast of Ireland, and here I am *en route* to Belfast. As you go farther you fare better in the way of fine scenery and interesting people. There is something about the greenness of Ireland which sanctifies its claim to be called the Emerald Isle. I have seen nothing anywhere else to rival the soft luxuriance of nature here. Grass, ivy, and flowers seem as indigenous as hospitable hearts. I was told that if you flung a clean-cut stick in a County Meath meadow, you might pick it up in a day or two covered with young lichens and moss; but this reminded me too much of the crow-bar planted in some other fertile country in the evening which sprouted out tenpenny nails in the morning. The very primroses have a depth of mellow beauty I never saw in England. Walking through the country you get a good insight into its social and political questions, and, whatever preconceptions you may have, you will be sure——if you have no bigotry in your bones and do not excite people about the burning questions of the hour——to carry from Ireland memories of its lovely scenery which nothing on earth can ever dispel.

PARIS AND ITS ATTRACTIONS.

HARRIET BEECHER STOWE.

[The city of Paris, the cynosure of European eyes, and the paradise of good Americans, calls loudly for a description at our hands. It is a call which can readily be answered. We suffer, indeed, from a superfluity of riches. Descriptions of every sort, shape, and complexion are so numerous that it is not easy to select with discretion. We take one that has the quality of enthusiastic admiration from the "Sunny Memories of Foreign Lands" of the author of "Uncle Tom's Cabin." It begins with her entrance into the city, after passing the easy ordeal of the custom-house officials.]

We rode through streets whose names were familiar, crossed the Carrousel, passed the Seine, and stopped before an ancient mansion, in the Rue de Verneuil, belonging to M. le Marquis de Brige. This Faubourg St. Germain is the part of Paris where the ancient nobility lived, and the houses exhibit marks of former splendor. The marquis is one of those chivalrous legitimists who uphold the claims of Henri V. He lives in the country, and rents his hotel. Mrs. C. occupies the suite of rooms on the lower floor. We entered by a ponderous old gate-way, opened by the *concierge*, passed through a large paved quadrangle, traversed a short hall, and found ourselves in a large, cheerful parlor, looking out into a small flower garden. There was no carpet, but what is called here a parquet floor, or mosaic of oak blocks, waxed and highly polished. The sofas and chairs were covered with light chintz, and the whole air of the apartment shady and cool as a grotto. A jardinière filled with flowers stood in the centre of the room, and around it a group of living flowers—mother, sisters, and daughters—scarcely less beautiful. In five minutes we were at home. French life is different from any other. Elsewhere you do as the world pleases; here you do as you please yourself; my spirits always rise when I get among the French....

Monday, June 6.—This day was consecrated to knick-knacks. Accompanied by Mrs. C., whom years of residence have converted into a perfect

Parisienne, we visited shop after shop and store after store. The politeness of the shopkeepers is inexhaustible. I felt quite ashamed to spend a half-hour looking at everything and then depart without buying; but the civil Frenchman bowed and smiled, and thanked us for coming.

In the evening we rode to L'Arc de Triomphe d'Etoile, an immense pile of massive masonry, from the top of which we enjoyed a brilliant panorama. Paris was beneath us, from the Louvre to the Bois de Boulogne, with its gardens and moving myriads, its sports, and games, and light-hearted mirth,—a vast Vanity Fair, blazing in the sunlight. A deep and strangely-blended impression of sadness and gayety sunk into our hearts as we gazed. All is vivacity, gracefulness, and sparkle to the eye; but ah, what fires are smouldering below! Are not all these vines rooted in the lava and ashes of the volcano-side?...

Wednesday, June 8.—A day on foot in Paris. Surrendered H. to the care of our fair hostess. Attempted to hire a boat at one of the great bathing establishments for a pull on the Seine. Why not on the Seine as well as on the Thames? But the old Triton demurred. The tide *marched* too strong,—"*Il marche trop fort.*" Onward, then, along the quays; visiting the curious old book-stalls, picture-stands, and flower-markets. Lean over the parapet and gaze upon this modern Euphrates, rushing between solid walls of masonry through the heart of another Babylon. The river is the only thing not old. These waters are as turbid, tumultuous, unbridled, as when forests covered all these banks,—fit symbol of peoples and nations in their mad career, generation after generation. Institutions, like hewn granite, may wall them in, and vast arches span their flow, and hierarchies domineer over the tide; but the scorning waters burst into life unchangeable, and sweep impetuous through the heart of Vanity Fair, and dash out again into the future the same grand, ungovernable Euphrates stream. I do not wonder Egypt adored her Nile and Rome her Tiber. Surely, the life artery of Paris is this Seine beneath my feet! And there is no scene like this, as I gaze upward and downward, comprehending in a glance the immense panorama of art and architecture,—life, motion, enterprise, pleasure, pomp, and power. Beautiful Paris! What city in the world can compare with thee?

And is it not chiefly because, either by accident or by instinctive good taste, her treasures of beauty and art are so disposed along the Seine as to be visible at a glance to the best effect? As the instinct of the true *Parisienne* teaches her the mystery of setting off the graces of her person by the fascinations of dress, so the instinct of the nation to set off the city by the fascinations of architecture and embellishment. Hence a chief superiority of Paris to London. The Seine is straight, and its banks are laid out in broad terraces on either side, called *quais*, lined with her stateliest palaces and gardens. The Thames forms an elbow, and is enveloped in dense fog and smoke. London lowers; the Seine sparkles; London shuts down upon the Thames, and there is no point of view for the whole river panorama; Paris rises amphitheatrically, on either side the Seine, and the eye from the Pont d'Austerlitz seems to fly through the immense reach like an arrow, casting its shadow on everything of beauty or grandeur Paris possesses.

GRAND OPERA-HOUSE, PARIS

Rapidly now I sped onward, paying brief visits to the Palais de Justice, the Hôtel de Ville, and spending a cool half-hour in Notre Dame. I love to sit in these majestic fanes, abstracting them from the superstition which does but desecrate them, and gaze upward to their lofty, vaulted arches, to drink in the impression of architectural sublimity, which I can neither analyze nor express. Cathedrals do not seem to me to have been built; they seem, rather, stupendous growths of nature, like crystals, or cliffs of basalt. There is little ornament here; that roof looks plain and bare; yet I feel that the air is dense with sublimity. Onward I sped, crossing a bridge by the Hôtel Dieu, and, leaving the river, plunged into narrow streets, exploring a quadrangular market; surveyed the old church of St. Genevieve, and the new, now the Pantheon; went onward to the Jardin des Plantes, and explored its tropical bowers. Many things remind me to-day of New Orleans and its Levee, its Mississippi, its Cathedral, and the luxuriant vegetation of the Gulf. In fact, I seem to be walking in my sleep in a kind of glorified New Orleans, all the while. Yet I return to the gardens of the Tuileries and the Place Vendôme, and in the shadow of Napoleon's Column the illusion vanishes. Hundreds of battles look down upon me from their blazonry.

In the evening I rested from the day's fatigue by an hour in the garden of the Palais Royal. I sat by one of the little tables and called for an ice. There were hundreds of ladies and gentlemen eating ices, drinking wine, reading the papers, smoking, chatting; scores of pretty children were frolicking and enjoying the balmy evening. Here six or eight midgets were jumping the rope, while papa and mamma swung it for them. Pretty little things, with their flushed cheeks and sparkling eyes, how they did seem to enjoy themselves! What parent was ever far from home that did not espy in every group of children his own little ones,—his Mary or his Nellie, his Henry or Charlie? So it was with me. There was a ring of twenty or thirty singing and dancing, with a smaller ring in the centre, while old folks and boys stood outside. But I heard not a single oath, nor saw a rough or rude action, during the whole time I was there. The boys standing by looked on quietly, like young gentlemen. The best finale of such a toilsome day of sight-seeing was a warm bath in the Rue de Bac, for the trifling sum of fifteen sous. The cheapness and convenience of bathing here is a great recommendation of Paris life. They will bring you a hot bath at your house for twenty-five cents, and that without bustle or disorder. And nothing so effectually as an evening bath, as my experience testifies, cures fatigue and propitiates to dreamless slumber....

After visiting the Luxembourg, I resorted to the gardens of the Tuileries. The thermometer was at about eighty degrees in the shade. From the number of people assembled, one would have thought, if it had been in the United States, that some great mass convention was coming off. Under the impenetrable screen of the trees, in the dark, cool, refreshing shade, are thousands of chairs, for which one pays two cents apiece. Whole families come, locking up their door, bringing the baby, work, dinner, or lunch, take a certain number of chairs, and spend the day. As far as eye can reach you see a multitude seated, as if in church, with other multitudes moving to and fro, while boys and girls without number are frolicking, racing, playing ball, driving hoop, etc., but contriving to do it without making a hideous racket.

How French children are taught to play and enjoy themselves without disturbing everybody else is a mystery. "*C'est gentil*" seems to be a talismanic spell; and "*Ce n'est pas gentil ça*" is sufficient to check every rising irregularity. Oh, that some *savant* would write a book and tell us how it is done! I gazed for half an hour on the spectacle. A more charming sight my eyes never beheld. There were gray-headed old men, and women, and invalids; and there were beautiful demoiselles working worsted, embroidery, sewing; men reading papers; and, in fact, people doing everything they would do in their own parlors. And all were graceful, kind, and obliging; not a word or an act of impoliteness or indecency. No wonder the French adore Paris, thought I; in no other city in the world is a scene like this possible. No wonder that their hearts die within them at thoughts of exile in the fens of Cayenne!

But under all this there lie, as under the cultivated crust of this fair world, deep abysses of soul, where volcanic masses of molten lava surge and shake the tremulous earth. In the gay and bustling Boulevards, a friend, an old resident of Paris, pointed out to me, as we rode, the bullet-marks that scarred the houses,—significant tokens of what seems, but is not, forgotten.

At sunset a military band of about seventy performers began playing in front of the Tuileries. They formed an immense circle, the leader in the centre. He played the octave flute, which also served as a baton for marking time. The music was characterized by delicacy, precision, suppression, and subjugation of rebellious material.

I imagined a congress of horns, clarionets, trumpets, etc., conversing in low tones on some important theme; nay, rather a conspiracy of instruments, mourning between whiles their subjugation, and ever and anon breaking out in a fierce *émeute*, then repressed, hushed, dying away, as if they had heard of Baron Munchausen's frozen horn, and had conceived the idea of yielding their harmonies without touch of human lips, yet were sighing and sobbing at their impotence. Perhaps I detected the pulses of a nation's palpitating heart, throbbing for liberty, but trodden down, and sobbing in despair.

[A *salon* experience is next described, followed by a visit to Versailles. Then our authoress plunges into the world of art at the Louvre.]

At last I have come into dream-land; into the lotos-eater's paradise; into the land where it is always afternoon. I am released from care; I am unknown, unknowing; I live in a house whose arrangements seem to me strange, old, and dreamy. In the heart of a great city I am as still as if in a convent; in the burning heats of summer our rooms are shadowy and cool as a cave. My time is all my own. I may at will lie on a sofa, and dreamily watch the play of the leaves and flowers in the little garden into which my room opens; or I may go into the parlor adjoining, whence I hear the quick voices of my beautiful and vivacious young friends.

You ought to see these girls. Emma might look like a Madonna, were it not for her wicked wit; and as to Anna and Lizzie, as they glance by me, now and then, I seem to think them a kind of sprite, or elf, made to inhabit shady old houses, just as twinkling harebells grow in old castles; and then the gracious mamma, who speaks French or English like a stream of silver, is she not, after all, the fairest of any of them? And there is Caroline, piquant, racy, full of conversation, sharp as a quartz crystal, how I like to hear her talk! These people know Paris, as we say in America, "like a book." They have studied it æsthetically, historically, socially. They have studied French people and French literature, and studied it with enthusiasm, as people ever should who would truly understand. They are all kindness to me. Whenever I wish to see anything, I have only to speak; or to know, I have only to ask. At breakfast every morning we compare notes and make up our lists of wants. My first, of course, was the Louvre. It is close by us. Think of it. To one who has starved all a life, in vain imaginings of what art might be, to know that you are within a stone's throw of a museum full of its miracles; Greek, Assyrian, Egyptian, Roman sculptors and modern painting, all there!...

It was, then, with a thrill almost of awe that I approached the Louvre. Here, perhaps, said I to myself, I shall answer fully the question that has long wrought within my soul. What is art? and what can it do? Here, perhaps, these yearnings for the ideal will meet their satisfaction. The ascent to the picture-gallery tends to produce a flutter of excitement and expectation. Magnificent staircases, dim perspectives of frescoes and carvings, the glorious hall of Apollo, rooms with mosaic pavements, antique vases, countless spoils of art, dazzle the eye of the neophyte, and prepare the mind for some grand enchantment. Then opens on one the grand hall of paintings arranged by schools, the works of each artist by themselves, a wilderness of gorgeous growths.

I first walked through the whole, offering my mind up aimlessly to see if there were any picture there great and glorious enough to seize and control my whole being, and answer at once the cravings of the poetic and artistic element. For any such I looked in vain. I saw a thousand beauties, as also a thousand enormities, but nothing of that overwhelming, subduing nature which I had conceived. Most of the men there had painted with dry eyes and cool hearts, thinking only of the mixing of their colors and the jugglery of their art, thinking little of heroism, love, faith, or immortality. Yet when I had resigned this longing, when I was sure I should not meet there what I sought, then I began to enjoy very heartily what there was.

In the first place, I now saw Claudes worthy of the reputation he bore. Three or four of these were studied with great delight,—the delight one feels who, conscientiously bound to be delighted, suddenly comes into a situation to be so. I saw, now, those atmospheric traits, those reproductions of the mysteries of air and of light, which are called so wonderful, and for which all admire Claude, but for which so few admire Him who made Claude, and who every day creates around us in the commonest scenes effects far more beautiful. How much, even now, my admiration of Claude was genuine, I cannot say. How can we ever be sure on this point, when we admire what has prestige and sanction, not to admire which is an argument against ourselves? Certainly, however, I did feel great delight in some of these works.

One of my favorites was Rembrandt. I always did admire the gorgeous and solemn mysteries of his coloring. Rembrandt is like Hawthorne. He chooses simple and every-day objects, and so arranges light and shadow as to give them a sombre richness and a mysterious gloom. The House of the Seven Gables is a succession of Rembrandt pictures, done in words instead of oils. Now, this pleases us, because our life really is a haunted one; the simplest thing in it is a mystery, the invisible world always lies around us like a shadow, and therefore this dreamy golden gleam of Rembrandt meets somewhat in our inner consciousness, to which it corresponds. There were no pictures in the gallery which I looked upon so long, and to which I returned so often and with such growing pleasure, as these. I found in them, if not a commanding, a drawing influence, a full satisfaction for one part of my nature.

There were Raphaels there which still disappointed me, because from Raphael I asked and expected more. I wished to feel his hand on my soul with a stronger grasp; these were too passionless in their serenity, and almost effeminate in their tenderness.

But Rubens, the great, joyous, full-souled, all-powerful Rubens! there he was, full as ever of triumphant, abounding life; disgusting and pleasing; making me laugh and making me angry; defying me to dislike him; dragging me at his chariot-wheels; in despite of my protests forcing me to confess that there was no other but he....

I should compare Rubens to Shakespeare for the wonderful variety and vital force of his artistic power. I know no other mind he so nearly resembles. Like Shakespeare, he forces you to accept and to forgive a thousand excesses, and uses his own faults as musicians use discords, only to enhance the perfection of harmony. There certainly is some use even in defects. A faultless style sends you to sleep. Defects rouse and excite the sensibility to seek and appreciate excellences. Some of Shakespeare's finest passages explode all grammar and rhetoric like sky-rockets,—the thought blows the language to shivers....

The halls devoted to painting of which I have spoken give you very little idea of the treasures of the institution. Gallery after gallery is filled with Greek, Roman, Assyrian, and Egyptian sculpture, coins, vases, and antique remains of every description. There is also an apartment in which I took a deep interest, containing the original sketches of ancient masters. Here one may see the pen-and-ink drawings of Claude, divided into squares to prepare them for the copyist. One compares here with interest the manners of the different artists in jotting down their ideas as they rose, some by chalk, some by crayon, some by pencil, some by water-colors, and some by a heterogeneous mixture of all. Mozart's scrap-bag of musical jottings could not have been more amusing.

On the whole, cravings of mere ideality have come nearer to meeting satisfaction by some of these old mutilated remains of Greek sculpture than anything I have met yet. In the paintings, even of the most celebrated masters, there are often things which are excessively annoying to me. I scarcely remember a master in whose works I have not found a hand, or foot, or face, or feature so distorted, or coloring at times so unnatural, or something so out of place and proportion in the picture as very seriously to mar the pleasure that I derived from it. In this statuary less is attempted and all is more harmonious, and one's ideas of proportion are never violated.

My favorite among all these remains is a mutilated statue which they call the Venus de Milo. This is a statue which is so called from having been dug up some years ago, piecemeal, in the island of Milos. There was a struggle for her between a French naval officer, the English, and the Turks. The French officer carried her off like another Helen, and she was given to Paris, old Louis Philippe being bridegroom by proxy. *Savans* refer the statue to the time of Phidias, and as this is a pleasant idea to me, I go a little further, and ascribe her to Phidias himself.

The statue is mutilated, both arms being gone, and part of the foot. But there is a majesty and grace in the head and face, a union of loveliness with intellectual and moral strength, beyond anything which I have ever seen. To me she might represent Milton's glorious picture of unfallen, perfect womanhood, in his Eve.

Compared with this matchless Venus that of Medici seems as inane and trifling as mere physical beauty always must by the side of beauty baptized and made sacramental, as the symbol of that which alone is truly fair.

TRAVEL IN FRANCE FIFTY YEARS AGO.

CHARLES DICKENS.

[It hardly seems to us, to whom the works of Dickens are household words, that his fame as a writer began more than half a century ago. Yet such is the case. The "Pictures from Italy," from which we make the following selection, was published in 1846, while his first book saw the light ten years earlier. We give here his story of how France and French life appeared to him on a journey southward from Paris.]

On a fine Sunday morning in the midsummer time and weather of eighteen hundred and forty-four it was, my good friend, when—don't be alarmed; not when two travellers might have been observed slowly making their way over that picturesque and broken ground by which the first chapter of a Middle Age novel is usually attained—but when an English travelling carriage of considerable proportions, fresh from the shady halls of the Pantechnicon near Belgrave Square, London, was observed (by a very small French soldier, for I saw him look at it) to issue from the gate of the Hôtel Meurice in the Rue Rivoli at Paris.

I am no more bound to explain why the English family travelling by this carriage, inside and out, should be starting for Italy on a Sunday morning, of all good days in the week, than I am to assign a reason for all the little men in France being soldiers and all the big men postilions, which is the invariable rule. But they had some sort of reason for what they did, I have no doubt, and their reason for being there at all was, as you know, that they were going to live in fair Genoa for a year; and that the head of the family purposed in that space of time to stroll about wherever his restless humor carried him.

And it would have been small comfort to me to have explained to the population of Paris generally that I was that Head and Chief, and not the radiant embodiment of good-humor who sat beside me in the person of a French courier,—best of servants and most beaming of men. Truth to say, he looked a great deal more patriarchal than I, who, in the shadow of his portly presence, dwindled down to no account at all.

There was, of course, very little in the aspect of Paris—as we rattled near the dismal Morgue and over the Pont Neuf—to reproach us for our Sunday travelling. The wine-shops (every second house) were driving a roaring trade; awnings were spreading, and chairs and tables arranging, outside the cafés, preparatory to the eating of ices and drinking of cool liquids later in the day; shoeblacks were busy on the bridges; shops were open; carts and wagons clattered to and fro; the narrow, uphill, funnel-like streets across the river were so many dense perspectives of crowd and bustle, parti-colored nightcaps, tobacco pipes, blouses, large boots, and shaggy heads of hair; nothing at that hour denoted a day of rest, unless it were the appearance, here and there, of a family pleasure-party, crammed into a bulky old lumbering cab, or of some contemplative holiday-maker in the freest and easiest dishabille, leaning out of a low garret window, watching the drying of his newly-polished shoes on the little parapet outside (if a gentleman), or the airing of her stockings in the sun (if a lady), with calm anticipation.

Once clear of the never-to-be-forgotten-or-forgiven pavement which surrounds Paris, the first three days of travelling towards Marseilles are quiet and monotonous enough. To Sens. To Avallon. To Châlons. A sketch of one day's proceedings is a sketch of all three, and here it is.

We have four horses and one postilion, who has a very long whip, and drives his team something like the courier of St. Petersburg in the circle at Astley's or Franconi's, only he sits his own horse instead of standing on him. The immense jack-boots worn by these postilions are sometimes a century or two old, and are so ludicrously disproportionate to the wearer's foot that the spur, which is put where his own heel comes, is generally half-way up the leg of the boots. The man often comes out of the stable-yard with his whip in his hand and his shoes on, and brings out, in both hands, one boot at a time, which he plants on the ground by the side of his horse with great gravity, until everything is ready. When it is—and oh, Heaven! the noise they make about it!—he gets into the boots, shoes and all, or is hoisted into them by a couple of friends; adjusts the rope harness, embossed by the labors of innumerable pigeons in the stables; makes all the horses kick and plunge; cracks his whip like a madman; shouts "En route—hi!" and away we go. He is sure to have a contest with his horse before we have gone very far; and then he calls him a thief, and a brigand, and a pig, and what not, and beats him about the head as if he were made of wood.

There is little more than one variety in the appearance of the country for the first two days,—from a dreary plain to an interminable avenue, and from an interminable avenue to a dreary plain again. Plenty of vines there are, in the open fields, but of a short, low kind, and not trained in festoons, but about straight sticks. Beggars innumerable there are, everywhere, but an extraordinarily scanty population and fewer children than I ever encountered. I don't believe we saw a hundred children between Paris and Châlons. Queer old towns, drawbridged and walled, with odd little towers at the angles, like grotesque faces, as if the wall had put a mask on, and were staring down into the moat; other strange little towers, in gardens and fields, and down lanes and in farm-yards; all alone, and always round, with a peaked roof, and never used for any purpose at all; ruinous buildings of all sorts; sometimes an hôtel de ville, sometimes a guard-house, sometimes a dwelling-house, sometimes a château with a rank garden, prolific in dandelion, and watched over by extinguisher-topped turrets and blink-eyed little casements, are the standard objects, repeated over and over again.

Sometimes we pass a village inn, with a crumbling wall belonging to it, and a perfect town of out-houses; and painted over the gate-way, "Stabling for sixty horses," as indeed there might be stabling for sixty score, were there any horses to be stabled there, or anybody resting there, or anything stirring about the place but a dangling bush, indicative of the wine inside, which flutters idly in the wind, in lazy keeping with everything else, and certainly is never in a green old age, though always so old as to be dropping to pieces. And all day long strange little narrow wagons, in strings of six or eight, bringing cheese from Switzerland, and frequently in charge, the whole line, of one man, or even boy,—and he very often asleep in the foremost cart,—come jingling past; the horses drowsily ringing the bells upon their harness, and looking as if they thought (no doubt they do) their great blue woolly furniture, of immense weight and thickness, with a pair of grotesque horns growing out of the collar, very much too warm for the midsummer weather.

Then there is the diligence, twice or thrice a day, with the dusty outsides in blue frocks, like butchers; and the insides in white nightcaps; and its cabriolet head on the roof, nodding and shaking like an idiot's head; and its Young-France passengers staring out of window, with beards down to their waists, and blue spectacles awfully shading their warlike eyes, and very big sticks clinched in their national grasp. Also the malle-poste, with only a couple of passengers, tearing along at a real good daredevil pace, and out of sight in no time. Steady old curés come jolting past, in such ramshackle, musty, rusty, clattering coaches as no Englishman would believe in; and bony women dawdle about in solitary places, holding cows by ropes while they feed, or digging and hoeing, or doing field-work of a more laborious kind, or representing real shepherdesses with their flocks,—to obtain an adequate idea of which pursuit and its followers, in any country, it is only necessary to take any pastoral poem, or picture, and imagine to yourself whatever is most exquisitely and widely unlike the descriptions therein contained.

You have been travelling along, stupidly enough, as you generally do in the last stage of the day; and the ninety-six bells upon the horses—twenty-four apiece—have been ringing sleepily in your ears for half an hour or so; and it has become a very jog-trot, monotonous, tiresome sort of business; and you have been thinking deeply about the dinner you will have at the next stage; when down at the end of the long avenue of trees through which you are travelling the first indication of a town appears, in the shape of some straggling cottages; and the carriage begins to rattle and roll over a horribly uneven pavement, ... and here we are in the yard of the Hôtel de l'Écu d'Or....

The landlady of the Hôtel de l'Écu d'Or is here; and the landlord of the Hôtel de l'Écu d'Or is here; and the femme de chambre of the Hôtel de l'Écu d'Or is here; and a gentleman in a glazed cap, with a red beard like a bosom friend, who is staying at the Hôtel de l'Écu d'Or, is here; and Monsieur le Curé is walking up and down in a corner of the yard by himself, with a shovel-hat upon his head, and a black gown on his back, and a book in one hand, and an umbrella in the other; and everybody, except Monsieur le Curé, is open-mouthed and open-eyed for the opening of the carriage-door. The landlord of the Hôtel de l'Écu d'Or dotes to that extent upon the courier that he can hardly wait for his coming down from the box, but embraces his very legs and boot-heels as he descends. "My courier! My brave courier! My friend! My brother!" The landlady loves him, the femme de chambre blesses him, the garçon worships him.

The courier asks if his letter has been received. It has, it has. Are the rooms prepared? They are, they are. The best rooms for my noble courier. The rooms of state for my gallant courier; the whole house is at the service of my best of friends! He keeps his hand upon the carriage-door, and asks some other question to enhance the expectation. He carries a green leathern purse outside his coat, suspended by a belt. The idlers look at it; one touches it. It is full of five-franc pieces. Murmurs of admiration are heard among the boys. The landlord falls upon the courier's neck and folds him to his breast. He is so much fatter than he was, he says. He looks so rosy and so well!...

The rooms are on the first floor, except the nursery for the night, which is a great rambling chamber, with four or five beds in it; through a dark passage, up two steps, down four, past a pump, across a balcony, and next door to the stable. The other sleeping apartments are large and lofty; each with two small bedsteads, tastefully hung, like the windows, with red and white drapery. The sitting-room is famous. Dinner is already laid in it for three; and the napkins are folded in cocked-hat fashion. The floors are of red tile. There are no carpets, and not much furniture to speak of; but there is abundance of looking-glass, and there are large vases under glass shades filled with artificial flowers, and there are plenty of clocks. The whole party are in motion. The brave courier in particular, is everywhere, looking after the beds, having wine poured down his throat by his dear brother the landlord, and picking up green cucumbers,—always cucumbers; Heaven knows where he gets them,—with which he walks about, one in each hand, like truncheons.

Dinner is announced. There is very thin soup; there are very large loaves,—one apiece; a fish; four dishes afterwards; some poultry afterwards; a dessert afterwards; and no lack of wine. There is not much in the dishes, but they are very good, and always ready instantly. When it is nearly dark, the brave courier, having eaten the two cucumbers, sliced up in the contents of a pretty large decanter of oil and another of vinegar, emerges from his retreat below, and proposes a visit to the Cathedral, whose massive tower frowns down upon the court-yard of the inn. Off we go; and very solemn and grand it is in the dim light; so dim at last that the polite old lantern-jawed sacristan has a feeble little bit of candle in his hand to grope among the tombs with, and looks, among the grim columns, very like a lost ghost who is searching for his own.

Underneath the balcony, when we return, the inferior servants of the inn are supping in the open air, at a great table; the dish, a stew of meat and vegetables, smoking hot, and served in the iron caldron it was boiled in. They have a pitcher of thin wine, and are very merry; merrier than the gentleman with the red beard, who is playing billiards in the light room on the left of the yard, where shadows with cues in their hands and cigars in their mouths cross and recross the window constantly. Still the thin curé walks up and down alone, with his book and umbrella. And there he walks, and there the billiard-balls rattle, long after we are fast asleep.

We are astir at six the next morning. It is a delightful day, shaming yesterday's mud upon the carriage, if anything could shame a carriage in a land where carriages are never cleaned. Everybody is brisk, and as we finish breakfast the horses come jingling into the yard from the post-house. Everything taken out of the carriage is put back again. The brave courier announces that all is ready, after walking into every room and looking all round it to be certain that nothing is left behind. Everybody gets in. Everybody connected with the Hôtel de l'Écu d'Or is again enchanted. The brave courier runs into the house for a parcel containing cold fowl, sliced ham, bread, and biscuits for lunch, hands it into the coach, and runs back again.

What has he got in his hand now? More cucumbers? No. A long strip of paper. It's the bill.

The brave courier has two belts on this morning,—one supporting the purse, another a mighty good sort of leathern bottle, filled to the throat with the best light Bordeaux wine in the house. He never pays the bill till this bottle is full. Then he disputes it.

He disputes it now violently. He is still the landlord's brother, but by another father or mother. He is not so nearly related to him as he was last night. The landlord scratches his head. The brave courier points to certain figures in the bill, and intimates that if they remain there the Hôtel de l'Écu d'Or is thenceforth and forever an hotel de l'écu de cuivre. The landlord goes into a little counting-house. The brave courier follows, forces the bill and a pen into his hand, and talks more rapidly than ever. The landlord takes the pen. The courier smiles. The landlord makes an alteration. The courier cuts a joke. The landlord is affectionate, but not weakly so. He bears it like a man. He shakes hands with his brave brother, but he doesn't hug him. Still, he loves his brother, for he knows that he will be returning that way one of these fine days with another family, and he foresees that his heart will yearn towards him again. The brave courier traverses all round the carriage once, looks at the drag, inspects the wheels, jumps up, gives the word, and away we go!

[And so onward they go, passing Châlons, which excites little comment, and at length reaching Lyons.]

What a city Lyons is! Talk about people feeling at certain unlucky times as if they had tumbled from the clouds! Here is a whole town that has tumbled anyhow, out of the sky; having been first caught up, like other stones that tumble down from that region, out of fens and barren places, dismal to behold! The two great streets through which the two great rivers dash, and all the little streets whose name is Legion, were scorching, blistering, and sweltering. The houses, high and vast, dirty to excess, rotten as old cheeses, and as thickly peopled. All up the hills that hem the city in, these houses swarm; and the mites inside were lolling out of the windows and drying their ragged clothes on poles, and crawling in and out at the doors, and coming out to pant and gasp upon the pavement, and creeping in and out among huge piles and bales of fusty, musty, stifling goods, and living, or rather not dying till their time should come, in an exhausted receiver. Every manufacturing town melted into one would hardly convey an impression of Lyons as it presented itself to me, for all the undrained, unscavengered qualities of a foreign town seemed grafted there upon the native miseries of a manufacturing one, and it bears such fruit as I would go some miles out my way to avoid encountering again.

In the cool of the evening, or rather in the faded heat of the day, we went to see the Cathedral, where divers old women, and a few dogs, were engaged in contemplation. There was no difference in point of cleanliness between its stone pavement and that of the streets; and there was a wax saint, in a little box like a berth aboard ship, with a glass front to it, whom Madame Tussaud would have nothing to say to, on any terms, and which even Westminster Abbey might be ashamed of. If you would know all about the architecture of this church, or any other, its dates, dimensions, endowments, and history, is it not written in Mr. Murray's Guide-Book, and may you not read it there, with thanks to him, as I did?

For this reason, I should abstain from mentioning the curious clock in Lyons Cathedral, if it were not for a small mistake I made in connection with that piece of mechanism. The keeper of the church was very anxious it should be shown; partly for the honor of the establishment and the town, and partly, perhaps, because of his deriving a percentage from the additional consideration. However that may be, it was set in motion, and thereupon a host of little doors flew open, and innumerable little figures staggered out of them, and jerked themselves back again, with that special unsteadiness of purpose, and hitching in the gait, which usually attaches to figures that are moved by clock-work. Meanwhile, the sacristan stood explaining these wonders, and pointed them out, severally, with a wand. There was a centre puppet of the Virgin Mary; and close to her a small pigeon-hole, out of which another and a very ill-looking puppet made one of the most sudden plunges I ever saw accomplished; instantly flopping back again at sight of her, and banging his little door violently after him. Taking this to be emblematic of the victory over Sin and Death, and not at all unwilling to show that I perfectly understood the subject, in anticipation of the showman, I rashly said, "Aha! The Evil Spirit. To be sure. He is very soon disposed of." "Pardon, monsieur," said the sacristan, with a polite motion of his hand towards the little door, as if introducing somebody,—"the Angel Gabriel!"

Soon after daybreak next morning we were steaming down the arrowy Rhone, at the rate of twenty miles an hour, in a very dirty vessel full of merchandise, and with only three or four other passengers for our companions; among whom, the most remarkable was a silly, old, meek-faced, garlic-eating, immeasurably polite Chevalier, with a dirty scrap of red ribbon hanging at his button-hole, as if he had tied it there to remind himself of something; as Tom Noddy, in the farce, ties knots in his pocket-handkerchief.

For the last two days we had seen great sullen hills, the first indications of the Alps, lowering in the distance. Now, we were rushing on beside them; sometimes close beside them; sometimes with an intervening slope, covered with vineyards. Villages and small towns hanging in mid-air, with great woods of olives seen through the light open towers of their churches, and clouds moving slowly on, upon the steep acclivity behind them; ruined castles perched on every eminence; and scattered houses in the clefts and gullies of the hills, made it very beautiful. The great height of these, too, making the buildings look so tiny that they had all the charm of elegant models; their excessive whiteness, as contrasted with the brown rocks, or the sombre, deep, dull, heavy green of the olive-tree, and the puny size and little slow walk of the Liliputian men and women on the bank, made a charming picture. There were ferries out of number, too; bridges; the famous Pont d'Esprit, with I don't know how many arches; towns where memorable wines are made; Vallence, where Napoleon studied; and the noble river, bringing, at every winding turn, new beauties into view.

There lay before us, that same afternoon, the broken bridge of Avignon, and all the city baking in the sun; yet with an underdone-pie-crust, battlemented wall that never will be brown, though it bake for centuries.

FROM NORMANDY TO PROVENCE.

DONALD G. MITCHELL.

["Fresh Gleanings; or, A New Sheaf from the Old Fields of Continental Europe," an interesting and appreciative work of travel by the "Ik Marvel" of literary fame, presents us with the following picturesque account of some of the more interesting cities of Normandy and Southern France, which can scarcely fail to prove of interest to readers. Leaving Lyons, our traveller makes a diligence journey to Limoges, in which city we take up the thread of his route.]

We wish to take our stop at some not too large town of the interior, and which shall it be,—Châlons-sur-Saône, with its bridge, and quays, and meadows; or Dijon, lying in the vineyards of Burgundy; or Châteauroux, in the great sheep plains of Central France; or Limoges, still more unknown, prettily situated among the green hills of Limousin, and the chief town of the department *Haute Vienne*?

Let it be just by the Boule d'Or, in the town last named, that I quit my seat in the diligence. The little old place is not upon any of the great routes, so that the servants of the inn have not become too republican for civility, and a blithe waiting-maid is at hand to take our luggage.

A plain door-way in the heavy stone inn, and still plainer and steeper stair-way, conduct to a clean, large chamber upon the first floor. Below in the little salon some three or four are at supper. Join them you may, if you please, with a chop nicely done, and a palatable *vin dupays*.

It is too dark to see the town. You are tired with eight-and-forty hours of constant diligence-riding,—if you have come from Lyons, as I did,—and the bed is excellent.

The window overlooks the chief street of the place; it is wide and paved with round stones, and dirty, and there are no sidewalks, though a town of thirty thousand inhabitants. Nearly opposite is a café, with small green settees ranged about the door, with some tall flowering shrubs in green boxes; and even at eight in the morning two or three are loitering upon their chairs and sipping coffee. Next door is the office of the diligence for Paris. Farther up the street are haberdashery shops and show-rooms of the famous Limoges crockery. Soldiers are passing by twos, and cavalrymen in undress go sauntering by on fine coal-black horses; and the guide-book tells me that from this region come the horses for all the cavalry of France....

There are curious old churches, and a simple-minded, gray-haired verger, to open the side chapels and to help you spell the names on tombs. Not half so tedious will the old man prove as the automaton cathedral-showers of England, and he spices his talk with a little wit. There are shops, not unlike those of a middle-sized town in our country; still, little air of trade, and none at all of progress. Decay seems to be stamped on nearly all the country towns of France, unless so large as to make cities, and so have a life of their own, or so small as to serve only as market-towns for the peasantry....

Wandering out of the edge of the town of Limoges, you come upon hedges and green fields, for Limousin is the Arcadia of France. Queer old houses adorn some of the narrow streets, and women in strange head-dresses look out of the balconies that lean half-way over. But Sunday is their holiday time, when all are in their gayest, and when the green walks encircling the town, laid upon that old line of ramparts which the Black Prince stormed, are thronged with the population.

The bill at the *Boule d'Or* is not an extravagant one; for as strangers are not common, the trick of extortion is unknown. The waiting-maid drops a courtesy, and gives a smiling *bon jour*, not surely unmindful of the little fee she gets; but she never disputes its amount, and seems grateful for the least. There is no "boots" or waiter to dog you over to the diligence; nay, if you are not too old, or ugly, the little girl herself insists upon taking your portmanteau, and trips across with it, and puts it in the hands of the conductor, and waits your going earnestly, and waves her hand at you, and gives you another "*bonvoyage*" that makes your ears tingle till the houses of Limoges and its high towers have vanished, and you are a mile away, down the pleasant banks of the river Vienne.

Shall we set a foot down for a moment in the queer, interesting, busy old Norman town of Rouen, where everybody goes who goes to Paris, but where few stop for a look at what in many respects is most curious to see in all France? The broad, active quays, and the elegant modern buildings upon them, and the bridges, and the river with its barges and steamers, are, it is true, worth the seeing, and exposed to the eye of every passer, and give one the idea of a new and enterprising city. But back from this is another city—the old city—infinitely more worthy of attention.

Out of its midst rises the corkscrew iron tower of the Cathedral, under which sleeps Rollo, the first Duke of Normandy; and if one have the courage to mount to the dizzy summit of that corkscrew winding tower of iron, he will see such a labyrinth of ways, shut in by such confusion of gables, and such steep, sharp roofs, glittering with so many colored tiles, as that he will seem to dream a dream of the olden time.

And if he have an agricultural eye, it will wander delightedly over the broad, rich plains that there border the Seine, rich in all manner of corn-land and in orchards. And if he have an historic eye, it will single out an old castle or two that show themselves upon the neighboring hills; and the ruins, and the Seine, and the valley, and the town will group together in his imagination, and he will bear away the picture in his mind to his Western home in the wilderness; and it shall serve him as an illustration—a living illustration—to the old chronicles of wars, whether of Monstrelet, or Turner, or Anquetil, or Michelet, down through all the time of his thinking life. So, when he readeth of Norman plain blasted with battle, and knightly helmets glittering in the crash of war, he shall have a scene,—a scene lying clear as mid-day under the eye of steady memory,—in the which he may plant his visions of Joan of Arc, or of stout Henry V., or of drivelling Charles VI., or of *Jean sans peur*; for these—all of them, he knows—have trodden the valley of Rouen.

Whoever may have seen English Worcester or Gloucester will have a foretaste of what comes under the eye at Rouen; but to one fresh from the new, straight thoroughfares of America nothing surely can seem stranger than the dark, crowded ways of the capital of Normandy.

How narrow, how dirty, how cool! for even in summer the sun cannot come down in them—for the projecting balconies and the tallness of the houses; and between the fountains in the occasional open places and the incessant washings it is never dry. There is no pavement for the foot-goer but the sharp, round stones sticking up from side to side, and sloping down to the sluice-way in the middle. Donkeys with loads of cabbages, that nearly fill up the way, women with baskets on their heads, and staring strangers, and *gendarmerie* in their cocked hats, marching two by two, and soldiers, and school-boys (not common in France), and anxious-faced merchants (still rarer out of the North), all troop together under gables, that would seem to totter were they not of huge oak beams, whose blackened heads peep out from the brick walls like faces of an age gone by.

What quaint carving! what heavy old tiles, when you catch a glimpse of the peaked roofs! what windings and twists! There are well-filled and sometimes elegant shops below, with story on story reeling above them.

Away through an opening, that is only a streak of light at the end, appears the ugly brown statue of the Maid of Orleans. There she was burned, poor girl!—and the valet, if you have the little English boy of the Hôtel de Rouen, will tell you how, and when, and why they burned her; and he will ring the bell at the gate of a strange, old house close by, and beckon you into the court, where you will see around the walls the bas-reliefs of the Cloth of Gold. St. Owens too, which, after Strasburg Cathedral, is the noblest Gothic church in France, is in some corner of the never-ending curious streets. And on a fête day, what store of costume on its pavement! What big, white muslin caps,—

flaring to left and right! What show of red petticoats, and steeple-crowned hats, and clumping sabots, and short-waisted boys, and little, brown men of Brittany!...

Many—many dull diligence—days lie between Rouen and the sunny southern town of Nismes; yet with the wishing we were there at once.

Where was born Guizot,—where are Protestant people,—where are almost quiet Sundays,—where there is a Roman Coliseum, dropped in the centre of the town,—there are we. On a December day, when I was there, it was as warm and summer-like,—the sunny side of that old ruin,—and the green things peeped out from the wall as fresh and blossoming, as if Merrie May had commenced her time of flowers. And the birds were chattering out of all the corridors, and the brown stone looked as mellow as a russet apple in the glow of that rich southern atmosphere.

The trees along the Boulevard—running here through the town—wore a spring-like air (there must have been olives or evergreen oaks among them), and though I cannot say if the peach-trees were in bloom, yet I know I picked a bright red rose in the garden by the fountain,—the great Roman fountain which supplies the whole town with water,—and it lies pressed for a witness in my journal yet. And there were a hundred other roses in bloom all around,— and a little girl was passing through the garden at the time, with one in her hair, and was playing with another in her hand. And the old soldier who limps, and lives in the little cottage at the gate of the garden, as patrol, was sunning himself on the bench by the door; and a canary-bird that hung over it was singing as blithely in his cage as the sparrows had been singing in the ruin.

And what was there in that charming garden spot of Nismes, with its wide walks and shade of trees, and fresh with the sound of running water and the music of birds? There was an old temple of Diana, and fountain of the Nymphs. Both were embowered in trees at the foot of the hill which lords it over the town.

The fountain rises almost a river, and alone supplies a city of forty thousand inhabitants. The guide-books will tell one that it is some fifty or sixty feet in depth, and surrounded with walls of masonry,—now green with moss and clinging herbs; and from this, its source, it passes in a gushing flood over the marble floors of old Roman baths, as smooth and exact now as the day on which they were laid. The old soldier will conduct you down and open the door-way, so that you may tread upon the smooth marble where trod the little feet of the unknown Roman girls. For none know when the baths were built, or when this temple of Diana was founded. Not even of the great arena, remarkable in many respects as the Roman Coliseum, is there the slightest classic record. Nothing but its own gigantic masonry tells of its origin.

Upon the top of the hill, from whose foot flows the fountain, is still another ruin,—a high, cumbrous tower. And as I wandered under it, full of classic fervor, and looked up,—with ancient Rome in my eye, and the gold Ægis, and the banner of triumph,—behold, an old woman with a red handkerchief tied round her head was spreading a blue petticoat over the edge of the tower to dry.

But from the ground beneath was a rich view over the town and valley. The hill and the garden at its base were cloaked with the deep black green of pines and firs; beyond was the town, just veiled in the light smoke of the morning fires; here peeped through a steeple, there a heavy old tower, and looming with its hundred arches and circumference of broken rocks—bigger than them all—was the amphitheatre of the Latin people, whose language and monuments alone remain. Beside the city—through an atmosphere clear as a morning on the valley of the Connecticut—were the stiff velvety tops of the olive-orchards and the long brown lines of vineyards;—away the meadows swept, with here and there over the level reach an old gray town, with tall presiding castle, or a glittering strip of the bright branches of the Rhone.

But not only is there pleasant December sun and sunny landscape in and about the Provençal town of Nismes, there are also pleasant streets and walks; there is a beautiful Roman temple,—*La Maison Carrée,*—than which there is scarce a more perfect one through all Italy, among the neat white houses of the city. Within it are abundance of curiosities, for such as are curious about dates and inscriptions that cannot be made out; and there are Roman portals still left in the vestiges of the Roman walls....

There is the Grand Theatre for such as wish a stall for a month; and there is the grander theatre of the old Roman Arêne. True, the manager is dead, and the actors are but bats and lizards, with now and then a grum old owl for prompter. But what scenes the arched openings blackened by the fires of barbarians, and the stunted trees growing where Roman ladies sat, paint to the eye of fancy! What an orchestra the birds make at twilight, and the recollections make always!

It was better than Norma, it was richer than Robert le Diable, to sit down on one of the fragments in front of where was the great entrance and look through the iron grating, and follow the perspective of corridors opening into the central arena, where the moonlight shone on a still December night,— glimmering over the ranges of the seats and upon the shaking leaves. And there was a rustle, a gentle sighing of the night wind among the crevices, that one could easily believe was the echo of a distant chorus behind the scenes:— and so it was,—a chorus of Great Dead Ones,—mournful and slow,—listened to by no flesh ear, but by the delicate ear of Memory.

There are rides about Nismes. There is Avignon with its brown ramparts and its gigantic Papal towers bundling up from the banks of the Rhone, only a half-day's ride away; and half a day more will put one down at the fountain of Vaucluse; where, if it be summer-time,—and it is summer-time there three-quarters of the year, you may sit down under the shade of a fig-tree, or a fir, and read—undisturbed save by the dashing of the water under the cliff—the fourteenth Canzonet of Petrarch....

Coming back at nightfall, [the traveller] will have a mind to hunt through the narrow, dim-lighted streets of Avignon in search of the tomb of Laura, and he will find it embowered with laurels and shut up by a thorn hedge and wicket; and to get within this, he will ring the bell of the heavy, sombre-looking mansion close by, when a shuffling old man with keys will come out and do the honors of the tomb. He will take a franc,—not absolutely disdainfully, but with a world of *sang-froid,* since it is not for himself (he says) but for the poor children within the mansion, which is a foundling hospital. He puts the money in his red waistcoat-pocket, suiting to the action a sigh, *"Mes pauvres enfans!"* Perhaps you will add in the overflowing of your heart, "Poor children!"

As you go out of the garden, a box at the gate, which had escaped your notice, solicits offerings in behalf of the institution from strangers visiting the tomb. The box has a lock and key; the old man does not keep the key. You have a sudden suspicion of his red waistcoat-pocket, and sigh as you go out, *Les pauvres enfans!*

Pont du Gard is the finest existing remain of a Roman aqueduct, and spans a quite deep stream, good for either fishing or bathing. Profusion of wild flowers grow about and over it, and fig-trees and brambles make a thicket together on the slope that goes down to the water.

One may walk over the top of the ruin—two yards wide, without parapet or rail—and look over into the depth three hundred feet below. The nerves must be strong to endure it, then the enjoyment is full. Less than half a day's ride will bring one from the Pont du Gard to the Hôtel du Luxembourg of Nismes.

Montpellier is in Provence, the city of summer-like winters, and upon the river is Arles, with its Arena, larger even than that of Nismes, but far less perfect; and its pretty women—famous all over France—wear a mischievous look about them, and the tie of their red turbans, as if coquetry were one of their charms.

It is a strange, mixed-up town, that of Arles,—ruins and dirt and narrowness and grandeur, an old church in whose yard they dig up Roman coffins, and a rolling bridge of boats. Not anywhere in France are there dirtier and more crooked streets, not anywhere such motley array of shops amid the filth, red turbans and meat, bread and blocks, old coins and silks. Within the museum itself are collected more odd scraps of antiquity than can be found elsewhere together; there are lead pipes and stone fountains, old inscriptions and iron spikes, and the noblest monument of all is a female head that has no nose; but the manager very ingeniously supplies with his hand the missing feature.

Opposite the doors of this museum stands an obelisk of granite, which was fished out of the Rhone, and boasts a high antiquity, and upon its top is a brilliant sun with staring eyes. To complete the extraordinary grouping, upon another side of the same square is a church with the strangest bas-relief over its central door-way that surely madcap fancy ever devised. It is a representation of the Last Judgment; on the right, the angels are leading away the blessed in pairs, and on the left a grinning devil with horns, and with a stout rope passed over his shoulder and clinched in his teeth, is tugging away at legions of condemned souls.

There is rare Gothic sculpture within some old cloisters adjoining, and a marble bas-relief within the church, with a Virgin and Child in glory, was—I say it on the authority of an ingenious *valet de place*—of undoubtedly Roman origin.

Ancient sarcophagi may be seen here and there in the streets, serving as reservoirs at the fountains; and many a peasant of the adjoining country makes the coffin of a Roman noble his water-trough.

There belongs another antiquity to Provence besides that of Roman date,—it is that of the gay, chivalrous times of William IX., Count of Poitou, and all the gallant Troubadours who came after him. Then helmets glittered over the Provençal plains, and ladies wove silken pennants in princely halls. Then the tournament drew its throngs, and knights contended not only with their lances for martial fame but with their songs for the ears of love. Even monarchs—Barbarossa and Cœur de Lion—vied with Troubadours, and the seat of the Provençal court was the great centre of Southern chivalry. Arles had its court of love, more splendid than now, and its *arrêt d'amour* was more binding than the charms of the brightest eyes that shine in Provence to-day.

Little remains of the luxurious tastes of the old livers at Arles. The café, dirty and dim, assembles the chivalry of the city, and a stranger Western knight, in place of baronial hall, is entertained at the Hôtel du Forum, where, with excess of cheatery, they give him for St. Peray a weak, carbonated Moselle.

Let no one judge of the flat sand surface of Provence by the rich descriptions of the Mysteries of Udolfo, nor let the lover of ballad poetry reckon upon the peasant *patois* as having the sweet flow of Raymond or Bertrand de Born.

A FRENCH FARMER'S PARADISE.

M. BETHAM-EDWARDS.

[So many woful stories are told us of the penury and strife for bare existence of the agriculturists of Europe that it is pleasant to read of happier scenes and more plentiful larders. M. Betham-Edwards, than whom few are better able to speak of the conditions of life in rural France, has drawn for us, in her "Holidays in Eastern France," a cheerful picture of such a scene, which we take pleasure in reproducing. We are here taken out of the beaten track of ordinary travel into "fresh scenes and pastures new."]

How delicious to escape from the fever, heat, and turmoil of Paris during the Exhibition to the green banks and sheltered ways of the gently undulating Marne! With what delight we wake up in the morning to the noise—if noise it can be called—of the mower's scythe, the rustle of acacia-leaves, and the notes of the stock-dove, looking back as upon a nightmare to the horn of the tramway conductor and the perpetual grind of the stonemason's saw! Yes, to quit Paris at a time of tropic heat, and nestle down in some country resort, is, indeed, like exchanging Dante's lower circle for Paradise. The heat has followed us here; but with a screen of luxuriant foliage ever between us and the burning blue sky, and with a breeze rippling the leaves always, no one need complain.

With the cocks and the hens, and the birds and the bees, we are all up and stirring betimes; there are dozens of cool nooks and corners, if we like to spend the morning out of doors, and do not feel enterprising enough to set out on an exploring expedition by diligence or rail. After the mid-day meal every one takes a siesta, as a matter of course, waking up between four and five o'clock for a ramble. Wherever we go we find lovely prospects. Quiet little rivers and canals, winding in between lofty lines of poplars, undulating pastures, and amber cornfields; picturesque villages, crowned by a church spire here and there; wide sweeps of highly cultivated land, interspersed with rich woods, vineyards, orchards, and gardens; all these make up the scenery familiarized to us by some of the most characteristic of French painters.

Just such tranquil rural pictures have been portrayed over and over again by Millet, Corot, Daubigny; and in this very simplicity often lies their charm. No costume or grandiose outline is here, as in Brittany; no picturesque poverty, no poetic archaisms; all is rustic and pastoral, but with the rusticity and pastoralness of every day.

We are in the midst of one of the wealthiest and best cultivated regions of France, moreover, and, when we penetrate beneath the surface, we find that in manner and customs, as well as dress and outward appearance, the peasant and agricultural population generally differ no little from their remote country-people, the Bretons. In this famous cheese-making country, the "Fromage de Brie" being the specialty of these rich dairy-farms, there is no superstition, hardly a trace of poverty, and little that can be called poetic. The people are wealthy, laborious, and progressive. The farmers' wives, however hard they may work at home, wear the smartest of Parisian bonnets and gowns when paying visits. I was going to say, when at church, but nobody does go there!

It is a significant fact that in the fairly well-to-do educated district, where newspapers are read by the poorest, where well-being is the rule, poverty the exception, the church is empty on Sunday, and the priest's authority is *nil.* The priests may preach against abstinence from church in the pulpits, and may lecture their congregation in private; no effect is thereby produced. Church-going has become out of date among the manufacturers of Brie cheese. They amuse themselves on Sundays by taking walks with their children, the *pater-familias* bathes in the river, the ladies put on their gala dresses and pay visits, but they omit their devotions.

Some of these tenant-farmers—many of the farms being hired on lease, possessors of small farms hiring more land—are very rich, and one of our neighbors whose wealth has been made by the manufacture of Brie cheese lately gave his daughter one hundred thousand francs as a dowry. The wedding-breakfast took place at the Grand Hotel, Paris, and a hundred guests were invited to partake of a sumptuous collation. But in spite of fine clothes and large dowries, farmers' wives and daughters still attend to the dairies, and when they cease to do so doubtless farming in Seine et Marne will no longer be the prosperous business we find it. It is delightful to witness the wide-spread well-being of this highly-farmed region.

"There is no poverty here," my host tells me, "and this is why life is so pleasant."

True enough, wherever you go you find well-dressed, contented-looking people; no rags, no squalor, no pinched want. Poverty is an accident of rare occurrence, and not a normal condition, every one being able to get plenty of work and good pay. The habitual look of content written upon every face is very striking. It seems as if in this land of Goshen life were no burden, but matter of satisfaction only, if not of thankfulness. Class distinction can hardly be said to exist; there are employers and employed, masters and servants, of course, but the line of demarcation is lightly drawn, and we find an easy familiarity wholly free from impoliteness, much less vulgarity, existing between them.

The automatic demureness characterizing English servants in the presence of their employers is wholly unknown here. There are households with us where the servants might all be mutes for any signs of animation they give, but here they take part in what is going on, and exchange a word and smile with every member of the household, never dreaming that it should be otherwise. One is struck, too, here by the good looks, intelligence, and trim appearance of the children, who, it is plain, are well cared for. The houses have vines and sweet peas on the walls, flowers in the windows, and altogether a look of comfort and ease found nowhere in Western France. The Breton villages are composed of mere hovels, where pigs, cows, and poultry live in close proximity to their owners, a dung-hill stands before every front door, and, to get in-doors and out, you have always to cross a pool of liquid manure. Here order and cleanliness prevail, with a diffusion of well-being hardly, I should say, to be matched out of America.

Travellers who visit France again and again, as much out of sympathy with its people's institutions as from a desire to see its monuments and outward features, will find ample to reward them in Seine et Marne. On every side we have evidence of the tremendous natural resources and indefatigable laboriousness of the people. There is one point here, as elsewhere in France, which strikes an agriculturist with astonishment, and that is the abundance of trees standing amid cornfields and miscellaneous crops, also the interminable plantation of poplars that can be seen on every side, apparently without any object. But the truth is, the planting of apple- and pear-trees in fields is no extravagance, rather an economy, the fruit they produce exceeding in value the corn they damage, whilst the puzzling line of poplars growing beside canals and rivers is the work of the government, every spare bit of ground belonging to the state being planted with them for the sake of the timber. The crops are splendid, partly owing to the soil, and partly to the advanced system of agriculture. You may see exposed for sale, in little towns, the newest American agricultural implements, while the great diversity of products speaks volumes for the enterprise of the farmers.

As you stroll along, now climbing, now descending this pleasantly undulated country, you may see growing in less than an acre, a patch of potatoes here, a vineyard there, on one side a bit of wheat, oats, rye, and barley, with fruit-trees casting abundant shadow over all; on the other Indian-corn, clover, and mangel-wurzel in the green state, recently planted for autumn fodder; farther on a poppy-field, three weeks ago in full flower, now having full pods ready for gathering,—the opium poppy being cultivated for commerce here. All those and many more are found close together, and near them many a lovely little glen, copse, and ravine, recalling Scotland

and Wales, while the open hill-sides show broad belts of pasture, corn, and vineyard. You may walk for miles through what seems one vast orchard, only, instead of turf, rich crops are growing under the trees. This is indeed the orchard of France, on which we English folk largely depend for our summer fruits. A few days ago the black-currant-trees were being stripped for the benefit of Parisian lovers of *cassis*, a liqueur in high repute.

We encounter on our walks carts laden with plums packed in baskets and barrels on their way to Covent Garden. Later on, it will be the peach and apricot crops that are gathered for exportation. Later still, apples, walnuts, and pears; the village not far from our own sends fruit to the Paris markets valued at one million francs annually, and the entire valley of the Marne is unequalled throughout France for fruitfulness and abundance.

But the traveller must settle down in some delicious retreat in the valley of the Marne to realize the interest and charm of such a country as this. And he must above all things be a fairly good pedestrian, for, though a land of Goshen flowing with milk and honey, it is not a land of luxuries, and carriages, good, bad, or indifferent, are difficult to be got. A countless succession of delightful prospects is offered to the persevering explorer who, each day, strikes out in an entirely different direction. I have always been of the opinion that the best way to see a country is to make a halt in some good central point for weeks at a time, and from thence "excursionize." By these means much fatigue is avoided, and the two chief drawbacks to the pleasure of travel, namely, hotels and perpetual railway travel, are avoided as much as possible.

Seine et Marne, if not one of the most picturesque regions in France, abounds in those quiet charms which grow upon the sympathetic traveller. It is not a land of marvels and pictorial attractions like Brittany. There is no costume, no legendary romance, no stone array of Carnac to entice the stranger, but, on the other hand, the lover of nature in her more subdued aspects, and the archæologist also, will find ample to repay them....

THE LUMINOUS PALACE Champ De Mars, Paris, 1900

My rallying-point was a pleasant country house at Couilly, offering easy opportunity of studying agriculture and rural life, as well as of making excursions by road and rail. Couilly itself is charming. The canal, winding its way between thick lines of poplar-trees towards Meaux, you may follow in the hottest day of summer without fatigue. The river, narrow and sleepy, yet so picturesquely curling amid green slopes and tangled woods, is another delightful stroll; then there are broad, richly-wooded hills rising above these, and shady side-paths leading from hill to valley, with alternating vineyards, orchards, pastures, and cornfields on either side. Couilly lies in the heart of the cheese-making country, part of the ancient province of Brie, from which this famous cheese is named.

[The French *département* of Seine et Marne possesses but two important historical monuments, the Château of Fontainebleau and the Cathedral of Meaux, though it contains archæological remains from the Mediæval to the Celtic Age. Fontainebleau is too well known to need description here, so we shall conclude by following our traveller to Meaux.]

The diligence passes our garden gate early in the morning, and in an hour and a half takes us to Meaux, former capital of the province of La Brie, bishopric of the famous Bossuet, and one of the early strongholds of the Reformation. The neighboring country, *pays Meldois* as it is called, is one vast fruit and vegetable garden, bringing in enormous returns. From our vantage-ground—for, of course, we get outside the vehicle—we survey the shifting landscape, wood and valley and plain, soon seeing the city with its imposing Cathedral, flashing like marble, high above the winding river and fields of green and gold on either side. I know nothing that gives the mind an idea of fertility and wealth more than this scene, and it is no wonder that the Prussians, in 1871, here levied a heavy toll; their sojourn at Meaux having cost the inhabitants not less than a million and a half of francs. All now is peace and prosperity, and here, as in the neighboring towns, rags, want, and beggary are not found. The evident well-being of all classes is delightful to behold.

Meaux, with its shady boulevards and pleasant public gardens, must be an agreeable place to live in, nor would intellectual resources be wanting. We strolled into the spacious town library, open, of course, to all strangers, and could wish for no better occupation than to con the curious old books and the manuscripts that it contains. One incident amused me greatly. The employé, having shown me the busts adorning the walls of the principal rooms, took me into a side closet, where, ignominiously put out of sight, were the busts of Charles the Tenth and Louis Philippe.

"But," said our informant, "we have more busts in the garret,—the Emperor Napoleon III., the Empress, and the Prince Imperial."

Naturally enough, on the proclamation of the republic, these busts were

considered at least supererogatory, and it is to be hoped they will stay where
they are.

CORDOVA AND ITS MOSQUE.

S. P. SCOTT.

[The following selection we owe to Scott's "Through Spain: A Narrative of Travel and Adventure in the Peninsula," a work of unusual interest, and which reproduces in picturesque language most of the attractions of that favored peninsula. The Moorish inhabitants of Spain have left in that country numerous monuments of their graceful architecture, notably the Alhambra of Granada and the Mosque of Cordova. The latter, to the description of which this selection is mainly devoted, is one of the most magnificent examples of Saracenic architecture extant, and despite the efforts of ecclesiastics to ruin it, still remains a worthy object of pilgrimage for the lovers of art.]

Once more we turn our faces southward over the bleak and lifeless plains. Estremadura and La Mancha are soon left behind, as the flying train darts through the passes of the Sierra Morena, and descends into the beautiful province of Andalusia. It is almost like another world. The country is thickly settled, green fields take the place of the barren steppes, hedges of aloe and cactus enclose the extensive olive plantations, and, here and there, overtopping the orange groves, are seen the feathery branches of the palm. The costumes grow bright and odd, and the people become more swarthy in complexion.

The water-carrier, with her Arab alcarazza lightly poised upon her head, approaches the car window, and deals out the crystal fluid to the thirsty traveller at the moderate price of one-fifth of a cent a drink. A few miles farther, and, entering a long and irregular city, with tortuous streets reeking with villanous smells—each of which seems considerably worse than the one you have just escaped—and squares overrun with indefatigable beggars, all startling specimens of horrible and loathsome deformity, we are informed that this is at last the renowned capital of the Khalifs.

If Cordova at first sight is so unprepossessing, a better acquaintance is hardly calculated to produce a more favorable impression upon the stranger.

It is a sleepy old town, substantially paved with stone blocks laid down by the Moors, whose notions of comfort and taste are further manifested in the shady courts, surrounded by latticed galleries resting upon graceful horseshoe arches,—peculiarities of the Arab style of architecture. The innumerable canals, aqueducts, and fountains that embellish the various squares reveal the predilection of its ancient citizens for an abundant supply of water, an advantage not recognized by the present inhabitants. The streets are so crooked, and pay such a disregard to the points of the compass, that three minutes after you have left the hotel you are helplessly lost, and wonder whether you will be able to find any one of whom to ask the way. You approach one of the houses that, barred like so many castles, line the streets, and knock. After some delay the gate opens, and discloses the leather-clad *portero* rubbing his eyes, and half asleep. You explain your misfortune; he laughs, and with a volubility that is perfectly amazing delivers himself of a string of directions intended to be explicit, but which soon involve you more deeply in the labyrinth than before. Then you commit yourself to the tender mercies of a boy who has providentially appeared, and who knows nothing of what you wish to see, but will gladly repel the attacks of the beggars, a service which no one who has had the benefit of it will be disposed to underrate.

The bigoted character of the people of Cordova is betrayed by the number of shrines, and the swarms of well-fed priests that congregate in the neighborhood of the Cathedral and the parish churches. In the Jewish quarter—where the Hebrews, persecuted by other nations, enjoyed complete liberty of worship, as well as the confidence of their Saracen rulers—stands the mosque. It is on the shore of the Guadalquivir, and opposite the Alcazar of the Khalifs, which is now a military prison, and destitute of even a suspicion of its ancient grandeur. It is impossible to realize that this spot, now steaming with noxious vapors, smeared with filth of every description, and haunted by ghastly representatives of vice and misery, was once the abode of science and art, the seat of the wealthiest court of mediæval Europe, the refuge of the oppressed of every creed in Christendom, and the home of the most polished society of the age.

The city contains but little to attest its former greatness, whose story reads like an exaggerated romance of the Orient. The mosque remains, indeed, sadly defaced by the hand of religious fanaticism; a few of the baths are intact, though long disused and abandoned; the wheels of the primitive stone mills are still turned by the rapid current of the Guadalquivir; and the venerable bridge erected by Augustus has survived the uninterrupted traffic and strange vicissitudes of nearly twenty centuries. There are a few handsome palaces, once curious on account of their minute and grotesque ornamentation, but now weather-beaten and decayed. The orphan asylum, built in the sixteenth century, offers the best example of the Gothic, but the churches are abominable, with the exception of San Nicolas, which possesses the only minaret left out of the seven hundred that once adorned the Saracen metropolis. The sight of the crumbling relics of an empire which once overshadowed all Europe with its power naturally recalls the circumstances under which that power was obtained, and suggests a brief notice of the wonderful civilization that, emanating from a people but a few removes from the Bedouins, communicated new life to the nations brought within the sphere of its authority, contributing so much of value to the common stock of human knowledge, and imparting an extraordinary impulse to scientific thought.

[This historical notice we omit, and proceed with a description of the celebrated mosque of Cordova.]

There has probably never been an edifice erected by the piety of any sect whose materials were gathered in as many different countries, or which could boast such a variety of superb decorations, as the *Djalma* of Cordova. The stones for its foundations were transported upon the shoulders of Christian captives from Narbonne in France. Pagan altars and Romish churches were alike despoiled of their precious marbles. Barbary gave her odoriferous woods, Egypt her ivory, Syria her stuccoes, Persia her tapestry, Constantinople her elegant mosaics.

The expenses of construction were defrayed by the appropriation of one-fifth of the spoils of battle, which amount, important in itself, was from time to time largely increased by contributions from the wealthy, tribute of conquered nations and munificent gifts from the royal treasury. The building measured six hundred and forty-two feet from north to south by four hundred and sixty-two feet from east to west; the walls were generally thirty-five feet high, except on the side towards the river, where they reached an altitude of seventy feet and a thickness of nearly twenty. They were strengthened by buttresses and crowned by battlements painted in brilliant colors. Over all towered the shapely minaret of Abderrahman III., inlaid with sculptured stone-work and enamelled tiles, and bearing upon its summit three huge gilded apples of bronze rising from the petals of silver lilies, the whole surrounded by a pomegranate of massy gold.

There were twenty-one entrances, encircled by legends from the Koran, interspersed with scarlet and gilded arabesques; the doors were very heavy, and covered with plates of polished brass. A subdued light came through the interstices of marble lattices, carved in fantastic patterns, imparting a mystic solemnity to the vast interior.

A spacious garden or court, called then, as now, the Court of the Oranges, planted with choice exotics and tropical trees, contained the fountains where the Moor performed the ablutions prescribed by his religion. One of these basins, still perfect, is a monolith hewn in the quarries of the distant sierra, and requiring the combined efforts of seventy oxen and hundreds of men to convey it to its present position. The nineteen naves of the mosque opened upon the court, none of them had doors,—and through the fretted arcades were wafted odors of rose and jasmine, which, mingling with incense and the smoke of perfumed tapers, gave to the fanatic believer a reminiscence of

Araby the Blest. Some of these tapers weighed sixty pounds, and the largest chandelier, used only during the feast of Ramadan, held fourteen hundred and fifty-four lights. Lamps of gold and silver were suspended from the richly-ornamented ceiling, and among them, memorable trophies of the conquest of Galicia, swung the bells of the church of Santiago.

Stretching around on every side was an endless forest of columns, the horseshoe arches arranged in tiers increasing the resemblance to a grove of palms,—that most primitive of temples,—which evidently served as a model for the interior of the mosque. Not far from the centre was the tribune, where, on Fridays, the Imam called the worshippers to prayer. Elevated a few feet above the floor, it was surrounded by engrailed, interlacing arches, and stood opposite the Kiblah, or point facing Mecca. The latter was indicated by three chapels, the Mihrab being placed in the central one.

The Byzantine mosaics, with which both walls and domes are incrusted, give to this part of the mosque an indescribably gorgeous appearance. They contain no piece larger than the top of a lead-pencil, and, being coated with glass like those of the church of St. Mark at Venice, which are of about the same date, have been preserved in all their original beauty. A noble horseshoe arch, opening in the mosaic, forms the entrance to the Mihrab, a little grotto faced with marble slabs, towards which the Moslem always turned to pray, and then made its circuit seven times upon his knees; the evidences of this act of devotion remaining, deeply furrowed in the pavement, after the lapse of six centuries. The Mihrab is hexagonal in shape, and twelve feet in diameter. Exquisitely carved, as became its sacred character, and the reverence with which it was universally regarded, the skill of its architects was exhausted upon its panels and its vaulted ceiling, cut from a single block of snowy marble in the exact representation of a shell. Here was kept the most precious relic of Mohammedan Spain, the Koran written by the Khalif Othman, which he was reading when assassinated. It was studded with jewels of immense value, and was so heavy that it required four men to lift it.

Great and important are the changes that have taken place in the arrangements of the mosque since the Spanish domination.

It was first purged of its heretical pollutions by the assembled clergy, and then lined with chapels presided over by ugly idols glittering with tinsel.

The marble pavement was next removed and replaced by coarse red tiles. The minaret, damaged by a storm in the sixteenth century, has been metamorphosed into an ordinary spire; thirteen of the exterior entrances, and sixteen of those in the Court of the Oranges, have been walled up; and many of the mosaics and stuccoes have been so daubed with whitewash that both colors and designs have disappeared. The carved ceiling was long since removed, and sold to guitar-makers and carpenters; the balustrades, inlaid with mother-of-pearl and tortoise-shell, were utilized as fuel. The outside has suffered less, and there still remain numerous tokens of its Oriental origin,— the flame-shaped battlements of Persia, typical of the adoration of fire; the

Syrian ornamentation of the door-ways, where can also be traced familiar symbols of ancient Egypt; and the suastika, or Indian cross, a mysterious emblem of the highest antiquity, which Layard found upon the palaces of Nineveh, Cesnola in the tombs of Cyprus, and Schliemann on the walls of Troy.

But even these "purifications" were not sufficient to satisfy the demands of an orthodox and iconoclastic priesthood. In 1523 a zealous bishop of Cordova, named Manriquez, wishing to distinguish himself, determined to build a cathedral in the very centre of the mosque. The people in vain protested against this outrage; the bishop appealed to the emperor, who sustained him; and though Charles afterwards, when visiting Cordova for the first time, sharply criticised the action of the prelate, the remonstrance came with a bad grace from one who had wrought such irreparable mischief in the Alhambra. The church was built, and, though in itself elegant, has destroyed the proportions of the unique structure, once the model of Saracen architecture and the pride of all Islam....

The Moorish city of Cordova was divided into five wards, each isolated by a fortified wall. Beyond these were the twenty-one suburbs, which— as well as the central part of the capital, where were located the palace and the Djalma—were paved and lighted, and furnished with mosques and markets. To accommodate a population that exceeded a million there were nine hundred public baths, more than are now to be found in all Europe.

Of the suburbs, that of Medina-Azzahrá was the most celebrated. It enclosed a palace built by An-Nassir for a favorite of his harem, and we are told that its decorations surpassed those of the mosque at the period of its greatest magnificence. The most expensive marbles and jaspers were used in its construction; Byzantine mosaics covered its walls; the ceilings of its pavilions were composed of alternate plates of gold and silver. In the principal hall stood a porphyry basin full of quicksilver, so contrived that it could be agitated by hidden mechanism, reflecting the rays of the sun with dazzling brilliancy, and striking with terror the mystified beholders. Over this curious toy was a miniature temple, with a dome of ebony and ivory, incrusted with pearls and rubies, and sustained by columns of polished crystal. Attached to the palace were delightful flower-gardens, orchards, labyrinths, lakes, and fountains. There were six thousand three hundred women of all ranks in An-Nassir's harem, who were guarded by an army of twelve thousand eunuchs clothed in silk, and wearing girdles of gold. In the neighborhood of the Khalif's residence stood the villas of the nobility, which, with the houses of their slaves and retainers, constituted of themselves a town of no inconsiderable dimensions.

Having read much of Medina-Azzahrá, I was naturally desirous to visit the site of this luxurious retreat of the Khalifs, which is known as "Cordoba la Vieja," or Old Cordova; and taking a carriage, the driver of which assured me he was perfectly familiar with the locality, I rode out to the mountains, a distance of about three miles. The carriage stopped; I got out, and, seeing a few steps away a low wall of masonry, evidently the enclosure of a pasture, I asked the driver what place this was.

Touching his hat, he replied, "This, señor, is Cordoba la Vieja."

"But the ruins you promised to show me,—where are they?"

"The ruins, señor—yes—there they are!" And he pointed to a row of dilapidated stables in the centre of the pasture, not far from where a herd of fierce Andalusian bulls were grazing. I would not have crossed that field for all the antiquities in Spain.

"And this is all that is to be seen here?"

"Yes, señor, this is all."

Re-entering the carriage, I returned to the city, with a feeling of disgust, which was not diminished by my honest coachman's demanding an exorbitant fee for his services as guide....

Among the many revolutions which have affected the manners and formed the society of Europe, none is entitled to more credit, or has been more completely ignored, than the occupation of Spain by the Saracens. This neglect is almost inexplicable, considering the prestige the invaders acquired by their extensive conquests, long a menace to the peace of Christendom, as well as by their invaluable services to literature, whose influence is even now to be traced in the language, the theology, the science, and the laws of distant countries, loath to acknowledge the debt they owe to this most ingenious and polished people. For the ambition and versatility of the Moor were boundless, and he labored with the same persevering energy in the solution of some abstruse mathematical problem as in the prosecution of every useful discovery and the encouragement of every branch of trade.

The importance of his foreign commerce is shown by the wealth and size of his seaports. Of these Almeria stood first in rank; its merchants not only maintained the closest intimacy with the nations of the Mediterranean, but penetrated as far as Persia and China. It employed three thousand eight hundred looms in the fabrication of damasks and brocades; the gardens and plantations of its environs embraced an area of four hundred square miles. Each city had its specialty: Baeza was famous for woollens, Murcia for coats of mail, Valencia for perfumes, Malaga for pottery and glass, Xativa for paper, Toledo and Seville for swords of perfect temper. In the early part of the twelfth century there were six hundred villages engaged in the manufacture of silk. Granada was the chief mart of this industry, and soon after the accession of Charles Fifth, when the Inquisition had already driven thousands of skilful artisans into exile, the crown revenues from this source alone amounted annually to one hundred and eighty-one thousand five hundred gold ducats, or seven hundred and twenty-six thousand dollars of our money.

The luxurious tastes of the East caused the introduction of many useful plants and fruits, among them the buckwheat, the sugar-cane, the peach, and the pomegranate, and the first palm ever seen in Andalusia was brought from

Damascus by Abderrahman, in memory of his native land. In his control over water, the most valuable treasure of his forefathers, the Moor displayed a power little short of marvellous, and a reverence as for something peculiarly sacred. Every drop of the precious fluid was utilized, and its distribution protected by a code of stringent regulations, causing its benefits to be felt in the remotest hamlets of the kingdom. This code is still in force in Valencia, and the ancient tribunal of seven judges, chosen from the farmers of the province, holds its sessions in that city every Thursday, the last day of the Mohammedan week, to hear and decide without appeal all questions involving the laws of irrigation.

The rapid progress made by the Spanish Arabs in those arts that tend to diminish the burdens and increase the enjoyments of life, unexampled as it was in history, was not more remarkable than the diligence with which they applied themselves to literary and scientific pursuits, studies destined to exert such lasting effects upon the happiness and well-being of mankind....

In the personal appearance and mode of life of the Andalusians, and particularly in those of the inhabitants of Cordova, can be detected unmistakable signs of their Arab ancestry. Their skins are darker, and the women especially have larger and more lustrous eyes than those of the other provinces of Spain. Their dialect, full of proverbial expressions, and unintelligible by its elision of consonants, seems a barbarous jargon to the Castilian of Salamanca or Valladolid. The popular cloak is the burnous; the hat of the muleteer a degenerate turban; the haick, under whose folds Eastern jealousy required the features of all females to be concealed, survives in the mantilla, that once covered the face, and does yet in certain towns, as Tarifa, and which has even travelled to Spanish America as the *tapada* of Lima. The sandal is much worn by the poorer classes, and the silken sash, or girdle, passes yet under its Arab name of *faja*. The irrigating apparatus, the cart, the plough,—which is nothing but a crooked stick,—are all Oriental; the mills were either actually built by the Moors, or modelled after those of that industrious people. Grain is still tramped out by cattle upon the primitive threshing-floor, and winnowed by the wind. The charcoal vender, with his panniers and his scales, is identical in all save costume with the vagrant charbonnier of Cairo.

The clapping of hands to call servants reminds one of the "Arabian Nights;" the seclusion of women savors strongly of the restraints of the harem.

Instances might be indefinitely multiplied to show the derivation of similar customs interwoven with every act of social and domestic life. And, notwithstanding the untold advantages and invaluable practical knowledge— the results of ages of experience—bequeathed by the Saracen to his conqueror, with the ruins of massive castles, and of palaces unrivalled in magnificent decoration, scattered all over the land; with the museums crowded with priceless relics of Arab art; with the fields watered by an ingenious yet simple system of irrigation, yielding prodigious returns with but trifling labor; it is the greatest insult you can offer a Spaniard to call him a "Moor," or insinuate that in his veins courses a drop of the blood of that despised race whose industry was once the boast, as its neglected souvenirs are now the glory, of his country.

THE SPANISH BULL-FIGHT.

JOSEPH MOORE.

["Outlying Europe and the Nearer Orient," by Joseph Moore, Jr., a work devoted to descriptive sketches of Egypt, the Holy Land, and the various countries of Europe, is the source of the following selection, which excellently delineates that ancient, though hardly time-honored, institution of Spain, which has long been its most distinctive form of public recreation. Happily, no other race than the Spanish has adopted this cruel sport.]

Nothing in the popular mind is more closely associated with Spain than the bull-fight. To travel in that country without witnessing the spectacle would imply the loss of an invaluable opportunity to study Spanish life. The people of all classes throughout the kingdom are unremitting in their enthusiasm for this favorite amusement, and no political or social prerogative could be guarded with more zealous devotion.

This species of gladiatorial contest took its origin at a remote period, and long before it assumed its present form exhibition combats of one bull against another were not uncommon. Pictorial sculptures at Beni Hassan and Thebes prove the latter to have been among the sports of the Egyptians nearly three thousand years before the Christian era. Strabo states that the bulls employed on these occasions were carefully trained for the purpose, and the encounters generally took place in the dromos, or avenue of approach to the temples. These displays, however, were probably abandoned under succeeding dynasties, as no such representations exist on walls of later periods. We have reasonable evidence to assume that bull-fights which included men and beasts as combatants were first instituted by the Thessalians more than three hundred years before Christ. As a people, they were skilled in horsemanship, and the spectacle was not unlike that of modern Spain. Julius Cæsar is believed to have noticed such exhibitions in Thessaly, which led to their appearance in Rome about B.C. 45. In later ages they were generally prohibited in the Latin empire, both by the emperors and the popes. Gibbon, however, describes a feast celebrated at Rome in 1332, which included a bull-fight in the Coliseum, with the Roman nobles as participants. The bull-fight was introduced into the Spanish peninsula by the Moors in the eighth century, and when those people were finally expelled in 1492 by Ferdinand and Isabella, Catholic Spain adopted the cruel sport of her Mohammedan predecessors. In the sixteenth century Pope Pius V. vainly decreed its extinction, and two hundred years later Charles III. practically failed to accomplish the same by persuasion. Late in the last century Charles IV. suppressed the bull-fight, but Joseph Bonaparte soon after restored the privilege to ingratiate himself with the nation whose throne he had usurped. Since then the ancient diversion has flourished despite the unanimous condemnation of the outer world. The present monarch, Alfonso XII., is said to favor its abolition, but such an attempt, it is declared, would be attended with the risk of engendering a revolution.

Bull-fights are popular throughout Spain, but, with the exception of Madrid, they are more frequent in the southern provinces. In fact, Seville is regarded as the centre of *tauromachia.* The season extends from the close of Lent to November, with Sundays and religious *fiestas* as the favorite days. The Plaza de Toros, or bull-ring, is an extensive hypæthral amphitheatre resembling the Coliseum on a reduced scale. The new one at Madrid is located near the driving-park, or Gardens of the Buen Retiro, and will seat about fifteen thousand people. That at Seville is an older building, situated near the Guadalquivir, and estimated to accommodate from ten to twelve thousand spectators. The stone Plaza de Toros of Jerez is credited with a capacity of thirteen thousand. The seats are of various grades, and the charges for them range from ten reales (fifty cents) to forty-six reales (two dollars and thirty cents). The choicest are those in the shade and in the boxes which form the upper tier. Not unfrequently during holy week in Seville the demand for places is such that speculators will realize fifty pesetas (ten dollars) for a single ticket.

The various breeds of Spanish bulls are easily distinguished by the practised eye, and the entire interest of the Spaniard is centred on the movements of the doomed beast. A savage, aggressive *toro* is an object of admiration, and one of timid demeanor of corresponding reproach. The fiercest of all are those of Andalusian blood. The stock of Navarre and the Castilian bulls on the Jarama, near Aranjuez, are likewise favorites, and the latter are generally used at Madrid. The proceeds of the bull-fights are usually devoted to religious or charitable purposes; those of the capital chiefly supporting the State hospital.

The actors in the bull-fights are of four classes: *matadores, banderilleros, picadores,* and *chulos,* their relative importance being in the order named. The word *torero* is a general term for bull-fighters on foot, while *toreador* is commonly applied to those on horseback. Before entering the ring a bull-fighter repairs to the chapel or confessional to be prepared for death should the merciless horns chance to reach his life.

Four o'clock in the afternoon is the usual time for the commencement of the spectacle, and but few seats are vacant when that hour approaches. The cheap circles are replete with boisterous humanity of both sexes, who loudly vent their impatience in case of delay. During the performance any failure of skill is greeted by the lower classes with energetic cries of condemnation, many of the epithets used being of an extremely vulgar character. The choicer sections contain a brilliant assemblage, the *señoritas* in full evening toilettes of delicate tints, white kid gloves, lace veils, fans, and opera-glasses. The *señores* wear a suit of black, except a vest of white, and pearl-colored gloves. Directly on the opposite side of the arena from the *toril*, or bull-door, is the enclosure reserved for the *autoridad*, or one in authority presiding on the occasion, just as a Cæsar did of old in the gladiatorial contests. In Madrid the king and his suite occupy this box, and the nobility cluster in the vicinity.

A few minutes before the performance opens, the floor of the arena is sprinkled to prevent any disturbance of the dust during the struggle. When this operation is completed, music by the band follows, and the king or the president of the day enters the reserved box. The excitement now becomes intense. A trumpeter stands awaiting the command to inaugurate the exhibition, and but a few seconds elapse before the notes are sounded. The band plays a march, a gate swings open, and a procession advances towards the royal loge. There it halts, and every performer salutes the occupant. The men on foot are in the Andalusian costume, richly elaborated,—flat hats, embroidered jackets, bright-colored knee-breeches, white stockings, and black slippers, and with the hair confined in nets. The horsemen are arrayed as Spanish knights of the olden time, with long buckskin breeches, under which the limbs are protected from injury by cork or tin leggings. The spurs of these combatants are provided with most cruel rowels to goad the timorous horses. The lance which the *picador* carries is of the usual length for a horseman, but the spear-head is purposely too short to inflict a very serious wound. The group of performers consists of six *chulos* on foot, with gay mantles, which they carry on the arm; two *matadores* in green, one with a red-hilted Toledo blade and the other with a mantle; three *banderilleros*, each with a pair of decorated barbed darts called *banderillas*; three *picadores* on blindfolded horses and armed with the lance; and, finally, some minor characters in charge of two brightly-caparisoned teams harnessed to crossbars.

After the salutation the teams withdraw, and the actors dispose themselves at various points in the ring. A horseman clad in black court costume, who has accompanied the procession and is called an *alguazil*, now gallops over to the box containing the authorities to receive the key of the *toril*, or bull-door. This he carries to the person in charge of that gate, and then hurriedly withdraws. The trumpet again sounds, the tumult becomes intensified, the toril-door opens, and the bull dashes into the arena. Upon his flank is a bright rosette with long ribbons, the *moña*, which is the prize of the victorious *matador*. For an instant "the lord of lowing herds" halts to survey the situation, but only an instant, and then the game of death commences. One of the *picadores*, mounted on a horse whose ears are filled with tow and whose eye towards the bull is covered, takes a position fronting the enemy, with his blunt spear in rest. The mighty brute hesitates a second, lowers his head, and charges. The spear is buried in the bull's shoulder, and the unprotected horse rears to escape the attack, but the deadly horns gore him, and all fall together. The bull's violence is instantly diverted by a *chulo*, who flaunts the red cape, and the *picador* is quickly extricated by vigilant satellites. The attention of a stranger is now instinctively directed to the horse, to discover the extent of the damage. Perhaps his hip bleeds, or there is a visible rent in his chest from which the blood jets forth, or a mass of entrails protrudes as he walks. In the first case the wound is stanched with clay, and the *picador* immediately remounts. If either of the latter happens, the horse is led towards the exit, but before reaching it he staggers and falls, in all probability dead. A subordinate called a *cachetero* then thrusts a stiletto into the brain, as though the bull had not wholly completed the tragedy.

In the mean while the infuriated bovine has been otherwise engaged. A *chulo* or two have flashed their bright-colored mantles in his face to madden him, or another *picador* has stood an attack. Then a *chulo* is pursued, greatly to the delight of the audience, and hastily retreats behind a short fence or refuge, built close to the ring and too narrow to admit the bull. In some *plazas* the refuges are entirely wanting, and instead the nimble actors leap the first of the two barriers. Occasionally the pursuing bull will likewise jump this outer fence, and must then be driven from the intervening circle back to the arena through a gate especially opened for the purpose.

Time passes, and the bull is wearied and bleeding. A *banderillero* now advances with a pair of the *banderillas*, or barbed darts, before mentioned. These instruments are rather less than a yard in length, and when necessary to aggravate a cowardly bull they are sometimes charged with explosives. The *banderillas* are whisked in the brute's face until he charges, which is the result desired. The *banderillero* quickly steps aside, the bull passes, and the javelins are thrust deeply into his shoulders, one on each side of the spine. The movement is as dexterous as it is dangerous, and never fails to excite a shout of admiration. The bull struggles to extricate himself from the darts, and perhaps one falls to the ground. A second adept immediately places a second pair in the bleeding shoulders, and then still another, making six in all. Now the bull is furious, and accordingly a *picador* again moves into position. A charge is made; all fall, and the horse is gored,—in all probability killed. The *chulos* again flaunt their red lures, and so the struggle continues until the bull retires some distance for a respite. Perhaps he will rest on his haunches, or lie upon the ground in utter exhaustion. A cry from the audience at this juncture is well understood. The skilled *matador* advances with his red-hilted Toledo blade and scarlet *muleta* to ask formal permission of the authority to despatch the foe. A duel ensues to display the dexterity and grace of the *espada.* Frequently but a single step is necessary to remove him from the approaching horns, so great is this actor's composure, and so thorough his mastery of his movements. The *matador*, to employ the technical parlance, "knows when the bull is right to kill;" and finally he deliberately aims a thrust which in an instant displays the sword transfixed almost to the hilt. If one blade is not sufficient, another sinks to the appointed spot.

"Where his vast neck just mingles with the spine,
Sheathed in his form the deadly weapon lies.
He stops—he starts—disdaining to decline;
Slowly he falls, amidst triumphant cries,
Without a groan, without a struggle, dies."

The victorious *matador* salutes the presiding dignitary, and Spain's sons and daughters unite in one mighty outburst of joy and noise. One of the teams is summoned; a rope is attached from the crossbar to the deadly horns; the whips are applied, and the dead monarch of the farm disappears with the galloping horses. Nothing is left of him save the blood-stained track which his weighty corse has marked on the soil. The trumpet again sounds; the toril-door swings on its hinges, and a second bull rushes into the arena. The entertainment consists of the death of six bulls, all by the original group of men, and is usually of three hours duration.

A remarkable fact to be noted is that injuries to the human combatants are not frequent, though occasionally one is killed and others are maimed. At Madrid we saw a *matador* thrown by the bull immediately after the sword had been fairly driven to the hilt. While the man lay upon his breast he received three passes from the frantic beast before the mantles of the *chulos* could distract the animal's attention. Strange to relate, the unfortunate performer escaped with no greater injury than bruises, and, indeed, he evinced a disposition to renew the contest; but his companions almost forcibly led him from the arena. An instant afterwards the bull commenced bleeding at the mouth from the internal sword wound, and in less than a minute dropped dead. In another case related by a spectator, a *chulo*, in his attempt to escape, slipped when close to the barrier. Upon falling the man quickly doubled himself into a ball, and, miraculous as it may seem, the bull's horns were driven into the wooden fence on each side of the huddled form, and the actor was saved. In an instant the lure of a brother *chulo* had diverted a second attack. Once when we were present a *cachetero* struck a dying bull with a stiletto before the tenacious vitality was wholly exhausted, and so suddenly did the brute resent the wound that the public butcher had his nether garment rent by the pursuing horns.

Words cannot describe the strange and engrossing excitement which the bull-fight inspires. The brain is probably in a whirl of agitation, when suddenly the heart ceases beating for an instant, as rider, horse, and bull clash in the deliberate encounter. The sympathy for the poor defenceless horse is without bounds, and with it comes a flush of indignation that so noble an animal should be cruelly butchered to make a Spanish holiday. It is true the horses thus devoted to immolation are of little value; but they are nevertheless horses, and their wanton slaughter will admit of no justification. The destruction of so many bulls is equally to be condemned, and charity for the brute should not be wanting because he employs the weapons and exhibits the propensities with which the Creator endowed him. The stranger is also impelled to contemplate the fact that those of the gentler sex, the famed beauty of Spain, regard these combats with sufficient partiality to insure their presence, and to behold with the utmost composure a death-stricken horse trailing his vitals before their very eyes. In extenuation it must be considered that their training and the traditions of the country pronounce the bull-fight a legitimate amusement. Travellers, however, are almost unanimous in their conclusion that pleasure is vainly sought in frequenting the *corrida de toros.* Yet

> "Such the ungentle sport that oft invites
> The Spanish maid, and cheers the Spanish swain."

SEVILLE, THE QUEEN OF ANDALUSIA.

S. P. SCOTT.

[We have already given one selection from Scott's "Through Spain." The work is so worthy that we feel impelled to offer other extracts from its well-filled pages. Seville, in many respects the most attractive city in Spain, offers a charm to the traveller which few can resist, while in respect to the treasure of Moorish architecture, possessed by many of the cities of Spain, it has to show its richly-decorated Alcazar, or citadel, its *Torre del Oro*, or Golden Tower, and its minaret, the Giralda, whose lofty summit looks down in pride upon the modern cathedral. But we must leave this story to our author's pen.]

Of all the cities of Spain, there is none that can compare in general attractiveness with the beautiful Andalusian capital. In the feudal towns of old Castile will be found much of interest to the student of history: in Madrid can be witnessed the pompous ceremonial of the court; Cordova has her mosque; Merida, her Roman, and Tarragona her Cyclopean, remains; Granada, her peerless Alhambra. But in Seville—inferior to none of these in the number and value of her antiquities—alone can be studied to advantage the singular manners of a society in some respects highly civilized yet in others manifesting unmistakable traces of barbarism, more noticeable here than in any other city of the kingdom.

It is a place of wonderful contrasts. On one side are stately avenues lined with magnificent palaces and gardens; on the other rise gloomy Moorish habitations, reached by winding passage-ways so narrow that an ordinary umbrella, when raised, will barely clear the walls. As in Oriental communities, the different sects are separated; the Jews are restricted to one quarter, the Moors to another, the gypsies to a third, and nowhere outside of Cairo and Damascus is exhibited such an array of outlandish costumes. In the surging crowds of the promenades the uniform of the soldier and the cowl of the friar are especially conspicuous, the one the sign of a jealous military despotism, the other the badge of an order fast passing away.

Seville has the first and grandest bull-fights of the season; her majos are the most extravagant in dress, her women the most witty and beautiful, her religious festivals the most expensive and splendid in the world. It is here, then, that we must look for the characteristic types of Andalusia, that favored land where the ancients placed their Elysian Fields and Garden of the Hesperides.

The city lies very low upon the Guadalquivir, which, overflowing with every freshet, has frequently submerged the streets and seriously damaged buildings situated a long distance from its banks.

The visitor, wandering along the substantial quays, will not fail to notice a curious, isolated tower, whose loop-holes and battlements resemble those of some feudal castle. It is the *Torre del Oro*, or Golden Tower, one of the landmarks of Moorish Seville, and was named from the shining yellow tiles that originally incrusted it, and which Spanish taste has thoroughly "improved" with a coat of plaster. It once guarded a bridge by which the city was supplied with provisions from the *Ajarafe*, the rich territory that extended for fifty miles up and down the river, and was under the most perfect cultivation.

From the Golden Tower, an irregular wall, whose summit is on a level with the roofs of the surrounding houses, can be traced for nearly a quarter of a mile, till it terminates in the Alcazar, or citadel. The date of the foundation of the Alcazar is too remote to be fixed with certainty, although it is known that a palace stood here about the time of the first Saracen invasion. The walls are fifty feet high and in excellent preservation. Within the principal gate is the room where the kadi, and after him Peter the Cruel,—who has left a deeper impress of his individuality upon Seville than any other monarch, Christian or Moslem,—exercised the office of judge. Beyond the grand court, which is large enough for the review of a considerable body of troops, is a smaller one enclosing the façade erected by Don Pedro in 1364. This, as well as much of the interior, was the work of the finest artists of Granada, sent to Don Pedro by his friend the Moorish king. Successive and ill-advised alterations have modernized the inner apartments, and what vandalism and whitewash could not accomplish has been effected by the stupidity of those intrusted with the repairs, who have awkwardly tried to imitate the delicate tile-work with paint, and have inserted many Arabic inscriptions upside down.

The Patio de las Doncellas was the central court of the seraglio, and the place where the annual tribute of one hundred Christian maidens was delivered by the vassals of the sultan. Its arches are festooned and pointed, or ogive, denoting the period of transition between the horseshoe of Cordova and the symmetrical curves of the Alhambra.

The Hall of the Embassadors, in all probability the most gorgeously decorated chamber in the world, opens upon this *patio*. Its dazzling walls are crowned with a carved wooden dome, or *artesonado*, colored in blue and scarlet, and studded with golden stars. Charles V. and Isabella of Portugal, mother of Philip II., were married here March 12, 1526....

Scarcely a stone's throw from the Alcazar is the cathedral, overtopped by the old Moorish minaret, the Giralda, which was built by the Sultan Yacub Al-Mansur in 1184. It rests upon a triangular base composed of all the statues of pagan deities and other idolatrous fragments of antiquity that could be collected by the zealous iconoclasts who founded it. The tower is fifty feet square, and the original height was two hundred cubits; modern additions, however, have increased it somewhat, and it now measures three hundred and fifty feet from the pavement to the head of the statue. For eighty-seven feet the walls are of polished blocks of stone; above this the material is brick, relieved by tracery and arabesques of the most capricious designs, different on each side, yet so artfully combined and blended that it requires close observation to detect the variations. The interior is lighted by double windows, divided by columns of white marble and alabaster. The Giralda is ascended by a series of ramps, or inclined planes, so wide, and of such easy slope, that two horsemen with lances poised could ride to the top and back again without dismounting, a feat that was more than once accomplished by the wild cavaliers of the Spanish court.

The Campanile of St. Mark's at Venice has similar ramps, the invention being of Byzantine origin. It is curious that the walls increase in thickness as the summit is approached, an anomaly which has never been satisfactorily explained.

Late in the fourteenth century the upper portion of the Giralda was injured by an earthquake, and remained half ruined until 1568, when the present belfry was built. It is encircled by the biblical quotation, "Fortissima turris nomen Domini," and supports a colossal bronze statue of Faith, which acts as a weathercock, moving with the lightest breath of air.

The Court of the Oranges, with the walls enclosing its northern and eastern sides, compose the existing portions of the mosque, upon whose site the cathedral was erected. It contains cool arcades, a grove, and a battered marble fountain, which for three hundred years served the Moor for his ablutions, and where now the sturdy water-carriers fill their kegs, trudging away with their cheerful "*A 'ua! a 'ua! quien quiere a 'ua?templ'a y muy 'uena!*"[A] a cry that is most welcome upon a sultry day.... ·

A suite of rooms in the upper story of the old mosque contains the precious collection of books and manuscripts bequeathed by Don Fernando Columbus to the cathedral. Of rare interest is this library, the greater number of whose musty volumes, bound in vellum, were once the property of the most renowned of navigators. In a glass case are preserved the original journals of Columbus, partly written in the dungeons of the Inquisition, and the "Travels of Marco Polo," his *vade-mecum* during his voyages.

This book, which bears evident marks of study and hard usage, is said to have been the first that suggested to him the probable existence of another world. There is scarcely a page that is not enriched with notes jotted down from time to time by this wonderful man, whose handwriting is as legible as print, the ink he used being but little faded after a lapse of four hundred years. I should have been glad to have examined these memorials more closely, and tried to induce the custodian to unlock the case; but the tempting bribe I offered failed, to my surprise, to accomplish the desired end, as he sorrowfully informed me that he was not intrusted with the key.

The Cathedral of Seville is worthy of its reputation as the grandest in Spain, and one of the most elaborate ever constructed. Inside the walls it measures three hundred and seventy-nine by two hundred and seventeen feet, the central dome rising one hundred and seventy-three feet from the floor. Begun in 1402, it is not yet finished, the delay affording a convenient pretext for continually soliciting funds, which, by a pious fiction, are presumed never to be adequate for the purpose.

The enormous pillars, disposed in groups, impart an air of great solidity to the edifice, whose dimensions, like those of all similar structures, are not at the first glance appreciated. To several of the pillars are attached iron coffers as large as ordinary trunks, for the reception of donations for holy uses. Little is dropped into them now but copper; but, at the time when the treasures of a world were pouring into Seville, they were too small for the piles of doubloons with which returning adventurers hoped to purchase immunity for revolting crimes against God and man.

Just inside the main entrance is the grave of Don Fernando Columbus, the last of his illustrious race, who died in 1539. A simple marble slab covers his remains; the Latin epitaph recites his own and his father's deeds,—deeds that were so ill requited by the jealousy and ingratitude of his sovereign.

The three caravels which achieved the discovery of the Bahamas are sculptured there, with the unique device, a globe belted with the famous motto,—

"A Castilla y á Leon

Nuevo mundo dió Colon."...

Seville possesses many ancient mansions, whose patios, perfumed with the blossoms of choice exotics and vines twining about their marble columns, and echoing to the songs of birds and the music of plashing fountains, afford pictures little to be expected from the severely plain exterior. In general one must be content with a passing glimpse of these luxurious dwellings, for the haughty grandee resents all intrusion, and guards his home with Oriental jealousy. There are, however, two palaces, the hereditary seats of the Dukes of Montpensier and Alba, splendid representatives of their class, where vagabond curiosity may enter and range at will, provided it is well watched. The first is called San Telmo, and is on the Guadalquivir, where the son of Louis Philippe lives in regal state. His halls are full of elegant furniture, costly paintings, and bronzes, embracing elegant masterpieces produced in the palmy days of France and Spain; and his grounds are very extensive, containing, in addition to the rare plants which grow with tropical luxuriance, acres of valuable orange-trees.

The palace of the Duke of Alba is semi-Moorish, and, being in an unfashionable neighborhood, is seldom occupied by its owner. It is approached by a fine gate-way, over which the arms of the house of Alba, emblazoned in colored tiles, are encircled by flags taken in many hard-fought battles, the insignia of the Golden Fleece, and the significant motto, "Tu in ea ego pro ea." The crest, an angel holding in one hand the globe and cross and in the other a flaming sword, is typical of the position which the bulwark of the monarchy, the oppressor of the Netherlands, and the doughty champion of the Faith, maintained to the last in the affections of the suspicious and bigoted Philip,—

"Wie Gottes Cherub vor dem Paradies,
Steht Herzog Alba vor dem Thron."

The ordinary houses of Seville are Oriental in plan, and well-fitted to resist the scorching heat of the climate. The heavy gates admit to the *zaguan*, a short hall having at the farther end an iron grating opening upon the patio, or court. The zaguan is the place where the young ladies receive calls. It would be a flagrant breach of etiquette for the lover to be admitted to the parlor, so he takes his place on one side of the grating, his dulcinea posting herself on the other. No chairs are permitted in this airy drawing-room, for, if they were furnished, the cavalier might never go away. As it is, it is not unusual to see couples standing together at midnight, sometimes with the rain blowing in upon them,—as the zaguan affords but slight protection from the weather,— and apparently oblivious of all the world save themselves. These protracted interviews are only allowed after betrothal, and the sighing gallant, at first the embodiment of devotion and sentiment, is usually transformed into the most imperious of husbands before the expiration of the honeymoon, for he never allows himself to forget the amusing proverb of his countrymen, "He who becomes a lieutenant upon his wedding-day will never be promoted."

Every court, even those belonging to the dwellings of the most modest pretensions, has one or more fountains, and a flower-bed in the centre. Overhead, covering the entire area, an awning—which is frequently sprinkled with water—is stretched during the summer months to temper the burning atmosphere, as the heat is so intense that an omelet can be cooked in a few minutes if exposed to the rays of the mid-day sun. In the old-fashioned Spanish houses the kitchen is always situated near the front door, giving one the full benefit of the garlic and saffron odors as soon as he enters, but preventing their diffusion through the parlors and sleeping-apartments. The latter are constructed with lofty ceilings, have no more windows than are absolutely necessary, and are often paved with white marble, and finished with brilliant *azulejos*, or Moorish tiles. They are delightfully cool in summer, but damp and cheerless at all other seasons....

The great fair, held here in April, is famous, and the people who visit it exhibit the best types of the Andalusian peasantry to be found in the province. A perfect city of booths is raised in the suburb of San Bernardo, each section, or ward, being assigned to a separate class of merchants, as in the bazaars of the East. One quarter is set apart for the nobility, many of whom have their private tents, which, as well as those of the numerous civil and military organizations, are fitted up in the most sumptuous manner.

As the interiors are open to view, the scenes, especially at night, when thousands of colored lamps and gas-jets make everything as light as day, are extremely charming and novel. Dancing, love-making, and flirting are going on on all sides, and down the broad avenues, upon gayly-caparisoned horses, ride troops of majos and majas, the dandies and coquettes of Andalusia, radiant in their beautiful national costume. The click of the castanet mingles with the music of the bands and the chants of the itinerant singers, who, standing in groups, compose impromptu ballads, like the ancient troubadours; the brazen-lunged showman recounts the wonderful feats of his dwarfs and educated ape, while above all sounds rises the uproar from the canvas theatre, whose tottering seats are packed to their utmost capacity with an appreciative audience that, never tiring of the oft-repeated and not over-decent comedies, regard this day as the brightest of their monotonous existence. It is a veritable pandemonium.

The picturesque gypsies are present in crowds, some wandering from booth to booth telling the *buena ventura* to the credulous, others selling specifics for the evil eye, a superstition whose influence is not limited to the ignorant, and against which holy water, generally so potent, is universally conceded to be of no avail.

These brown-skinned maidens, with their heads wreathed with flowers, occupy one entire avenue, where they range themselves in lines, and solicit all passers-by to taste their *buñuelos*, a kind of insipid doughnuts boiled in olive oil. The presence of Moors and Jews from Tangier and other cities of Morocco, who come for trade, offering so-called Oriental curiosities, mostly manufactured in Paris and Birmingham, adds not a little to the attractiveness of the great fair of Andalusia....

The natives of Seville, even in Roman times, were noted for their frivolity, their indisposition to labor, and their love of pleasure, qualities which they have transmitted in an exaggerated degree to their descendants.

Venus was then, as now, their favorite goddess; her image was borne during her festivals upon the shoulders of women of patrician rank, and certain rites of the Phœnician Astarte, her prototype, survive in the ceremonies of modern holidays.

Some strange performances are to be witnessed on St. John's eve, identical with the summer solstice, when numbers of both sexes assemble in the parks and along the promenades, to dance around the fires of Cybele, and leap over them when the clock strikes twelve; and at daybreak run in crowds to gather the mysterious vervain, associated with the religious observances of so many nations of antiquity. The coquettish graces and fascinations of the Sevillian ladies,—

"Skilled in the ogle of a roguish eye,
Yet ever well inclined to heal the wound,"—
the lively, semi-Oriental dances, the groups of grotesque maskers and musicians, the jaunty smugglers and bull-fighters, and the general air of gayety and enjoyment that pervades all classes, make it well worth while to lose a few hours' sleep on the merry eve of St. John.

Seville, the "Queen of Andalusia," the depository of the glories and crimes of a dozen distinct races, and nearly as many conflicting religions, is slowly emerging from the darkness with which priestly domination and Inquisitorial tyranny have enveloped her for centuries. Her age of discovery and victory, of sentimental gallantry, of chivalric devotion, is past,—the age "when dreams of conquest, and tales of golden lands beyond the ocean, were wafted on every breeze;" the age when Isabella, clad in shining armor, set forth at the head of her knights to besiege Granada; the age when Alonso de Ojeda fastened the scarf of the queen upon the dizzy pinnacle of the Giralda, and Ponce de Leon threw himself, sword in hand, into the lion's den, in search of his lady's glove; the age when Cortes and Pizarro, penniless adventurers, sailed upon expeditions destined to immortal fame; the age when Sebastian de Elcano, the lieutenant of Magellan, was received with royal honors after his circumnavigation of the earth.

Of the glorious deeds whose renown once filled the world the fruits were recklessly wasted, the memory alone survives. And now the proud old city, waking from the lethargy in which she has so long slumbered, conscious of her great natural advantages, seems determined to again reap their benefit and, if possible, recover her lost prestige. Her commerce is yearly increasing, fleets of shipping are anchored in the muddy Guadalquivir, and an infusion of foreign blood seems to have imparted new life to the deserted streets, where the treasures of America and Asia were once paraded, and bands of victorious soldiers of fortune landed from the galleons that, freighted with the wealth of Ormus and of Ind, were unloading their precious cargoes at the docks of the chief emporium of Spain.

STREET SCENES IN GENOA.

AUGUSTA MARRYAT.

["Genova la Superba," the great seaport city of mediæval Italy, and retaining still much of the beauty and grandeur of its days of greatness, is amply worthy of attention in these modern times. We give here, therefore, a picturesque account of what Genoa retains for the eye of the traveller after its centuries of decline.]

The town of Genoa is bustling and full of movement, and one that grows upon the visitor, since each day discloses new beauties of situation, and he is struck with increased admiration for the splendor of the palaces. The streets are narrow, and the tops of the tall houses nearly meet, so that the sun is jealously kept from even a glimpse of the passers-by, who without other protection than a white muslin covering for the head, or a fan by way of parasol, can walk in safety from its scorching rays. These streets are too narrow to admit of a carriage, but mules with jingling bells upon their headstalls, and laden with birch brooms, or live kids in panniers on their backs, hustle along with the greatest *sang-froid*, regardless whose toes they may crush in their progress. There is a market held in an open space near the Carignano bridge, where ladies with their heads dressed (and undergoing dressing) in the latest Parisian fashion superintend the sale of peas and potatoes. A brisk trade apparently is done in fowls, as there are baskets and baskets of them on all sides. They are kept in their hampers by means of netting placed over a framework of osier, and pass an idle hour, squabble with and peck at one another, and make as much noise as if they were at a show of prize poultry instead of in momentary anticipation of death and the spit.

In the Vico del Duca a lot of girls sit in a row, each having a little *chauffrette*, with a gridiron on it, before her, busily employed frying snails; and if ever martyrdom made canonization deserved the Genoese snail is entitled to that distinction. The poor things are first trimmed with a knife, then crammed into a small bird-cage to prevent their crawling away, and finally set to bubble and frizzle and splutter, as they are roasted alive.

THE GROTTO OF THE SIBYL, TIVOLI

The Cathedral of Genoa very much resembles that of Florence, being built of alternate blocks of black and white marble, and the façade is remarkable for the beauty of its design. Inside some few monuments have survived the fury of the revolution that destroyed so many relics of the republic, but they are much mutilated. Here also is kept the celebrated emerald vase called the Sano-calino, found at Cæsarea, and chosen by the Genoese, in 1101, in preference to any other spoil. It was broken on its return from Paris, and has since been mounted in gold. It is said to have been presented to Solomon by the Queen of Sheba (the same queen, the cicerone added, who caused St. John the Baptist's head to be cut off), and was used by our Saviour at the Last Supper. The vase is composed of green bottle glass, and the only extraordinary thing about it is that any people could have labored under such a delusion during seven centuries.

Every one who has ever visited Genoa is familiar with the Via degli Orefici,—its quaint small shops, its stalls, and its marvels of elegance in filigree-work, and its wealth of bonbons and cakes. The beautiful mild face of the Madonna in the picture belonging to the Goldsmiths' Company still gazes placidly down from her shrine on the traffic below.

The artist who painted this picture was called Pellegrino Piola, and was a pupil of Castello, who, it is said, caused him to be assassinated from motives of jealousy. A prize had been offered by the Goldsmiths' Company for the best painting of a Holy Family, and Pellegrino, who was only twenty-two years of age at the time, was the one to gain it.

Every shop in the Via degli Orefici that is not filled with jewelry is full of sweets; and chemists, grocers, and basket-makers are all confectioners, or sweet-stuff sellers, as well. The little girls in their white dresses and veils, who have just made their first communion, carry baskets of bonbons in their hands, and one, too poor in station, perhaps, to possess so extensive a present, wears a necklace of nuts round her throat, with a cake by way of locket. The owner of the big Bologna sausage, decorated with a pink camellia, has just placed a small white-napkin-covered table in the door-way of his shop, so that he may eat his dinner in a position to see and be seen by his friends in the street. The Genoese salesman does not allow his domestic arrangements to interfere with his business; and a young lady who was cooking the mid-day meal at a little charcoal stove has just removed a saucepan from the fire to tell the price of a counterpane.

The lemonade seller has pitched his tent in the sunniest corner of the Piazza delle Fontane Amorose, and calls aloud to thirsty thousands as they pass, "Fres-ca, fres-ca." His emporium is very like a small four-post bedstead, and its chintz curtains are wreathed with lemons on boughs. And lemons bob up and down in cool-looking tin tanks filled with water, but the lemonade itself seems guiltless of such an article, except for a minute portion of the peel of one which floats in it.

When tired of the gold and silver filigree-work, and the coral ornaments, let the wanderer turn into the Street of Palaces. Here his eyes will not be distracted by stalls of fluttering shawls and handkerchiefs, or his progress impeded by stoves for the roasting of chestnuts or baking of apples, but even in this aristocratic quarter of the town mules will obstinately dispute the right of road with him, and some agility is required to keep clear of them and of the carriages. There are no pavements in Genoa, excepting in the new streets, and the heads of the horses belonging to the grand carriages are so bedecked with long horse-hair tassels and fur trimmings, and their tails tied up with such smart satin ribbons, that they cannot be expected to think of anything besides their personal appearance, much less the pedestrian's feet.

The Serra Palace is famous for its "golden" room, the panels of which are of lapis lazuli. The Brignole is famous for its pictures, especially some wonderfully beautiful Vandykes. This gallery is now joined to that once belonging to the Durazzo Palace, but which by death became the property of the former, and the two are united in the Palazzo Rosso, or Brignole. The Café della Concordia is opposite, and is entered by a flower-shop, up a marble staircase, and through a court with a fountain and statue and weeping-willows that make a pleasant shade, and where you can sit amidst orange-trees and myrtles and eat your breakfast or dinner, if you prefer it to going inside. The Concordia is the prettiest little place imaginable, and the scent of the flowers and the splashing of the water are very refreshing coming in from the hot dusty street. There is also the Café Mathurin in the Piazza San Carlo Felice, good and reasonable in price, but more bustling and far less romantic than the weeping-willowy Concordia. The Royal Palace is handsomely furnished, and contains some valuable pictures amidst a great deal of rubbish. The rooms are fairly proportioned, and the furniture, though somewhat faded, is in good taste....

The once powerful family of Doria are possessed of numerous palaces and villas in and about Genoa. The Palazzo Doria, just outside the Porta di San Tomaso, however, is the one in which the great Andrea Doria lived. It was given to him in 1522, when he rebuilt and improved it. It is now very much out of repair, and the only portions of it shown to strangers are the rooms formerly inhabited by him. There is not much furniture of any kind in the old Admiral's bedroom; but the blue and white plates he was in the habit of using at dinner are ranged in rows, at the back of a large fireplace, on a thing somewhat resembling a kitchen dresser. A large gilt arm-chair, once the property of Charles V., is in the drawing room. It is a heavy-looking article, with a red velvet seat. It was this monarch who granted Doria the title of "Il Principe." Life-sized frescoes of him and of his sons appear in a gallery leading to a terraced garden outside, and in these the portrait of Andrea is that of a very brown old gentleman, with white hair and beard, and but small allowance of clothes on. The sons, who are also in "semi-heroic" costume, imitate Adam before the fall, except that each wears a helmet and leans on a shield.

These frescoes are the work of Pierino del Vaga, who, having been obliged to seek refuge at Genoa from the calamities of Rome in 1527, was patronized by the great Doria, and intrusted to decorate his palace. Genoa has been the birthplace of many painters, and art was in its most flourishing condition in this city in the fifteenth century, during which time Giovanni Cambiaso lived. At this epoch, so many persons of noble family were painters, that the Genoese, by a special decree, raised painting from a trade to a profession, declaring that it was a liberal art, and might be practised without derogating from nobility. The reason of the sudden decline of the Genoese school is attributed to the plague in 1657, when many of its chief painters fell victims to the disease. Lazzaro Calvi, who lived one hundred and five years, was born in 1502, and therefore died just fifty years prior to the epidemic, so that his country may congratulate itself that he was not cut off prematurely in the flower of his youth by that scourge.

At the back of the palace is the grave of Andrea's dog, Roldano, given to him by Charles V., and over it is the following epitaph, or something like it: "Here lies the Great Roldano, a dog belonging to Prince Gio. Andrea Doria, who, for his fidelity and goodness, was considered to merit this memorial. In life, for years, he nobly obeyed both these laws. In death we must place his ashes by the side of those of the beast that perishes. A companion worthy indeed of his regal donor. Died at 11 years and 10 months of age, in September of 1605, the 8th day, at 8 o'clock at night."

In the centre of the garden, facing the sea, and from whence Prince Doria may have looked on his fleet of twenty-two galleys at anchor in the harbor, is a fountain, and in it a statue in which he is represented as Neptune. Doria's tomb is in the crypt beneath the high altar of the church of San Matteo, and it is here also that the sword he received, in 1535, from Paul III., for the services he had rendered the church, is deposited. In the piazza adjoining there is a house with an inscription over it, to the effect that it was given to Andrea Doria by the republic. Here he once lived, and it was in an open square in front of it that he assembled his fellow-citizens to consult with them on the best way of repulsing the French, when they besieged Genoa in 1528. The house is now used as a shop,—for pictures and old furniture on the ground floor, and for stationery on the upper story. It, and the church of San Matteo, which has always been under the patronage of the Dorias, are both built of alternate layers of black and white marble. This magpie style of construction was confined to public edifices, but four patrician families—the Doria, Grimaldi, Spinola, and Fieschi—were allowed the privilege of using it....

If Genoa is a fair city by day, she is a still fairer one by night, when the innumerable lights on all sides make it look as if the stars had come down from heaven, and give the whole place an appearance of fairy-land. There are lights all round the harbor and on the quays; lights above the hills, and below in the old town; lights in the gardens of the cafés and in the streets, making them, and the gay company that crowds them, more brilliant than when seen in the full glare of mid-day. The fireflies flit and flicker, but never rest as they hold their evening revels among the bushes and trees, and over the grass and flowers.

A charity bazaar was held every night on the Acqua Sola, when the fountains were illuminated with gas, and rings of light spanned the trunks of the great trees, and darling arches were placed over the garden paths. All the decorations were exceedingly pretty and light, as they were of gas arranged to represent branches of laurel, or lyres, or such like devices. There were not many stalls,—two dozen, perhaps; but these were in the fanciful shape of chalet or kiosk, and the Genoese ladies, in their temporary character of shopwomen, sat within them, with no covering on their heads but a white veil, and a rose at one side.

The orthodox band played inside the fair, for part of the garden was walled off, so only to admit of those who had tickets; whilst another band just outside appeared to be trying hard to outblow it. A little farther on, at the Café d'Italie, the band of the Guides, in their light blue and silver uniform, charm the eaters of ice and drinkers of lemonade by their music, and make them linger at their little tables.

This place is a favorite resort in the evening of the Genoese men (where they put all the women is a mystery, as the streets are crowded with the nobler sex of every class, whilst scarce any Italian fair ones of any kind are to be seen), and it is, for light and brilliancy, a very transformation scene. The lamps gleam from amidst beds of flowers and groves of orange-trees that make the air faint with their sweetness; and in the centre of the garden, under a kind of tent, is a large cocoanut-tree, with a branching green head and a cluster of lamps beneath to represent the fruit. And from the statues and fountains, and trees and arches, rose-colored and white lamps are hung, and being all of ground glass, they shed a subdued, mysterious light around the idlers who crowd the seats and benches. In fact, Genoa never looks as if she intended to go to bed at all; and the cool summer nights, the stars, the lamps, the sweet scent of the flowers, and the bands of music make it so pleasant a time that one cares not to think of to-morrow.

THE ALHAMBRA.

S. P. SCOTT.

[Among the many marvels of architecture left by the Mohammedans, as landmarks of their outflow over the earth, none have elicited more admiration than the remains of the Alhambra at Granada. This celebrated group of Saracenic edifices has suffered little from time, but much from ignorance and vandalism, of which the most deplorable Instance is the demolition due to the Emperor Charles V., in his insane effort to better the work of the Moors. This palace and fortress of the Moorish caliphs of Spain is eloquently described in the following selection.]

Few readers need to be told that the kingdom of Granada at the period of the Conquest was one of the richest and most flourishing countries in the world. Its fertile valleys embraced the garden of the Peninsula; its industrious population had carried agriculture to a degree of perfection unknown to modern times; its mountains yielded great quantities of the precious metals; its manufactures of silk and porcelain found a ready market in the courts of semi-barbaric Europe; the commerce of Almeria and Malaga, its principal seaports, extended to the Indies. As the victorious arms of Castile and Aragon gradually encroached upon the provinces of Andalusia, the remains of that extraordinary civilization which, in the ninth and tenth centuries, had raised the Western khalifate to such a height of prosperity and renown, took refuge in Granada. To the beautiful capital, that included within its walls nearly half a million souls,—among them many thousand Jews and Christians,—fled the exiles of the conquered cities, bringing with them that advanced knowledge of the natural and exact sciences which, after surviving the vicissitudes of four hundred years of revolution and invasion, the ferocious bigotry of the Spanish clergy, more intolerant by far than the rude barbarism of Africa, threatened with utter extinction.

Here, under the protection of a race of sovereigns who rivalled each other in promoting the happiness of their subjects, a new impulse was imparted to the study of astronomy and medicine, and literature and the mechanical arts found in the tastes and habits of a luxurious people an ample field for their development. And here began the third and most glorious period of Arab art as displayed in its application to architecture, which, appropriating to itself all that was valuable in the experience of former ages,—ages which had witnessed the erection of the Mosque of Cordova and the Giralda of Seville,—soon disclosed a splendor and variety of decoration peculiarly its own, and, after filling the kingdom with its monuments, attained its climax in the creation of that masterpiece of human skill, the fairy palace of the Alhambra....

The Alhambra, the stronghold of a prince who united the triple functions of civil, military, and religious head of his people, stands on an isolated hill five hundred feet above the plain, or Vega. This hill, which romantic native writers love to compare to a *granada*, or pomegranate, thence deriving the name of their favorite city, is half a mile long by eight hundred feet wide, and is entirely surrounded by walls. Traversing a grove of elms that covers the slope nearest the Genil, we reach the Gate of Justice, a massive tower forming the entrance to the fortress. The seat of the *kadi*, or civil magistrate, who here settled all disputes not deemed important enough to be carried before the sultan, the Gate of Justice was regarded with peculiar veneration by the Moors. Innumerable are the legends connected with this spot, many of them traceable to the mysterious hand and key carved upon the outer and inner arches of the portal. The hand, an unfailing talisman against the evil eye, was symbolical of the five precepts of Islam,—prayer, fasting, alms, ablution, and the pilgrimage to Mecca; the key referred to the dominion given to the Prophet over heaven and hell, and was the badge of the kings of Andalusia. The old gate is well preserved; the cement covering the masonry is as smooth as when laid on; the ponderous bronze doors which opened to admit the Christian armies on the memorable 2d of January, 1492, are still in their places, so also are the racks that sustained the lances of the Moorish guard.

We next enter the Plaza de los Algibes, a square of comparatively modern date, which lies between the palace and the Alcazaba or citadel,—these two portions of the sultan's residence having been originally separated by a wall, of which the gate, now called the Puerta del Vino, alone remains. Fronting the venerable Moorish battlements rises the façade of the palace of Charles V., with the arms and trophies of the most arrogant and crafty of emperors.

[This structure was erected with the aid of money wrung from the Moors themselves, as a bribe to the emperor and his officials to suspend the work of the Inquisition.]

The winter residence of the Moors, that seems to have equalled the remainder in magnificence, and was probably of greater extent, was razed, the fountains were removed, the doors and balustrades broken up, and the stuccoes carted away as rubbish. Founded thus in the misery of the most intelligent and thrifty portion of his subjects, and upon the ruins of that unrivalled palace,—the boast and glory of the Western empire of the Khalifs,—the ill-omened design of Charles V. was destined never to be carried to completion. His attention soon became engrossed by the discovery and conquest of Mexico and Peru, and this costly toy, neglected and forgotten, was long utilized as a ring for bull-fighting, being now degraded to the vilest uses of the beggars of Granada.

The gorgeousness of Moorish architecture, which, with its enamelled tile-work, its gilded domes and filigree arcades, speaks so eloquently of Oriental luxury, bursts suddenly upon us as we pass, by a narrow gate-way opened in the seventeenth century, from the Plaza de los Algibes into the Court of the Myrtles. On the right is the portico of what was once the winter palace, on the left the Tower of Comares, containing the Hall of the Embassadors, the largest apartment of the Alhambra. The great basin occupying the centre of the court is bordered by hedges of myrtle interspersed with orange-trees. Arabic inscriptions cover the walls and galleries, and in the latter appear the identical jalousies which once screened from vulgar gaze the voluptuous charms of the wives and favorites of the sultan. This court, the only part of the building to which the public were ever admitted, was the theatre of frequent intrigues of the hostile factions that contended for the mastery even while the common enemy was thundering at the gates, and to whose bitter feuds, as much as to the valor of the Christian arms, should be attributed the downfall of the kingdom. In the Court of the Myrtles were received the flower of the Castilian chivalry, who upon grand occasions came to compete for the prize of knightly skill and courtesy in the famous Plaza de la Bibarrambla; here were entertained the picturesque envoys of the distant East, bringing greeting from the lords of Cairo and Ispahan; here the captive bishop of Jaen defied the monarch, and was sent to labor with his fellow-slaves upon the fortifications of the city; and here the fiery old Abul Hacen, surrounded by his harem, listened with gloomy forebodings to the predictions of the astrologer announcing the loss of his empire and the extinction of his race, and endeavored to forget his fears in the stirring ballads of his ancestors, or in the caresses of the beautiful Zorayda, the "Star of the Morning."

The Hall of the Embassadors occupies the whole of the Tower of Comares, and was used for coronations and royal festivals. From the balconies which replace the curious Moorish lattices of its alcoves we look down upon the gypsy quarter of the Albaycin, and the cypress groves that fringe the banks of the Darro, so named from its sands of gold. In this brilliant hall, during the closing days of the siege, Aixa, the mother of Boabdil, learned for the first time that he had been arranging for a capitulation; and, leading him to one of the windows, she threw open the gilded lattice and bade him look below. The last rays of the sun disappearing behind the Sierra Elvira lighted up the landscape, and through the purple haze, which hung like a veil over the lovely Vega, sparkled the domes of mosque and villa and the battlements of many a shapely tower and minaret. It was the hour of prayer, and the shrill tones of the muezzin, as turning towards each point of the compass he summoned the faithful to their devotions, mingling with the clash of arms and the cheers of the populace as they hailed the return of some valiant band from the successful foray, rose faintly to the lofty ramparts of the castle. A wilderness of orchards and vineyards which the ravages of war had spared still covered the mountain-side. The score of palaces with which the voluptuous Alhamares had embellished the environs of the capital still displayed their wonted beauty; though over more than one floated the hated banner of the infidel, whose intrenched lines appeared in the distance, encircling like a band of steel the walls of the devoted city. The quaint houses, red and white, with terraced roofs, and embowered amid verdant groves, recalled the simile of the poet who likened Granada to "a silver vase full of hyacinths and emeralds." The Genil and the Darro, which the ancient Syrian invader had pronounced rivals of Abana and Pharpar, rivers of Damascus, could be traced for leagues, as, after turning the wheels of more than three hundred mills, they distributed their refreshing waters, until lost in the innumerable canals that, like a net-work of glittering threads, spread far and wide over the fertile plain.

As the cowardly king gazed in silence on a scene which, including the fairest portion of his dominions, offered a view unequalled in the world, his mother, who united the courage of a soldier with the vindictiveness of the renegade, indignantly said, "See what you are about to surrender, and remember that all of your ancestors died kings of Granada, and that their line will end with you." The tears stood in Boabdil's eyes as he turned away, but the remonstrance had come too late. The truce was already signed; and three days later, attended by his mournful retinue, he left the fortress by the Gate of the Seven Stories, and departed for his little principality in the Alpujarras.

The Court of the Lions, which communicates with the Court of the Myrtles by means of a short passage, is rectangular in form, and is surrounded by galleries and pavilions supported by columns of white marble. To the right is the Hall of the Abencerrages, where, tradition says, the chiefs of this noble tribe were beheaded one by one in the presence of Boabdil; and beyond is the Hall of Justice, noted as the place where the rites of the Christian religion were first celebrated after the Conquest. It was used as a chapel while the cathedral was building, and differs in plan from the other halls, being divided into a suite of rooms crowned with little cupolas. The ceilings of its alcoves are covered with rude paintings of unknown origin, almost obliterated by time and neglect.

The Court of the Lions, renowned in ballad and chronicle, is the culminating point of the beauties of the Alhambra. No pen can describe them, no pencil can delineate them. The strange Cufic letters, the lace-work of the graceful arches, the stalactitic pendants of the domes blazing with scarlet and gold, the texts of the Koran meeting the glance at every turn, the long colonnades through which slant the rays of sunlight from the jalousies above, the chequered floors, the gorgeous tiles incrusting pilaster and wall, dazzle the eye with their splendor. And if now, with their ornaments cracked and faded, stained with damp and defaced by vandal travellers, these scenes can so enthrall the mind, what were they in the days of their glory, when the gilded arcades rang with the laughter of the houris imprisoned here, and black eunuchs, in silken robes and armed with jewel-hilted scimitars, guarded with jealous care these treasures of the harem!

On the north side of the court is the Hall of the Two Sisters, unsurpassed in the elegance of its decorations. Its divans are models of taste and richness, its enamels are the most curious in Spain. The broad inscriptions, that, twined with buds and leaves, are so conspicuous, are poems in praise of the builder, and amid the snowy arabesques appears at frequent intervals his shield, bearing the devout motto of the Alhamares, "There is no conqueror but God."

Did space permit, much might be said of the subterranean apartments of the Alhambra,—the cisterns, the baths, the dungeons, the magazines; of the little oratories or mosques, mementos of the piety of the Moslem; of the isolated towers, each forming a miniature palace, with guard-room and courts and hall of state, their boudoirs cooled by the spray from alabaster fountains, their walls incrusted with precious mosaics resembling tissues of brocade. In the corridor under the Tower of Comares the two discreet statues immortalized by Irving gaze yet upon the niche where the treasure was discovered by the little Sanchica. Unlike most of the legends to which Moorish fancy has given rise, this story is substantially true, for three immense jars of finished workmanship and full of coins and jewels were found here soon after the Conquest. Two of them were afterwards lost by neglect; the third, the famous vase of the Alhambra, unique in design, is preserved, though in a damaged condition, in a room near the Court of the Lions.

Of the numerous suburban villas that offered rest and seclusion to the princes of Granada, but one, the Generalife, or Garden of the Architect, now exists. It is situated much higher than the adjoining fortifications, and, completely commanding the city, was a point of the greatest strategic importance during the siege. Owned by a descendant of Boabdil, who has not entirely forgotten the customs of his princely line, the grounds of the Generalife present not a few of the distinctive characteristics of Moorish horticulture. Most prominent in the landscape are the venerable cypresses which have stood here for centuries, and by the trunk of the largest well-founded tradition says the daring Aben Hamet whispered words of illicit love in the ears of the frail sultana.

So extensive are the alterations which ignorance and barbarism have made in the Alhambra that its original plan cannot now be determined. We know that it contained five grand courts, of which only two remain, and that of the area enclosed by the outer wall scarce a foot of space was not occupied by buildings, the latter as late as 1625 affording shelter to six thousand souls who in that year attempted to turn the palace into a ribbon-factory. The royal residence was divided into several departments, each having its *alcalde*, or mayor, who was responsible to the governor of the fortress. One quarter was assigned to the sultan's family, another to the religious functionaries and doctors of the law, another to the garrison. Upon the highest point of the hill were lodged the *muftis*, or expounders of the Koran, and in the midst of their dwellings rose the tapering minarets of the great mosque, whose rare marbles and columns with capitals of massy silver caused it to be justly regarded as one of the wonders of the Moslem world. Instead of the coarse tiles whose weight is crushing the galleries, the roofs were covered with thin plates of porcelain corresponding with the gay mosaics of the pavements and the walls. The taste of the Oriental was visible everywhere, in cascades and fountains, in groves where myrtle and cypress were trimmed in all manner of fantastic shapes,— pyramids, grottoes, obelisks, stalactitic arches,—in aromatic hedges diffusing a succession of delicate perfumes, in beds where flowers of glowing colors traced texts and legends on a ground of brightest green. Seventy thousand gold ducats—one hundred and forty thousand dollars, equal to four times that amount at the present day—were expended annually upon the palace, to which additions were made by each succeeding monarch, until arrested by the fatal dissensions that heralded the overthrow of the Saracen power.

No Arab names of the apartments of the Alhambra have come down to us: those by which they are at present designated are modern and entirely imaginary. We are even ignorant as to the uses of many rooms, and it is sometimes difficult to separate the parts of the original structure from those of later date erected with materials taken from the demolished winter palace. These mutilations, that, under the pretext of "improvements," were effected in the reign of Charles V. and his immediate successors, have rendered a complete restoration impossible. Enough remains, however, to show the immense progress made by the Moors in architecture during the latter half of the fourteenth century, appropriately named the Hispano-Arab age of gold. The changes undergone by the various orders before the arch peculiar to Granada was developed are clearly defined and worthy of attention; and not less interesting is the study of the fragile and elaborate arabesques.

It is remarkable that such magical results were produced by the simplest means; for Arab ornamentation, far from being as complicated as it appears, is subject to certain plain geometrical rules. The figures, which at first sight show but a maze of lines and curves, can be easily resolved into the square and the circle; the shawls of Cashmere have afforded the patterns of the intricate floral designs lavished in such bewildering variety; the stalactitic cornices and domes are modelled after the sections of a pomegranate divested of its seeds. All the countries which the armies of Islam had overrun in their wonderful career seem to have furnished suggestions to the architects of the Alhambra. The huge stone blocks of the gates, fitted with perfect accuracy, are copied from the masonry of the Roman, who built for eternity; the hanging gardens are the gardens of Babylon; the lions that support the basin in the famous court are Phœnician; the fountain itself is an imitation of the brazen laver of Solomon, mentioned in the thirty-fourth *sura* of the Koran; the *tarkish,* or stucco-work, was invented at Damascus; the hand of the Persian artist is visible upon the glittering walls of the Tower of Comares. Nor did the Moor, ever proud of his origin and tenacious of the prejudices of his race, though separated hundreds of leagues from the home of his ancestors and domiciled for centuries in a foreign land, reject the influence of their traditions in the decoration of his palaces. The lotus of Egypt and the palm of Arabia are interwoven in the foliage of every fretted hall; the letters of the Cufic alphabet—singularly adapted to ornament—proclaim the doctrines of Islam from cornice and capital; while the profusion of water and verdure proves that the Saracen, though surrounded by the luxuriant vegetation of the Vega, beheld a grove or a fountain with the same emotions as did the weary camel-driver when, uttering a prayer of thanksgiving to Allah, he hailed with delight the refreshing oasis shining amid the dull gray sands of the desert.

"Quien no ha visto Granada
No ha visto nada,"—[B]

so saith the Andalusian proverb; but, aside from the Alhambra, the city boasts but few attractions. The streets are filthy beyond description, and so narrow that two persons can hardly ride abreast; the houses have a dilapidated appearance, and the people an air of dejected poverty. Long Venetian blinds hang over the balconies, and through their interstices peer the charming *Granadinas*, displaying in lustrous eyes and jet-black tresses their Moorish ancestry. At the side of almost every door is an altar, where a plaster image, arrayed in blue and tinsel, amid a cloud of votos and paper flowers, stares vacantly at the passer-by.

The Granadan dress is wholly Spanish, far different from that of the western provinces, where Parisian fashions are fast supplanting the showy national costume. The ladies wear lace mantillas and close-fitting skirts of light-colored silk, and are never seen without the coquettish fan, which no one knows how to wield so well as the charming Spanish woman. As for the men, they are almost invariably muffled in a cloak that hides them to the very eyes, except on some grand holiday, when they appear in all the splendor of plush jacket and scarlet sash, adding much to the brilliancy of the gay and noisy throng. When riding, the lady usually mounts behind her lover, and, with nothing to steady her but a scarf fastened to the crupper, will gallop unconcernedly over mountain-roads and through crooked lanes at the greatest speed. At the festivals is exhibited to the best advantage the character of the idle and music-loving Andalusian, from the lounging dandy, praising in bad extempore verses the beauty of some bar-maid in the little wine-shop, to the dishevelled gypsy, equally ready to sing a song or pick the pocket of the careless and admiring stranger.

INDEX.

Footnotes:

[A] "Water! water! Who wants water? tepid and good!"
[B] "Who hath not Granada seen
Is no traveller, I ween."

www.ingramcontent.com/pod-product-compliance
Lightning Source LLC
LaVergne TN
LVHW011223190726
843642LV00004B/1301